Saving Social Security

Saving
Social Security

A Balanced Approach

Peter A. Diamond
Peter R. Orszag

BROOKINGS INSTITUTION PRESS
Washington, D.C.

Copyright © 2004
THE BROOKINGS INSTITUTION
1775 Massachusetts Avenue, N.W., Washington, D.C. 20036
www.brookings.edu

Library of Congress Cataloging-in-Publication data

Diamond, Peter A.
    Saving Social Security : a balanced approach / Peter A. Diamond and Peter R. Orszag.
    p.   cm.
Includes bibliographical references and index.
    ISBN 0-8157-1838-1 (cloth : alk. paper)
    1. Social security—United States. 2. Retirement income—Government policy—United States. 3. Old age pensions—United States. I. Orszag, Peter R. II. Title.
    HD7125.D525 2004
    368.4'3'00973—dc22   2003022639

9 8 7 6 5 4 3 2 1

The paper used in this publication meets minimum requirements of the American National Standard for Information Sciences—Permanence of Paper for Printed Library Materials: ANSI Z39.48-1992.

Typeset in Sabon

Composition by Cynthia Stock
Silver Spring, Maryland

Printed by R. R. Donnelley
Harrisonburg, Virginia

Contents

Acknowledgments   vii

1   Introduction   1

2   A Brief Overview of Social Security   14

3   Goals for Social Security Reform   27

4   Social Security's Long-Term Deficit   55

5   A Three-Part Plan to Shore Up
Social Security   79

6   Strengthening Social Security's
Effectiveness as Social Insurance   99

7   Implications for Benefits and Revenue   116

8   Individual Accounts   133

9   Questions and Answers about Our
Balanced Reform Plan   164

10   Conclusions   193

Appendixes

A   Social Security and National Saving   199

B   Trends in Retirement Age   205

C   How the Legacy Debt Arose: A Simplified Example   208

D   Characteristics of Tax-Favored Defined-Contribution
    Plans   210

E   Should the Trust Fund Invest in the Stock Market?   214

F   Comparisons with Models 2 and 3 of the President's
    Commission   217

G   Memorandum from the Office of the Chief Actuary   229

Notes   247

Index   281

Acknowledgments

We are grateful to our colleagues who dramatically improved the quality of our reform proposal and this book by reading initial drafts and discussing the ideas contained in them. Among those providing comments or engaging in helpful discussions were Henry Aaron, Gregory Anrig, Jon Bakija, Robert Ball, Lily Batchelder, Cheryl Bates-Harris, Barry Bosworth, Melanie Brunson, Gary Burtless, Robert Cumby, Irma Elo, Martha Ford, William Gale, Robert Greenstein, Kilolo Kijakazi, Richard Leone, Jeffrey Liebman, Maya MacGuineas, Matthew Mitchell, David Moss, Alicia Munnell, Kathryn Olson, Jonathan Orszag, Michael Orszag, Virginia Reno, Robert Reischauer, Alice Rivlin, John Rother, Bernard Saffran, Charles Schultze, Gerry Shea, Kirsten Smith, Gene Sperling, Eugene Steuerle, Joseph Stiglitz, Peter Temin, David Wilcox, and Ethel Zelenske.

Our research assistants, David Gunter, Jennifer Derstine, Matthew Hall, and Emil Apostolov, did an outstanding job on numerous aspects of this volume. We could not have completed the book without their excellent assistance.

We owe particular thanks to Stephen Goss, the Chief Actuary at the Social Security Administration, as well as

Seung An, Christopher Chaplain, Michael Clingman, William Piet, Lesley Reece, Jason Schultz, and Alice Wade in the Office of the Chief Actuary for providing crucial technical assistance and the official actuarial analyses of our reform plan. A memorandum from the Office of the Chief Actuary is included as appendix G to this volume.

The Brookings Institution Press was particularly accommodating. We thank Robert Faherty, Janet Walker, and Christopher Kelaher for overseeing the production process, and Michael Treadway for excellent editing.

Finally, we are especially grateful to our spouses, Kate and Cameron, for all the suggestions and support they have provided throughout this project.

1 Introduction

Social Security is one of America's most successful government programs. It has helped millions of Americans avoid poverty in old age, upon becoming disabied, or after the death of a family wage earner. As President Bush has emphasized, "Social Security is one of the greatest achievements of the American government, and one of the deepest commitments to the American people."[1] Despite its successes, however, the program faces two principal problems.

First, Social Security faces a long-term deficit, even though it is currently running short-term cash surpluses. Addressing the long-term deficit would put both the program itself and the nation's budget on a sounder footing.

Second, two decades have passed since the last significant changes in Social Security. Since then, as our economy and society have continued to evolve, some aspects of the program have become increasingly out of date. The history of Social Security is one of steady adaptation to evolving issues, and it is time to adapt the program once again.

Restoring long-term balance to Social Security is necessary, but it is not necessary to destroy the program in order to save it. To be sure, some analysts reject the view that Social Security's projected financial problems are serious enough to warrant any changes right now.[2] Others, in contrast, exaggerate the difficulty of saving Social Security to justify proposals that would shred the most valuable features of this exemplary program.[3] Our view is that Social Security's projected financial difficulties are real and that addressing those difficulties sooner rather than later would make sensible reforms easier and more likely. The prospects are not so dire, however, as to require undercutting the basic structure of the system. In other words, our purpose is to save Social Security both from its financial problems and from some of its "reformers."

In this book we present a plan for saving Social Security.[4] Our approach recognizes and preserves the value of Social Security in providing a basic level of benefits for workers and their families that cannot be decimated by stock market crashes or inflation, and that lasts for the life of the beneficiary. Our plan updates Social Security to reflect changes in the labor market and life expectancies. And it eliminates the long-term deficit without resorting to accounting gimmicks, thereby putting the program and the federal budget on a sounder financial footing.

Our plan to restore long-term solvency has three components, each of which addresses one of the factors that contribute to the long-term deficit in Social Security: improvements in life expectancy, increased earnings inequality, and the ongoing legacy debt that arises from the program's generosity to its early beneficiaries. Each component of our reform plan includes adjustments to both benefits and revenue to help close the long-term deficit.

The first of these components is the life expectancy component. Life expectancy at age 65 has risen by four years for men and five years for women since 1940, and it is expected to continue rising in the future. Increases in life expectancy make Social Security benefits more valuable to recipients, because the benefits are paid over more years. But for that very reason, increases in life expectancy also raise the cost of Social Security.

Many observers have recognized that it makes sense to adjust Social Security for the effects of increased life expectancy. Previous proposals to do this, however, have adopted the extreme view that all of the adjustment should occur through reductions in benefits.[5] Instead, we propose a balanced approach in which roughly half the life expectancy adjustment occurs through changes to benefits and the rest through changes to payroll taxes.

The second component of our plan addresses earnings inequality, which has risen substantially in the past two decades. Inequality of earnings across workers in the labor force affects Social Security in several ways. For example, the payroll tax is levied on earnings only up to a certain level (in 2003 that level, the maximum taxable earnings base, was $87,000). In each year over the past two decades, about 6 percent of workers have had high enough earnings that some of their earnings were above the maximum taxable earnings base and therefore not subject to the payroll tax. These higher-income workers have enjoyed disproportionately rapid earnings growth over that period, so that the share of economy-wide earnings not taxed for Social Security has risen substantially. In 1983, when the last major reform of Social Security was undertaken, 10 percent of all earnings were above the maximum taxable earnings base. By 2002 that share had risen to about 15 percent.

In addition to having more of their earnings escape taxation by Social Security, high-income workers have enjoyed increasing life expectancies relative to other workers. This increasing difference in life expectancy tends to diminish the progressivity of Social Security (that is, its provision of relatively more generous benefits to lower-earning workers) on a lifetime basis. The life expectancy adjustments in the first component of our plan are based on average increases in life expectancy for the entire population. Since life expectancy for higher earners is increasing more rapidly than the average, an additional adjustment just for higher earners is warranted.

To address the effect of earnings inequality on Social Security, our plan again includes a balance of revenue and benefit adjustments. First, we propose gradually raising the maximum taxable earnings base until the share of earnings that is above the base—and hence escapes the payroll tax—has returned to roughly its average level over the past twenty years. This change would gradually reduce the share of earnings not subject to the payroll tax until it reaches 13 percent in 2063, roughly halfway between its current level and its level in 1983. Second, to make Social Security somewhat more progressive, and thereby offset the effects of disproportionately rapid gains in life expectancy among higher earners, we propose a benefit reduction that affects only relatively high earners. Currently, about 15 percent of workers newly eligible for Social Security benefits have sufficiently high earnings that a portion of those earnings falls in the highest tier of the Social Security benefit formula. Our benefit adjustment for income inequality consists of a gradual, modest reduction in benefits that would affect only those with earnings in this highest tier.

The third component of our plan recognizes the legacy cost stemming from Social Security's history. The first generations of beneficiaries received far more in benefits than they had contributed in payroll taxes. Beneficiaries in the earliest years of the program, for example, contributed for only a few years of their career but then received full benefits over their whole retirement. The decision to provide ample benefits to these early beneficiaries is understandable: most of them had experienced hardship during the Great Depression, many had fought in World War I or World War II, and elderly poverty rates were unacceptably high. But those benefits did not come free: the iron logic of accounting requires that since those early retirees received more in benefits than they had paid in, later generations of retirees must receive less. In other words, the system's generosity to early beneficiaries generated an implicit debt, which we refer to in this book as Social Security's legacy debt. That debt can be defined as the accumulated difference between benefits and taxes (accumulated at the market rate of interest) for past and current beneficiaries. This legacy debt imposes an ongoing cost on participants in the program, which we call the legacy cost. (Box 1-1 further explains the origin of this legacy and how the burden it imposes on current and future beneficiaries can be understood as the cost of servicing an implicit debt.)

We all inherit a legacy from Social Security's history. Even if we wanted to, nothing we can do now could take back what was given to Social Security's early beneficiaries. In addition, most people are unwilling to reduce benefits for those already receiving them or nearing retirement. Those two facts determine the size of Social Security's legacy debt. And once that debt is determined, its cost cannot be avoided: the only issue is how we finance that cost across different generations.

Social Security's legacy is not new. It has been with us since the origins of the program itself. But the idea of a Social Security reform based in part on explicitly recognizing the need to share the cost of that legacy is new. We propose to reform the financing of the legacy debt through three changes:

—First, we would gradually phase in universal coverage under Social Security, to ensure that all workers bear their fair share of the cost of the nation's generosity to earlier generations. Currently, about 4 million workers, almost all of them in state and local governments, are not covered by Social Security. Their nonparticipation means that those workers escape any contribution to the financing of the legacy debt.

—Second, we would impose a legacy tax on earnings above the maximum taxable earnings base, thereby ensuring that very high earners contribute to financing the legacy debt in proportion to their full earnings. The legacy tax above the base would start at 3.0 percent and gradually rise to 3.5 percent by 2080.

—Third, we would impose a universal legacy charge on future workers and beneficiaries, roughly half of which would be in the form of a benefit reduction for all beneficiaries becoming eligible in or after 2023, and the rest in the form of a very modest increase in the payroll tax from 2023 onward.[6] This universal legacy charge would gradually increase over time, so as to help stabilize the legacy debt as a share of taxable payroll.[7]

This approach to financing the legacy debt reflects a reasonable balance between current and distant generations, between lower earners and higher earners, and between workers who are currently covered by the program and workers who are not. As explained in more detail in later chapters, it is meant to keep the full cost of servicing the legacy debt from simply being pushed further into the future for our children and grandchildren to pay.

As an alternative to some of our proposals for benefit reductions or revenue increases, policymakers could dedicate revenue from another specific source to Social Security. For example, the estate tax could be reformed rather than eliminated entirely, as the Bush administration has proposed, and some or all of that revenue could be dedicated to Social Security. In other words, policymakers who object to certain elements in our plan could substitute for those elements a dedicated stream of revenue from a reformed estate tax.

Our three-part proposal would restore long-term balance to Social Security as that term is conventionally understood: actuarial balance over

Box 1-1. *Understanding the Legacy Cost in Social Security*

To see how the early history of Social Security gave rise to today's legacy cost, imagine that, many decades ago, your great-grandfather fell very ill. He had no accumulated assets and no health insurance, so he had to rely on his son, your grandfather, to pay his medical bills. Your grandfather agreed to do this, despite the financial burden, not only because he loved your great-grandfather and was grateful for his upbringing, but also because he was confident that his own son, your father, would similarly be willing to finance his (that is, your grandfather's) medical costs late in life. Your father fulfilled that expectation, but at the cost of running down his own assets, because he in turn was confident that he could rely on you to finance his health care expenses during retirement.

At this point, you inherit a family legacy in the form of an implicit debt, which originated with your great-grandfather's illness and has since been passed from one generation of your family to the next. If you accept the responsibility to finance your father's health care costs as he did his father's, you assume the debt imposed by that legacy, in the expectation that your own child will pay for your health care costs when you grow old. In this way the legacy of that initial decision to finance the health care costs of your great-grandfather is passed on to yet another generation.

What if you renege on your obligation to your father and refuse to pay his medical bills? In that case the legacy debt is eliminated, but your father is forced to bear the entire deferred cost of your great-grandfather's medical expenses as well as his own. In other words, canceling the legacy debt in this way requires a "transition generation"—in this case, your father—to pay a very heavy toll.

If the legacy debt simply gets passed from one generation to the next, in what sense is there any cost? In other words, if you pay for your father's health care when he is elderly and your child pays for your health care when you are elderly, aren't you just getting paid back when you are old what you paid in when you were young?

In fact, both you and your father and grandfather do bear a legacy cost, even though you are effectively repaid in retirement for the money you spent on your father when young. The reason is that you could have earned a market rate of interest on that money in the meanwhile. The legacy cost consists of the forgone returns you would have earned on those funds. Suppose, for example, that you spend $10,000 for your father's health care, and that you would otherwise have earned $1,000 in interest on that $10,000, for a total of $11,000. Suppose then that, decades later, your child spends $10,000 for your health care, paying you back for what you spent on your father.* It might seem that you have broken even, but in fact you are $1,000 poorer than you would have been otherwise. The $1,000 in interest that you would have earned had you not participated in this family arrangement is your legacy cost. And every future generation that partici-pates will bear a similar legacy cost, all stemming from your grandfather's initial decision to support your great-grandfather in his time of need.

This story, although simplified, is a close approximation to the history of Social Security—and a good description of the challenge for reform. Past and current beneficiaries received benefits disproportionate to their contri-butions, generating a legacy debt. Whatever the reasons for, and whatever the good that came of, the decision to provide those generous benefits, we all now face the burden of financing the debt created by that decision. That burden takes the form of our having to forgo the higher return that we could have earned on our payroll tax contributions.

The actual Social Security system resembles this simplified example in that we all would earn higher returns on our payroll tax contributions if those contributions could be invested at a market rate of return. That is not possible in reality, however, because our payroll taxes are mostly used to finance benefits for our parents' and grandparents' generations, and our retirement benefits in turn are financed by payroll contributions from sub-sequent generations.

We could earn a market rate of return on our payroll tax contributions if we failed to pay the benefits promised to the generations before us, but that would impose severe hardship on them. If we act responsibly and do not renege on the promises made to current beneficiaries, the "rate of return" we receive on our Social Security payroll taxes will be lower than the market rate of return. That difference reflects the legacy of Social Secu-rity's history and represents the cost that we must pay because of the pro-gram's justified generosity to early beneficiaries. The degree to which the rate of return on our contributions falls below a market rate of return determines how much of the cost of Social Security's legacy debt we bear, and how much we pass along to future generations.

To be sure, the legacy associated with Social Security is more compli-cated than this simplified story. In our example, a single generation accounts for the entire legacy debt; in reality, that debt accumulated over several generations. And unlike the real Social Security, our story did not assume any long-term projected deficit. That underscores an important point that we discuss further in chapter 4, namely, that the legacy debt and the long-term deficit are related, but are also two different things.

---

*To simplify the story, we assume that the cost of health care does not increase over time. Making the more realistic assumption that health care costs change over time complicates the story but does not alter the underlying conclusion: if some gen-erations received more than the market rate of interest on their payments, others will have to receive less.

a seventy-five-year horizon. Our plan would not only eliminate the seventy-five-year deficit in Social Security, but indeed would produce a modestly growing ratio of the Social Security trust fund to annual costs at the end of the seventy-five-year period. This is important because it makes it more likely that Social Security will not again face a seventy-five-year deficit for a long time to come.

Table 1-1 shows how each of the components of the plan contributes to restoring balance. Our plan combines revenue increases and benefit reductions—the same approach taken in the last major Social Security reform, that of the early 1980s, when Alan Greenspan chaired a bipartisan commission on Social Security. That commission facilitated a reform that included adjustments to both benefits and taxes.[8] Such a balanced approach was the basis for reaching a consensus between President Ronald Reagan and congressional Republicans on one hand and congressional Democrats led by House Speaker Thomas P. O'Neill on the other.

In addition to our three-part plan to restore long-term balance to Social Security, we propose improvements to Social Security's financial protections for certain particularly vulnerable beneficiaries. We focus on changes in four areas: benefits for workers with low lifetime earnings; benefits for widows and widowers; benefits for disabled workers and young survivors; and further protection for all beneficiaries against unexpected inflation. These changes would significantly improve Social Security's ability to provide cost-effective social insurance while maintaining long-term financial balance.

What do these various changes imply for the benefits that individual workers will receive and for the taxes they will pay? Workers who are 55 years old or older in 2004 will experience no change in their benefits from those scheduled under current law. For younger workers with average earnings, our proposal involves a gradual and modest reduction in benefits from those scheduled under current law for successive cohorts. For example, a 45-year-old average earner would experience less than a 1 percent reduction in benefits under our plan. A 35-year-old average earner would experience less than a 5 percent reduction. And a 25-year-old with average earnings would experience less than a 9 percent reduction in benefits (table 1-2). Higher earners would experience somewhat larger reductions in benefits than the average, and lower earners would

Table 1-1. *Summary of Effects of Proposed Reforms*

Percent

Proposed reform[a]	Effect on actuarial balance	
	As share of taxable payroll	As share of actuarial deficit[b]
Adjustments for increasing life expectancy		
Adjust benefits	0.26	13
Adjust revenue	0.29	15
Subtotal	0.55	29
Adjustments for increased earnings inequality		
Increase taxable earnings base	0.25	13
Reduce benefits for higher earners	0.18	9
Subtotal	0.43	22
Adjustments for fairer sharing of legacy cost		
Make Social Security coverage universal	0.19	10
Impose legacy tax on earnings over taxable		
maximum	0.55	29
Impose legacy charge on benefits and revenue	0.97	51
Subtotal	1.71	89
Reforms to strengthen social insurance functions[c]		
Enhanced benefits for lifetime low earners	−0.14	−7
Increased benefits for widows and widowers	−0.08	−4
Hold-harmless provisions for disabled workers		
and young survivors	−0.21	−11
Completion of inflation protection of benefits[d]	0.0	0
Subtotal	−0.43	−22
Interactions of above reforms	−0.26	−14
Total effect	2.00	104
Alternative: reform existing estate tax[e]	0.60	31

Source: Authors' calculations based on memorandum from the Office of the Chief Actuary.

a. See the text for details of specific proposed reforms.

b. The seventy-five-year deficit is currently estimated to be 1.92 percent of taxable payroll over that period. Numbers may not sum to totals because of rounding.

c. On these reforms and their separate impacts on actuarial balance, see chapter 6.

d. Not included in the package of reforms officially scored by the Office of the Chief Actuary, but should have de minimis actuarial effect.

e. This reform could be enacted in place of one of the other proposed reforms that affect primarily higher earners.

Table 1-2. *Benefit Reductions under Proposed Reform for Average Earners*

Age at end of 2004	Change in benefits from scheduled benefit baseline (percent)	Benefit at full benefit age (2003 dollars)[a]
55	0.0	15,408
45	−0.6	17,100
35	−4.5	18,200
25	−8.6	19,400

Source: Authors' calculations.

a. For a retired worker with scaled medium preretirement earnings pattern. This scaled earnings pattern allows wages to vary with the age of the worker but ensures that lifetime earnings are approximately equal to those of a worker with the average wage in every year of his or her career.

experience smaller reductions. These modest reductions in benefits are also in keeping with the tradition set in 1983. For example, the 1983 reform reduced benefits by about 10 percent for those 25 years old at the time of the reform, a slightly larger benefit reduction than under our plan for average earners age 25 in 2004.[9]

It is important to underline that the reductions just described are relative to currently scheduled benefits; they are not absolute reductions from what retirees receive today. (Box 1-2 discusses the use of alternative baselines in evaluating Social Security reform proposals.) Although today's younger workers would experience somewhat larger percentage reductions in scheduled benefits when they retire than older workers, those benefits would still be higher, even after adjusting for inflation, than those of the older workers. An average earner who is 25 years old in 2004, for example, would receive an annual inflation-adjusted benefit at retirement that is more than 25 percent higher than the inflation-adjusted benefit of an average earner who is 55 years old in 2004. The reason is that Social Security benefits increase when career earnings rise, and today's 25-year-olds are expected to have higher career earnings than today's 55-year-olds because of ongoing productivity gains in the economy. Even with the modest benefit reductions in our plan, the result is that inflation-adjusted benefits rise from one generation to the next.

Box 1-2. *The Baseline for Benefit and Revenue Comparisons*

Discussions of Social Security reform are often confused by the so-called baseline issue. Because the program currently faces a projected imbalance, the issue involves the appropriate basis of comparison for reform plans. One possibility is the "scheduled benefits" baseline, which assumes that all benefits payable under the current benefit formula will be paid, as they would be if full funding were provided. An alternative is the "payable benefits" baseline, which assumes that only those benefits that can be financed by the current payroll tax will be paid. Payable benefits are equal to scheduled benefits for the next few decades, but then they fall increasingly below scheduled benefits. Under the payable benefits baseline, Social Security does not face an imbalance, but that is because that imbalance has effectively been assumed away.

Proponents of some Social Security reform plans use these two baselines selectively to make their proposals seem artificially attractive. To do this, they measure their proposed changes in benefits relative to the payable benefit baseline, which assumes a reduction in benefits but no long-term imbalance. They then measure their proposed changes in the system's financing relative to the scheduled benefits baseline, which contains the projected imbalance. This is not only inconsistent but can leave the impression that benefits are being increased while the deficit is being reduced.

All of the benefit proposals in this book are measured relative to the scheduled benefits baseline. And even though it requires the use of language that could make our proposals appear less attractive, our proposed tax changes are described relative to the current tax structure, which is insufficient to finance scheduled benefits. This combination seems the most straightforward way to describe the changes we propose, to ensure that they are properly understood. In chapter 7, when we evaluate the payroll tax rate under our plan, we compare it both with the current payroll tax rate and with the rate that would be required to finance scheduled benefits.

Our plan balances its modest and gradual benefit reductions with a modest and gradual increase in the payroll tax rate. As table 1-3 shows, the employee share of the payroll tax under our plan would slowly increase from 6.2 percent in 2005 to 7.1 percent in 2055. Because employees and their employers each pay half of the payroll tax, the combined employer-employee payroll tax rate would rise from 12.4 percent today to 12.45 percent in 2015, 13.2 percent in 2035, and 14.2 percent in 2055. This gradual increase in the payroll tax rate helps ensure that

Table 1-3. *Payroll Tax Rates under Proposed Reform*
Percent of earnings

Year	Employee rate	Combined employer-employee rate
2005	6.20	12.40
2015	6.22	12.45
2025	6.35	12.69
2035	6.59	13.18
2045	6.84	13.68
2055	7.09	14.18

Source: Authors' calculations based on memorandum from the Office of the Chief Actuary.

Social Security continues to provide an adequate level of benefits that are protected against inflation and financial market fluctuations, and that last as long as the beneficiary lives.

In addition to explaining more fully the motivation for and the details of our plan, later chapters of this book discuss some changes to Social Security proposed by others that are not part of our plan. Some of these, such as diverting revenue from the traditional Social Security program into individual accounts, we regard as ill advised. Others we view favorably but exclude from our plan because they are highly controversial and would complicate the task of restoring actuarial balance and getting the less controversial improvements through Congress. Still others seem to have a worthy purpose but have not been sufficiently researched to justify including them at this point.

In summary, our plan differs from most other recent Social Security reform proposals, and in our view it represents the most auspicious way of reforming the program, for the following reasons:

—It balances benefit and revenue adjustments.

—It restores long-term balance and sustainable solvency to Social Security.

—It does not assume any transfers from general revenue.

—It does not rely on substantial reductions in disability and young survivor benefits to help restore long-term balance.

—It strengthens the program's protections for low earners and widows.

—It does not divert Social Security revenue into individual accounts.

—It preserves Social Security's core social insurance role, providing a base level of income in time of need that is protected against financial market fluctuations and unexpected inflation.

Despite our confidence in the plan's substantive merits, we are under no illusions regarding the political difficulties of enacting it. Social Security reform is controversial, as it should be. After all, Social Security plays a critical role in the lives of millions of Americans and in the federal budget. Reforms to such an important program *should* generate political interest and debate. Nonetheless, we hope that the simplicity and balance of our basic three-pronged plan demonstrate that Social Security can be mended without resorting to the most controversial and problematic elements included in some other recent reform plans.

The plan of the book is as follows. In chapter 2, we review how Social Security works. Chapter 3 considers the criteria that matter when evaluating reform proposals. Chapter 4 discusses the long-term Social Security deficit and its causes. Chapter 5 contains our proposals for restoring actuarial balance, and Chapter 6 our proposals for improving social insurance protections. Chapter 7 draws together the implications of the various pieces of our plan for Social Security revenue and benefits. Chapter 8 explains why we do not include individual accounts in our proposal. Chapter 9 raises and responds to questions that might be asked about our plan and our analysis. Chapter 10 offers a brief concluding discussion.

2 | A Brief Overview of Social Security

Social Security was created in 1935 and issued its first monthly retirement benefit payment, to Ida May Fuller of Ludlow, Vermont, in January 1940.[1] Over time, an increasing share of American workers have qualified for benefits under the program, and the number of beneficiaries has risen from 3.5 million in 1950 to 35.6 million in 1980 and 46 million in 2001. To comprehend the challenges facing Social Security today and to evaluate alternative reform packages, it is important to understand who receives Social Security benefits and how the program works to provide recipients with a base level of assured income, one that is protected against inflation, financial market fluctuations, and the risk of outliving one's assets.

Who Receives Social Security Benefits?

Although Social Security is typically thought of as a retirement program, it actually covers a broad array of beneficiaries. It provides benefits not only to retired workers but also to disabled workers, survivors of deceased workers, and family members of these beneficiaries. In addition to the prototypical retiree (or disabled worker) and spouse, some of those who qualify for Social Security benefits include

—Children of retired, disabled, or deceased workers. Recipients must be under the age of 18 (19 if enrolled in high school), or disabled before the age of 22.

—Spouses of disabled workers. The spouse must either be caring for a child under age 16 or a disabled child, or be at least 62 years old.

—Widows and widowers of covered workers. The recipient must be at least 60 years old, or be caring for a child under age 16 or a disabled child, or be disabled and at least 50 years old. Surviving divorced spouses may qualify if the marriage lasted at least ten years.

—Parents of a deceased worker. The parent must have been dependent on the deceased worker and be at least 62 years old.

Of the approximately 46 million Social Security beneficiaries in December 2001, 29 million were retired workers, 5 million were disabled workers, and 12 million were survivors of deceased workers or family members of other beneficiaries (table 2-1). To be sure, more than 90 percent of Americans over age 65 receive Social Security benefits. But the image of Social Security solely as a retirement program is inaccurate: almost 15 percent of beneficiaries are younger than 62.

For most beneficiaries, Social Security is an important source of income, and for some it is essential. Social Security benefits account for more than half of total income for almost two-thirds of beneficiaries over age 65. Even more striking, Social Security represents 90 percent or more of total income for almost one-third of elderly beneficiaries, and 100 percent of income for 20 percent of elderly beneficiaries. That last statistic is worth emphasizing: for one-fifth of all beneficiaries over 65, Social Security is their *only* source of income.

Notwithstanding their profound importance for so many of the nation's elderly, Social Security benefits were never intended to be sufficient to provide a comfortable retirement by themselves. Rather, they are meant to be a safe income *foundation* after retirement or disability. The average Social Security benefit amounts to only about $10,000 a year, and 20 percent of beneficiaries receive $7,000 a year or less. These

Table 2-1. *Social Security Beneficiaries by Type, December 2001*[a]

Type of beneficiary	Number (thousands)[b]	Percent of total
Retired workers and dependents	32,046	70
Retired workers	28,837	63
Spouses and children	3,209	7
Disabled workers and dependents	6,913	15
Disabled workers	5,274	11
Spouses and children	1,639	4
Survivors of deceased workers	6,918	15
All beneficiaries	45,878	100

Source: *Fast Facts and Figures about Social Security, 2002.*

a. Dually entitled beneficiaries (those who receive their own retirement benefit supplemented by a partial spousal benefit) are counted as retired workers.

b. Numbers may not sum to total because of rounding.

figures underscore the program's role in providing households with a minimum level of income following the retirement, disability, or death of a wage earner.

Social Security benefits are particularly valuable for their recipients' financial security because they are indexed for inflation and because they last for as long as the beneficiary lives. Beneficiaries therefore do not have to worry that they will exhaust the income flow from their assets before they die, nor do they have to worry that inflation will rob them of the standard of living supported by Social Security today. Social Security benefits represent what is called an inflation-adjusted annuity, a series of payments that maintain their purchasing power over time and that last as long as the worker (or his or her spouse) is alive. Annuities of this kind are virtually nonexistent in the private financial market, despite their substantial value as a form of insurance.[2]

By design, Social Security benefits are progressive: they replace a larger share of previous wages for those whose earnings were low during their working life than for those whose earnings were high. For example, in 2003, annual Social Security benefits replaced about 56 percent of previous wages for new beneficiaries who had earned 45 percent of the national average wage during their careers, but replaced only 41 percent of previous wages for those who had earned the national average wage. And for recipients who had earned the maximum amount of earnings taxable under Social Security, benefits replaced only 30 percent of previous earnings.[3]

This progressivity represents a form of social insurance and results from Social Security's benefit formula, described in the next section.[4] To understand why such progressivity is important, imagine a young worker just beginning her career. She expects her career to be financially rewarding, and indeed the prospects look good. But many things can change over the course of a career that may last forty or more years. For example, the occupation in which she chooses to specialize may gradually decline (perhaps as it is outmoded by new technology), forcing her to spend valuable time learning a new one. Or her prime earnings years may occur during a prolonged recession, substantially reducing her lifetime earnings.

The progressivity of Social Security's benefit formula provides some protection against this young worker's career not progressing as well as she hoped at the start, whether through bad luck or her own misjudgments. If her earnings turn out to be lower than she initially expected, Social Security benefits automatically become relatively more generous. This worker's benefits will be lower than they would have been had she earned more, but they will cushion the blow by declining less than proportionately with the shortfall in her earnings from what she expected. It is this feature of the benefit formula, along with the disability and other protections embedded in the program, that gives Social Security the character of social insurance. But to provide these relatively larger annual benefits for workers whose lifetime earnings turn out to be low, Social Security must provide smaller annual benefits (relative to previous earnings) for workers whose lifetime earnings turn out to be high.

How Retirement Benefits Are Determined

The mechanics of how Social Security benefits are determined can seem very complicated. But the basic principles are not: Social Security benefits depend on the beneficiary's past earnings, and, as just explained, they are designed to replace a larger share of previous earnings for lower earners than for higher earners. Social Security retirement benefits also depend on the age when one starts collecting benefits. To ensure that the value of lifetime benefits is little affected by whether one retires and first claims benefits at an earlier or a later age, the monthly benefit is raised for those who delay claiming benefits. Finally, for all beneficiaries, Social Security benefits increase each year in line with inflation.

More precisely, Social Security benefits are determined through a four-stage process:

—*Average earnings.* First, a worker's earnings history is used to compute that worker's average indexed monthly earnings (AIME). The worker's covered earnings in each year up to age 60 are indexed for the growth in national average wages that has occurred since that year.[5] For example, if a worker earned $5,000 in a given year three decades ago, and if average wages in the economy today are five times what they were then, those wages from three decades ago would be inflated to $25,000 for this purpose. This wage indexation means that the change in initial benefits from one generation to the next reflects ongoing earnings growth in the economy. Not all of the years in a worker's career are included in the AIME computation, however; instead only the highest earnings years up to a specific number of years are included. The number of years depends on the type of benefit being claimed; for retired workers it is thirty-five. The AIME is then computed by averaging the indexed earnings for those years (including zeros if the worker actually worked fewer than thirty-five years) and dividing by 12.

—*Primary insurance amount.* The second step in determining the monthly benefit is to compute the worker's primary insurance amount (PIA). The PIA formula is progressive: the PIA is larger as a share of earnings for lower earners than for higher earners. For example, for a worker with a calculated AIME of $1,000 becoming entitled to benefits in 2003, the PIA would have been $671, or 67 percent of the AIME.[6] For a worker with an AIME of $6,000, the PIA would have been $1,872, or 31 percent of the AIME.

—*Monthly benefit amount.* The third step is to compute an initial monthly benefit amount from the PIA. This is where the adjustment for early or late first claiming of benefits occurs. For retired workers the initial monthly benefit is equal to the PIA if benefits are claimed at the "full benefit age," which is discussed below. Retired workers who claim bene-

---

Box 2-1. *Indexation in Social Security*

Social Security has a number of features that adjust automatically in response to economic developments. For example, after benefits start, they increase each year in line with consumer prices, as described in the text. This protects benefits against being eroded by inflation. In calculating a worker's initial monthly benefit, however, that worker's past earnings are indexed not to inflation but to average earnings in the economy, also as described in the text. This indexing of past earnings, and thus the initial benefit, to economy-wide average earnings allows Social Security benefits to keep pace with wages over time; it means that the benefit replacement rate (the ratio of benefits to a worker's past earnings) remains roughly stable.* In keeping with this relationship between initial benefits and average earnings, the maximum level of benefits subject to the payroll tax is adjusted by the same average earnings index.

This kind of automatic indexing is widely held to be a useful feature of social security systems, both in the United States and abroad. Because the future paths of both prices and wages are not fully predictable, automatic adjustments reduce the frequency with which Congress needs to address Social Security reform. In this volume, we propose extensions of the automatic indexing in Social Security, so that the system becomes indexed to additional factors (life expectancy) and better indexed to existing factors (inflation).

*This statement strictly applies only after the already legislated increase in the full benefit age has fully taken effect. During the transition to the higher full benefit age, the replacement rate for each subsequent generation will decline.

---

fits before the full benefit age receive an initial monthly benefit that is smaller than the PIA, whereas those who wait until after the full benefit age to claim benefits receive a monthly benefit that is larger than the PIA.

—*Indexation for inflation.* After a worker becomes eligible for benefits, his or her PIA—and thus his or her monthly benefit—is increased each year by a cost-of-living adjustment (COLA). The COLA is based on the change in the consumer price index over the previous year and ensures that Social Security benefits are protected against the effects of inflation. (Box 2-1 further discusses the role of indexation in Social Security.)

Table 2-2. *Full Benefit Age and Retirement Benefit Received at Different Ages of Initial Claim*

Year worker turns 62	Full benefit age	Benefit at indicated age (percent of PIA)		
		62 years[a]	65 years	67 years
1999	65 years	80	100	113
2000	65 years, 2 months	$79\,^1/_6$	$98\,^8/_9$	$111\,^{11}/_{12}$
2001	65, 4 months	$78\,^1/_3$	$97\,^7/_9$	$111\,^2/_3$
2002	65, 6 months	$77\,^1/_2$	$96\,^2/_3$	$110\,^1/_2$
2003	65, 8 months	$76\,^2/_3$	$95\,^5/_9$	110
2004	65, 10 months	$75\,^5/_6$	$94\,^4/_9$	$108\,^3/_4$
2005–16	66 years	75	$93\,^1/_3$	108
2017	66, 2 months	$74\,^1/_6$	$92\,^2/_9$	$106\,^2/_3$
2018	66, 4 months	$73\,^1/_3$	$91\,^1/_9$	$105\,^1/_3$
2019	66, 6 months	$72\,^1/_2$	90	104
2020	66, 8 months	$71\,^2/_3$	$88\,^8/_9$	$102\,^2/_3$
2021	66, 10 months	$70\,^5/_6$	$87\,^7/_9$	$101\,^1/_3$
2022 and after	67 years	70	$86\,^2/_3$	100

Source: Committee on Ways and Means, U.S. House of Representatives, *2000 Green Book,* table 1-20, p. 60.

a. In all years, 62 years is the earliest age at which a worker is eligible to receive retirement benefits, and benefits do not increase with additional delay after age 70.

As the above description indicates, the full benefit age is an important element in calculating a recipient's initial monthly retirement benefit. The full benefit age is the age at which a retiring worker can claim retirement benefits and receive exactly the calculated PIA. The full benefit age was 65 years and 8 months for those turning 62 in 2003, but a reduced retirement benefit can be claimed as early as age 62. Under current law, the full benefit age will gradually increase over time until it reaches age 67 for those turning 62 in 2022 (table 2-2).

As explained above, retired workers who claim benefits before the full benefit age receive an initial monthly benefit that is smaller than the PIA. For example, a retiree initially claiming benefits at exactly age 62 in 2003 would have received a monthly benefit that is 23.33 percent less than the PIA.[7] Monthly benefits are higher than the PIA for workers who claim benefits after the full benefit age. This credit for delayed retirement applies through age 69 and gradually increases until it reaches 8 percent of the PIA for each year benefits are delayed past the full benefit age for those turning 62 in 2005 and thereafter. For example, a 62-year-old in 2003 who waits until age 70 to claim benefits would receive a monthly benefit that is 32.5 percent more than the PIA. After age 70, no additional credit is provided for further delaying benefits.

These adjustments are intended to be roughly actuarially fair. That is, the reductions and increases are intended to ensure that retired workers receive, on average, roughly the same lifetime benefits regardless of the age at which they first claim benefits. The higher monthly benefit offered to a worker who waits to start receiving benefits is calculated so that the additional lifetime benefits received approximately equal, in present value, the benefits forgone while the start of benefits is delayed.

The full benefit age is officially referred to as the "normal retirement age," but that terminology has led to frequent misunderstandings. Under Social Security, retired workers are allowed to elect retirement benefits as early as age 62, and benefits begin automatically once a worker reaches age 70. Furthermore, the full benefit age is not "normal" in any meaningful sense. Indeed, one of the most dramatic trends over the past several decades is the increasing proportion of Social Security beneficiaries who elect to begin receiving benefits at age 62. In 2001 some 54 percent of male workers and 58 percent of female workers (table 2-3) began receiving benefits at age 62. Roughly three-quarters of both men and women began to draw benefits before age 65.

How Benefits for Disabled Workers Are Determined

The determination of benefits for disabled workers is broadly similar to that for retired workers. To qualify as disabled, a worker must be so severely impaired as to be unable to perform any substantial gainful work. To be eligible for disability benefits, the disabled worker must also have worked and been covered by Social Security for a specified minimum period of time, and a sufficient amount of that covered work must have occurred in recent years.

For workers who qualify for disability benefits, the AIME is calculated over the period from age 21 until the worker became disabled, less a specified number of dropout years; this is a shorter period than the thirty-five

Table 2-3. *Workers Making Initial Retirement Benefits Claims by Age at Time of Claim*[a]

Percent of total

Year	Age at initial claim (years)			
	62	63–64	65	66 or older
Men				
1965	16.6	17.0	27.4	39.1
1975	29.2	26.1	36.2	8.5
1985	52.4	23.0	20.9	3.8
1995	55.9	20.2	17.9	6.1
2001	53.6	21.5	20.7	4.1
Women				
1965	33.6	18.7	17.4	30.3
1975	44.9	22.3	23.7	9.1
1985	63.7	18.9	13.4	4.0
1995	61.4	18.5	14.2	5.9
2001	57.6	20.9	14.4	7.2

Source: Social Security Bulletin, *Annual Statistical Supplement,* table 6.B5, and authors' calculations.

a. Figures exclude workers converting from disability benefits to retirement benefits at the full benefit age. Numbers for a given year may not sum to 100 percent because of rounding.

years for workers claiming retirement benefits. The initial monthly benefit for a disabled worker is equal to the PIA regardless of the age at which disability benefits are claimed; unlike retirement benefits, the initial monthly benefit is not adjusted for the age at claiming. As with retirement benefits, however, the benefit is increased each year thereafter for inflation.

How Benefits for Family Members Are Determined

Social Security also provides benefits to the families of covered workers. Like the worker's own benefits, these family benefits are based on the earnings record of the worker who has retired, become disabled, or died, and the specifics of their determination are broadly similar to those for worker benefits.

The following are some examples of family benefits available under Social Security. The spouse of a retired or disabled worker is eligible for a spousal benefit, equal to 50 percent of the worker's PIA, if the spouse has reached the full benefit age or is caring for a disabled child or a child under age 16. A spouse who is between age 62 and the full benefit age may claim a reduced benefit. The spouse of a worker who has died may claim survivor benefits, with the amount depending on both the age at which the surviving spouse claims benefits (the spouse must be at least age 60 if not disabled, or 50 if disabled) and, if relevant, the age at which the deceased worker first claimed benefits. If both the worker and the surviving spouse claimed benefits at the full benefit age, the benefit equals the PIA of the deceased worker. A child under age 18 who survives a deceased worker receives 75 percent of that worker's PIA. There are also benefits for divorced spouses and divorced surviving spouses, provided the previous marriage lasted at least ten years. After family members become eligible, their benefits are increased each year in line with inflation in the same way as other Social Security benefits.

Benefits to family members under Social Security are subject to certain limits, however. One of these applies when a person is eligible both for a family benefit and for a retirement benefit based on his or her own earnings records.[8] In such cases the rule is that the person shall receive a total benefit from all the various types of benefits equal to the largest of any benefits to which he or she is entitled. For example, as noted above, a retired worker's spouse who has never worked receives a spousal benefit equal to one-half of the PIA of the retired worker (assuming that the spouse first claims benefits at the full benefit age). If instead the spouse has worked long enough to be entitled to a retirement benefit based on his or her own earnings record, the total benefit is the larger of that retirement benefit or the spousal benefit. For a spouse with low enough earnings, the result is that work does not increase the total benefit in retirement. Any such work, however, could entitle the spouse to disability benefits if he or she should become disabled, or to retirement benefits if he or she retires before the higher-earning spouse retires.

How Social Security Is Financed

Social Security's central role in providing a financial safety net for American workers clearly has a cost: the benefits paid must be financed somehow. In 2003 Social Security was projected to pay about $475 billion in benefits. Administrative expenses were projected to be an additional $4.3 billion, or roughly 0.9 percent of benefits paid. That same year Social Security expected to collect $555 billion in taxes from the public, resulting in a surplus (excluding interest on the Social Security trust fund) of about $75 billion.

More than 97 percent of that $555 billion in tax revenue comes from a payroll tax on covered workers and their employers. The Social Security payroll tax is currently 12.4 percent of covered wages, legally imposed as a 6.2 percent tax on the employer and a 6.2 percent tax on the employee. Thus, for each $100 that an employee earns, the employer owes $6.20 and the employee owes $6.20. (Self-employed workers pay the full $12.40.) Despite this legal distinction, both economic theory and empirical evidence suggest that the employee effectively pays the full $12.40 in taxes, because the tax imposed on the employer reduces what he or she is willing to pay the employee by approximately the amount of the tax. (Exceptions to this outcome occur when the legal minimum wage is binding and, temporarily, for those with wage contracts when tax rates change.) In other words, if an employer is willing to hire an employee for $100 and pay $6.20 in Social Security taxes, and if the employee is willing to work for that wage, the employer and employee should be willing to agree instead on a wage of approximately $106 if the employee paid the entire Social Security tax.[9]

The Social Security payroll tax is imposed only up to a given level of earnings, called the maximum taxable earnings base, which is adjusted each year in line with growth in average wages. In 2003 the maximum taxable earnings base was $87,000. Social Security payroll taxes are not paid on earnings above that base.[10] Roughly 6 percent of workers covered by Social Security have earnings above the maximum taxable earnings base, and about 85 percent of aggregate earnings in covered employment was taxable (that is, below the maximum taxable earnings level) in 2002.[11] In other words, the untaxed earnings of the 6 percent of workers with earnings above the base (which was $84,900 in 2002) totaled 15 percent of aggregate earnings in that year.

The remainder of Social Security tax revenue comes from the partial taxation of Social Security benefits. Since 1984, a portion of benefits has been subject to federal income tax for those recipients whose income exceeds $25,000 for single taxpayers and $32,000 for married couples filing a joint return. Above these thresholds, up to 50 percent of benefits is included in taxable income if the income measure is below $34,000 for singles or $44,000 for joint filers. For those with higher incomes, legislation enacted in 1993 increased the maximum inclusion rate to 85 percent of benefits. Most of the revenue generated from the taxation of Social Security benefits is credited to the Social Security trust fund, but the additional revenue generated from the 1993 provision is credited to the Medicare Hospital Insurance Trust Fund. Because the above dollar thresholds are not indexed to inflation, the partial taxation of benefits is expected to play a growing role in the financing of Social Security and Medicare's Hospital Insurance program. Nonetheless, payroll tax revenue will remain overwhelmingly the predominant source of Social Security financing.

In addition to the $555 billion in tax revenue credited to Social Security in 2003, the Social Security trust fund was credited with roughly $90 billion in interest earnings. Since the early 1980s, Social Security has been running cash flow surpluses, which have been credited to a trust fund whose holdings now amount to more than $1.5 trillion.[12] The broader implications of the trust fund are controversial, and we defer further discussion of that topic to chapter 3. What is not controversial, however, is that Social Security will face increasing financial pressure in the future, and that without legislated changes the trust fund is extremely likely to be exhausted at some point over the next seventy-five years.

Conclusion

Social Security's success as a social insurance program is attributable to several basic features of the system. It provides participants with a well-defined, assured basic income that is protected against inflation, the risk of outliving one's assets, and financial market fluctuations. It is progressive, providing larger annual benefits (relative to previous wages) for lower earners than for higher earners. And it provides families with insurance against the disability or death of a wage earner, in addition to retirement benefits.

Because benefits for retired workers, for children whose parents have died, for disabled workers, for surviving spouses, and for other beneficiaries are all tied to the same Social Security benefit formula, changes to that formula intended to reduce retirement benefits would have the consequence of proportionately reducing benefits for these other beneficiaries, including many of the most vulnerable in society. Furthermore, as this chapter has documented, most elderly and disabled beneficiaries receive the majority of their income from Social Security. These two facts underscore the importance of designing reforms carefully to preserve Social Security as a cost-effective social insurance program.

3 Goals for Social Security Reform

S ocial Security is a huge and complex program, serving an array of purposes and affecting the lives of the vast majority of Americans. It plays a central role in the nation's retirement system, its social insurance system, and the federal budget. But the program also faces a long-term deficit and is in need of updating—the last significant reform of Social Security was two decades ago. Any such reform must strike an appropriate balance among many competing goals. This chapter examines five such goals: restoring Social Security to a sound financial footing, reducing the future burden from Social Security on the rest of the federal budget, sharing the ongoing costs of the program's past generosity in a fair manner, preserving and strengthening the program's social insurance functions, and ensuring that, on balance, the changes enhance the overall performance of the economy.

Putting Social Security on a Sound Financial Footing

Because Social Security faces a long-term deficit, the first task of any reform must be to restore fiscal soundness to

27

the program. The first question is what definition of "fiscal soundness" to apply.

Current Official Projections

The basis for evaluating the fiscal soundness of Social Security is a set of projections of the program's annual cash flows, done each year by the Office of the Chief Actuary of the Social Security Administration.[1] Figure 3-1 shows such a projection, taken from the 2003 annual report of the Social Security trustees.

The curve labeled "income rate" in figure 3-1 reports the tax revenue that, according to the projections, will be credited to Social Security in each year from now through 2080, as a share of projected taxable payroll in that year. (Taxable payroll is the aggregate value of earnings that will be subject to payroll taxation. This denominator is used because if the figures were presented in dollars, whether nominal or adjusted for inflation, the numbers spread over such a long period would be so staggering that it would be hard to make sense of them.) The curve excludes the interest earned on the Treasury bonds held in the Social Security trust fund. The curve labeled "cost rate" reports for each year the projected value of benefits paid to retirees, survivors, disabled workers, and their families, along with administrative costs, also as a share of projected taxable payroll. The cost rate reflects the full cost of providing benefits according to the benefit formulas in current law; this benefit projection is often referred to as "scheduled benefits."[2]

The figure reveals a fact that is familiar to students of Social Security: by 2018, under current law, scheduled benefits under Social Security will exceed the program's projected revenue. The reason is that although revenue is projected to change little relative to taxable payroll, in part because the payroll tax rate is not scheduled to change under current law,[3] expenditure is projected to rise sharply as the baby-boomers retire and to continue rising less steeply thereafter. This increase is mitigated somewhat by the provision, legislated in 1983, for a gradual increase in the full benefit age (see chapter 2). Chapter 4 discusses the causes of this long-term deficit in more detail.

Given the annual cash flow projection shown in figure 3-1, it is a matter of simple arithmetic to project the future balance of the Social

Figure 3-1. *Projected Cost and Income Rates, 2003–80*[a]

Percent of taxable payroll

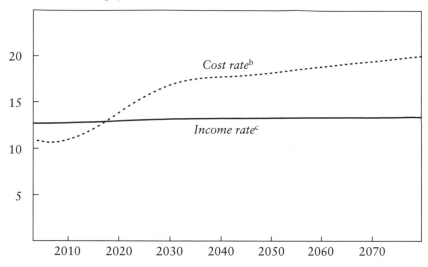

Source: *2003 Annual Report of the Board of Trustees of the Federal Old-Age and Survivors Insurance and Disability Insurance Trust Funds,* March 2003.
a. Projections are based on the Social Security trustees' intermediate cost assumptions.
b. Benefits plus administrative costs as a share of taxable payroll.
c. Tax revenue as a share of taxable payroll.

Security trust fund. From its current balance of roughly $1.5 trillion, the trust fund is projected to first rise and then fall, reaching zero in 2042. That is, under Social Security's intermediate cost projection, the revenue anticipated under current law plus the existing trust fund balance is not sufficient to cover all of the program's anticipated expenditure—benefits and administrative costs—beyond 2042.

At that time, however, revenue from payroll taxes and the income taxation of benefits would still be sufficient to cover 73 percent of projected expenditure. That fraction then declines slowly to 65 percent in 2077. Thus, although some observers refer to the "bankruptcy" of Social Security, in fact a substantial revenue flow would still be dedicated to Social Security even after the trust fund is exhausted. Thus concerns that there will be nothing from Social Security for future generations are misplaced.

Even so, everyone agrees that a serious political problem arises when the trust fund reaches zero: at that point, the system cannot pay all promised benefits given the existing revenue structure.

Some observers have argued that the problem arrives much sooner than that, when the flow of revenue from taxes first falls short of annual expenditure in 2018. We see no basis for attaching any significance to such a date, however, and are unaware of any rigorous presentation of an argument for why that date represents a crisis. A full discussion of this issue requires reviewing the pattern and meaning of cash flows between Social Security and the rest of the federal budget. We defer that discussion to appendix A at the end of this volume.

Seventy-Five-Year Actuarial Balance

The annual cash flow projections and the current level of the trust fund can be used to compute an "actuarial balance" figure. This measure reflects the degree to which the current trust fund and projected revenue over some period are sufficient to finance projected costs. The period conventionally chosen is seventy-five years. When the projection shows insufficient resources to pay scheduled benefits over that period, the Office of the Chief Actuary calculates what level of additional resources would be sufficient to close the gap and leave the trust fund with a projected balance (considered a "precautionary balance") equal to projected expenditure in the first year after at the end of the period.[4] This measure of the actuarial deficit, presented as a percentage of taxable payroll over the next seventy-five years, is the key traditional criterion for evaluating Social Security's finances.[5] One interpretation of this number is that it indicates what payroll tax increase would be sufficient to finance benefits over the seventy-five-year horizon (and leave a precautionary balance as defined above), provided the increase began immediately and remained in force for the full seventy-five years.

In the 2003 trustees' report, the actuarial imbalance was 1.92 percent of taxable payroll. However, reporting the imbalance in this way is not meant to recommend that the payroll tax rate be raised by this amount. Rather, it is a way of summarizing the magnitude of the financial difficulties at hand. People may disagree about whether a shortfall of 1.9 percent of taxable payroll is a large problem or a small one, but it is a

Box 3-1. *The Seventy-Five-Year Actuarial Balance in Dollars at Present Value*

For some purposes, it is useful to express the seventy-five-year actuarial imbalance in dollars rather than as a share of taxable payroll. But the Office of the Chief Actuary never reports a projected actuarial balance based simply on adding up revenue needs, in dollars, in different years. Instead it reports, in dollars, the present discounted value of the actuarial imbalance, in addition to reporting the imbalance as a share of payroll. For example, 1.92 percent of payroll, the actuarial imbalance in the 2003 report, corresponds to $3.8 trillion in present discounted value. In other words, if $3.8 trillion were set aside today, the principal plus interest (accruing at a Treasury bond interest rate) would be just enough to cover the projected shortfall over the next seventy-five years. Such a present discounted value calculation recognizes the time value of money: with a positive interest rate, a dollar received today is much more valuable than a dollar received seventy-five years from now. To put that $3.8 trillion number in perspective, GDP in 2002 was more than $10 trillion; thus the actuarial imbalance was roughly equal to one-third of one year's GDP at the beginning of the projection period.

Expressing the actuarial imbalance in dollars facilitates comparisons with other government actions that would have long-run financial effects, such as permanent income or estate tax cuts. For example, the 2001 and 2003 tax cuts, if continued over the next seventy-five years, would reduce revenue by about $12 trillion in present value, or roughly three times Social Security's actuarial imbalance over the same period.*

*See Peter Orszag, Richard Kogan, and Robert Greenstein, "The Administration's Tax Cuts and the Long-Term Budget Outlook," Center on Budget and Policy Priorities, March 19, 2003, for related estimates.

straightforward way to present the problem. (See box 3-1 for another measure of the actuarial imbalance.)

One of the primary goals of a Social Security reform plan should be to achieve seventy-five-year actuarial balance. But this should not be accomplished through the "magic asterisk" approach of simply assuming transfers from the rest of the budget (discussed in the next section). Nor should one adopt the deceptive approach of using the higher expected returns on stocks relative to bonds (discussed further in box 3-2) to eliminate the projected deficit.

Box 3-2. *Actuarial Balance over the Very Long Run*

Alternative measures of the long-term actuarial imbalance can be computed for periods that extend beyond the conventional seventy-five years. Indeed, the Office of the Chief Actuary has itself calculated a measure of the imbalance that sets no horizon at all. That calculation finds that, if the present discounted value of the shortfall is calculated for the indefinite future, the imbalance amounts to $10.5 trillion, or about 4 percent of taxable payroll over the indefinite future. That is more than 2 1/2 times the present value in dollars of the imbalance over the next seventy-five years ($3.8 trillion, as noted in box 3-1), and twice as large as the seventy-five-year imbalance as a share of payroll. (Similarly projected over an indefinite horizon, the 2001 and 2003 tax cuts reduce revenue by more than $15 trillion in present value.) The fact that the imbalance is much larger over an infinite horizon reflects several factors, including continuing increases in life expectancy.

Calculation of the imbalance over the indefinite future does provide useful information, but a key question is what horizon policymakers should adopt for the purpose of evaluating reform. Despite some theoretical attraction of the indefinite future or "permanent" imbalance measure, using it as the primary measure of Social Security's deficit would prove problematic in practice. The legislative process invariably places heavy weight on certain summary statistics, such as actuarial balance. If that balance is defined over an indefinite future, it could place excessive importance on what will happen in the more-distant (and harder to predict) future than on what will happen in the near future. Focusing exclusively on

---

The traditional use of a seventy-five-year horizon for measuring long-term balance in Social Security has recently come under attack from opposite directions: some would like to shorten the projection period, whereas others would like to extend it considerably. The choice of projection period in fact involves a trade-off. Ideally, it should be long enough to make sure Congress does not slight the valid concerns of future generations, but not so long that Congress is forced to address problems that, because of inaccuracies in the projections, may well never arise. It seems to us that a seventy-five-year projection period is a good compromise between these two concerns.

Plans that fail to achieve seventy-five-year actuarial balance may or may not include beneficial changes to the program, but they do not put Social Security on a firm long-term financial footing. Reforming Social

a very long horizon may also make it easier to employ gimmicks in order to achieve balance. For example, a massive tax rate increase scheduled for the years 2150 and beyond may technically be able to address the permanent imbalance, but it would be widely and correctly seen as having no credibility.* Besides, there is no reason for today's policymakers to try to fix Social Security once and for all time—future Congresses can and should respond to changing circumstances, and the legislative process today should give far more weight to concerns emerging 35 years from now than 135 years from now.

To be sure, longer projection horizons are beneficial for some purposes. They can alert us to serious drawbacks in reform proposals that might otherwise pass muster. But they should not play the central role in the political decisions to be made about Social Security's finances.

---

*Such a proposal might restore long-term balance to Social Security, but it would not pass the "test of long-range actuarial balance," which compares the balance over each of several subperiods from the present out to the seventy-five-year horizon against a deviation from balance that is deemed allowable for that subperiod. (For a discussion of this test, see 2003 *Annual Report of the Board of Trustees of the Federal Old-Age and Survivors Insurance and Disability Insurance Trust Funds,* hereafter referred to as the 2003 Trustees' Report, pp. 63–65.) Actuarial balance over seventy-five years (or solvency over seventy-five years) is neither necessary nor sufficient to meet this test.

Security is a difficult and complicated task. Policymakers are unlikely to be willing to undertake substantial reforms to the program every year or even every few years. It is therefore important that, when a reform is chosen and implemented, it puts the system on a sound basis for an extended period. Furthermore, today's workers deserve to have some sense of the program's structure in the future, so that they can plan for their own retirement and other financial needs. The seventy-five-year horizon provides a reasonable approximation to the life span of workers just entering the labor force: a 20-year-old worker today, for example, has less than a 5 percent chance of living past 95. Failing to achieve seventy-five-year solvency would leave too much uncertainty about the future course of the program. But extending the central measure of actuarial balance beyond seventy-five years also has its downside (box 3-2).

A final reason for retaining the seventy-five-year projection horizon is that, despite the recent criticisms, this traditional measure enjoys a surprising degree of bipartisan support among policymakers. Such bipartisan consensus is rare in the Social Security debate. Even if the optimal projection period were slightly shorter or slightly longer, any gains from changing it may not be worth opening up the Pandora's box of argument over precisely what that projection period should be.

The Terminal-Year Problem

Merely restoring seventy-five-year actuarial balance while preserving the current structure of Social Security's benefits and revenue would result in the reappearance of a seventy-five-year imbalance as the projection window rolls forward in time. This phenomenon is referred to as the "terminal-year problem." For example, the seventy-five-year window for the 2003 projections extends from 2003 through 2077. For the 2004 projection, the actual outcome in 2003 will be included in the initial trust fund balance, and the seventy-five-year window for the projection will shift to 2004 through 2078. The year 2003 will have been a year of positive cash flow for the system. But because retirees in the future are expected to live longer, and because the system is still transitioning to the effects of lower fertility and immigration rates (resulting in slower growth of the labor force), 2078 is projected to have a negative net cash flow. Thus the effect of adding 2078 is to increase the seventy-five-year actuarial imbalance.

The terminal-year problem can also be seen from figure 3-1: as the figure shows, the cost rate continues to rise over time, even after the last baby-boomers have died.[6] The higher cost rate reflects the ongoing increases in the life expectancy of retirees and the lagged effects of declines in fertility and immigration rates, noted above. The terminal-year problem results from the combination of these factors.

There are two ways to address the terminal-year problem. One is simply to move beyond a seventy-five-year horizon for the projections. As we explain in box 3-2, however, that approach raises problems of its own because of the important role played by the central actuarial projection in political discussions of reform plans. An alternative approach, and the one we prefer, is to continue using a seventy-five-year projection but to design reforms in a way that mitigates or eliminates the terminal-year problem as an issue.[7] For example, policymakers could aim to more than restore actuarial balance over seventy-five years (that is, to create an actuarial surplus). Then, if the balance becomes a little worse the following year, it may nonetheless remain positive. An even better approach would change some of the rules governing Social Security's benefit and revenue provisions, so that the cost rate and the income rate have more similar shapes over time. If the structure of Social Security were changed, policymakers could retain the seventy-five-year horizon, and the mere passage of time would not necessarily reintroduce an actuarial imbalance.

The bottom line is that any thorough reform of Social Security should restore seventy-five-year actuarial balance. Further, if the reform addresses the underlying causes of the terminal-year problem, there is no reason to extend the actuarial balance requirement beyond seventy-five years.[8]

Avoiding Burdens on the Rest of the Federal Budget

Merely restoring long-term financial balance to Social Security is not sufficient: Social Security reform should also avoid imposing burdens on the rest of the federal budget.[9] The nation faces substantial fiscal problems over the coming decades. The aging of the baby-boomers and lengthening life spans generally will place increasing pressure on the budget, not only through Social Security, but also in programs such as Medicare and Medicaid.[10] The projected long-term deficits in Medicare and Medicaid are indeed much larger than that in Social Security, and those programs will be harder to reform than Social Security because they may ultimately require far-reaching changes in the nation's system of health care.

In this context, claiming to restore long-term balance to Social Security in a manner that depends on substantial, unspecified transfers from general revenue amounts to a massive "magic asterisk."[11] Indeed, Congress could ostensibly erase the long-term deficit in Social Security without any other changes simply by legislating that the trust fund may draw upon general revenue as needed to finance scheduled benefits.[12] If no other budget changes were made, however, such legislation would raise serious questions about how the general revenue transfers could be financed when the need arrived. Since substantial deficits are forecast outside Social Security, simply assuming the availability of large transfers is highly problematic and could be regarded as fiscally reckless. The assumed transfers would put excessive pressure on the rest of the budget at a time when projections suggest the rest of the budget will be under extreme pressure.

Similarly, it might be proposed that revenue be made available for Social Security by diverting specific existing revenue sources away from the rest of the budget. Such proposals could amount to an accounting shell game, although the analysis is more complicated here because it depends on the alternative use of the funds. For example, a portion of the revenue from the taxation of Social Security benefits currently accrues to the Medicare system; transferring that revenue back to Social Security would, without other changes, only add to the large financial hole in Medicare.[13]

The complication in the analysis arises with regard to current revenue sources that may be reduced or eliminated through tax cuts in the future. For example, under legislation passed in 2001, the estate tax is currently scheduled to be repealed in 2010 and then, in 2011, to revert to the form in which it existed before the legislation was passed. The Bush administration and many members of Congress have proposed extending the estate tax repeal beyond 2010. If any estate tax revenue after 2010 were dedicated to Social Security, the rest of the budget would be held harmless if the alternative were repealing the estate tax after 2010. It would, however, harm the rest of the federal budget if the alternative were that the estate tax would be retained and used for general budgetary needs.

A similar argument could be made for the recent reductions in income tax rates, which are currently temporary but may become permanent. Since these tax cuts may not last beyond 2010, transferring the revenue from them to Social Security after that date may or may not affect the financial strength of the federal government to meet its other obligations, again depending on what the alternative is.

Inevitably, there is some uncertainty about the effects of Social Security reform on the rest of the budget, in part because the actual effect depends on how policymakers respond in the future to various changes made now. But, again, the principle at stake here is that Social Security reform should avoid placing burdens on the non–Social Security budget. To evaluate whether this principle is met in practice, it is important to compare realistic projections of the non–Social Security budget both with and without the proposed Social Security reform. Such an evaluation, for example, would require judgments regarding whether the repeal of the estate tax would be continued past 2010.

In general, the analysis is more straightforward with regard to new sources of revenue. Restoring actuarial balance to Social Security through decreases in future benefits or increases in payroll tax revenue, for example, would basically hold harmless the federal government's ability to fulfill its other goals. A similar conclusion holds for proposals to introduce a new federal tax dedicated to Social Security.[14] Even here, however, one would need to consider whether the new tax might have been introduced anyway and not dedicated to Social Security. In the end, evaluating proposed reforms on this principle requires some degree of political judgment.

Sharing the Legacy Debt Burden Fairly

The first generations of Social Security beneficiaries, including those receiving benefits today, received much larger benefits than could have been financed from the value of their contributions plus the returns on those contributions at a market rate of interest. As the next chapter explains in more detail, this history has left all subsequent generations with a "legacy debt" that must be financed. Later generations of recipients will finance that legacy debt through having to accept benefits that are lower than could have been financed by their contributions plus accumulated returns. We refer to the cost of financing the legacy debt in this way as the "legacy cost" of Social Security.

Social Security's legacy debt is similar in many ways to the explicit public debt. The public debt reflects the accumulated difference between spending and revenue from the beginning of the nation to the present; because spending has exceeded revenue in the past, we are left with a public debt. The cost of financing that public debt requires some combination of higher taxes and lower spending in the future than would have been necessary in the absence of the public debt. So, too, the legacy debt within Social Security reflects the accumulated difference between benefits and revenue for previous and current beneficiaries; the cost of financing that debt will require some combination of higher taxes and lower benefits than the system could otherwise afford for future generations. Social Security reforms, unless they reduce benefits for current retirees (which no one today is seriously proposing), will have only modest effects on the size of the legacy debt.[15] With the size of the legacy debt thus largely already determined, the type of reform enacted will instead determine how the resultant legacy cost is spread across generations.[16] In other words, how actuarial balance is restored will determine how the costs of the program's legacy debt are shared.

As one extreme example, imagine that benefits in the years after 2042 (when the trust fund is projected to be exhausted) are reduced so that they just equal incoming payroll revenue at the existing tax rate. Such an approach would pass most of the legacy debt along to distant generations. The reduction in benefits for those distant generations would have to be substantial, because little of the legacy debt would have been paid down in the meanwhile. At the other extreme, imagine that taxes are raised on current workers by enough to eliminate the entire legacy debt within a generation. Such an approach would transform Social Security into a fully funded system. It would leave generations in the distant future with no legacy debt, but it would impose a substantial burden on the transition generation.

Social Security reform should reflect a balance in the financing of the system's legacy debt between these two extremes of paying off the entire debt immediately and shifting all of it to future generations. The "appropriate" balance between them is clearly a subjective matter, but, as we see it, a sensible balance should reflect three principles:

—First, each generation should pay, over its lifetime, a legacy cost that is roughly similar, as a share of its total earnings, to that paid by other generations.

—Second, each generation should pay a legacy cost sufficient to stabilize the ratio of legacy debt to taxable payroll over time. As noted above, one analogy for thinking about the legacy debt is the nation's public debt. A country's ability to service its public debt depends on its national income and its citizens' willingness to pay taxes on that income. At a time of large deficits, stabilizing the ratio of public debt to income over time is a sensible initial goal. So, too, stabilizing the ratio of the legacy debt to taxable payroll over time is a sensible goal.

—Third, all workers within a generation should share in the legacy cost. Here the problem is that some groups are not covered by Social Security, and therefore do not currently bear a fair share of the legacy cost.

Evaluating how a reform would finance the legacy debt underscores one of the problems with relying on general revenue transfers not backed by a dedicated revenue source to restore actuarial balance. Compared with a reform without such transfers, the transfers must ultimately result in some combination of higher taxes in the future, reduced government services in the future, or higher fiscal deficits in the future (which would effectively push the legacy debt even further into the future). Which of these options is chosen has important implications for who bears the ultimate burden of the legacy debt. Unspecified general revenue transfers thus blur the distribution of that cost, and this further argues against financing Social Security reform in this manner.

Preserving and Improving the Social Insurance Character of Social Security

Reform should preserve and improve Social Security's important social insurance functions. After all, actuarial balance could be trivially achieved through the extreme step of eliminating the Social Security program—benefits and taxes alike. Guaranteeing financial balance thus does not guarantee that Social Security will continue to serve its social purpose of providing a basic, assured level of financial security during retirement or disability or after the death of a family's wage earner. Chapter 2 stressed how Social Security's structure provides beneficiaries with an income that is protected against inflation, the risk of outliving one's assets, and financial market fluctuations. Preserving and improving Social Security's role as a provider of social insurance involves several dimensions.

Accounting for Risk

The life and career experiences of workers and their families differ greatly both one from another and over time. Most of us do not and cannot know what is in store for us in the future. As was discussed in chapter 2, social insurance can therefore be very useful in mitigating the risks associated with our careers and other life experiences, when these may not turn out as we expect. Any reform of Social Security should ensure that it continues to provide benefits in a manner that protects workers in the face of significant individual uncertainty, and that reflects America's diverse population.

One type of risk involves individual experiences in the labor market. As people age, some find that work becomes more difficult and the opportunities for work more limited, while others find work ever more exciting and lucrative. Some people learn that they are not likely to live to a very old age, whereas others become increasingly optimistic about their chances of survival. Wages for some professions rise unexpectedly over time; others decline unexpectedly. The current structure of Social Security mitigates the effects of these individual labor market risks on income in retirement, both through its progressive benefit formula and because benefits are based on some but not all of a worker's historical earnings.[17] Social Security also offers a wide range of possible retirement ages, while relating benefits to retirement age in a way that neither punishes early retirement excessively nor rewards late retirement excessively.[18]

Another type of risk involves financial markets. People in general appear to be very sensitive to changes in their income or wealth that occur after they have formed their expectations, and possibly their plans, about retirement. To examine the magnitude of such changes under a system of individual accounts, Gary Burtless of the Brookings Institution studied the replacement rates that workers would have achieved if they had invested 2 percent of their earnings in stock index funds each year over a forty-year work career and converted the accumulated balance to a nominal retirement annuity upon reaching age 62. (A nominal retirement annuity would provide regular payments in retirement for the life of the retired worker, but the payments would not be indexed to inflation as Social Security benefits are.) Burtless found that these replacement rates would vary greatly over time. Workers reaching age 62 in 1968 would have enjoyed an initial 39 percent replacement rate of their peak career wage upon retirement; that is, the annual annuity payment in the first year of retirement would have equaled 39 percent of their highest previous annual earnings. By contrast, the initial replacement rate for workers retiring in 1974—only six years later—would have been only 17 percent, or less than half as much. A worker who retired in March 2000 would have received an initial replacement rate of 39 percent, but a worker retiring in March 2001 would have received a replacement rate of just 25 percent; in this case the replacement rate thus fell more than one-third in just twelve months.[19]

Shifting to individuals the financial market risks associated with providing, as Social Security does, the foundation of retirement income would thus be a mistake. A defined-benefit system, like the current Social Security system, instead spreads the risks across a broader population, because asset returns (such as those on the Treasury bonds held by the trust fund) affect Social Security as a whole, leaving time for adjustment and room to change later benefits and taxes for many generations, not just those holding the assets and nearing retirement. (See box 3-3 for a discussion of how stock market returns should be "scored" in assessing proposals for Social Security reform.)

Aggregate economic and demographic developments are not fully predictable and so also involve risk. Social Security does not make such aggregate risks disappear. It does, however, offer a mechanism for adjusting how those risks are borne in a way that is different from how they would be allocated in the absence of Social Security.

A final source of risk has been dubbed "political risk." For any system of retirement income, future legislative action affecting that system is uncertain. Perhaps the greatest uncertainty comes from having a system that is not in long-term actuarial balance, as is the case today. Workers know that Congress is likely to make some changes in currently legislated tax and benefit rules, because projected benefits under the current rules exceed projected revenue. But workers have little basis for predicting *how* Congress will restore actuarial balance. That is, failing to restore long-term actuarial balance within Social Security leaves current workers more uncertain about the future evolution of taxes and benefits than if actuarial balance were restored. Legislating a credible, sustainable plan that restores actuarial balance would thus greatly reduce political risk.[20]

When, instead, the point of departure is an actuarially balanced system, political risk becomes a more subtle concept. In particular, given actuarial balance, it is not clear whether the possibility of further legislation should be viewed as a political risk to be minimized or as a political hedge or safeguard to be preserved. The possibility of adapting Social

Box 3-3. *Stock Market Returns and Actuarial Solvency*

The actuarial scoring of Social Security reform plans is important in helping policymakers evaluate options and make good decisions. The methodology for such scoring has been developed over many years, and the Office of the Chief Actuary at Social Security enjoys bipartisan respect and support.

New reform proposals naturally raise questions as to how they will be scored and whether the method of scoring provides accurate input to the political decisionmaking process. For example, consider the proposal, embraced by both the Clinton administration and one faction of the 1994–1996 Advisory Council on Social Security, to allow the Social Security trust fund to invest in stocks rather than only in Treasury bonds as at present.

When the Office of the Chief Actuary scores the effect of such a proposed change in the trust fund's portfolio, its central projection reflects the expected return on stocks but makes no adjustment for the greater riskiness of stocks than of bonds. As explained in chapter 8, most if not all of the higher expected returns to stocks reflects that greater risk. The vast majority of economists would argue that, in reporting the projections, at least some adjustment should be made for this increased risk, and alternative actuarial projections produced by the Office of the Chief Actuary do make rough adjustments. The political process, however, relies mostly on the central forecast. In that forecast, allowing trust fund investment in stocks reduces the actuarial deficit simply by raising the projected rate of return on the trust fund. This scoring, in our opinion, makes stock investments seem more attractive than they really are from society's perspective.

A similar argument applies to any proposal that links Social Security in any way to the return earned on individual accounts. (See chapter 8 for some of the mechanisms through which this might be done.)

The bottom line is that we think actuarial balance should be restored without counting the added return from stocks in the central estimate. Alternative projections could then show the effects of higher expected returns from stocks without this adjustment for risk.

To be clear, even though we do not include them in our plan, we do favor some proposals to explicitly or implicitly invest part of the trust fund in the stock market. Social Security has the ability to absorb some stock market risks through adjustments in benefits and revenue. However, we do not think that the higher expected returns from such investment should be used to reduce the amount of actuarial imbalance to be corrected by tax and benefit changes. That is, actuarial balance, in our view, should be restored without counting any gain from investment in equities rather than Treasury bonds. We would continue to embrace such proposals even if the Office of the Chief Actuary were to score stock returns as if they were bond returns. Such proposals may make sense, but they should not be presented as a free lunch.

Security to changing circumstances in the future may actually make it *more* valuable to society, not less. Thus it should not necessarily be viewed as a "risk," with the negative connotations thereby implied. In particular, it is important to distinguish changes that respond merely to shifts in political circumstances from changes that respond to shifts in the underlying economic or demographic circumstances. If Social Security's long-term actuarial deficit were eliminated, only the response to shifts in political power would truly represent political risk.

Furthermore, any such "political risks" are not unique to Social Security. They also arise in our private tax-preferred retirement system and in the individual accounts systems that have replaced defined-benefit social security programs in other countries. For example, Chile has altered the rules governing its individual accounts system several times, and here in the United States the rules governing 401(k) plans and Individual Retirement Accounts (IRAs) have been revised almost continuously.[21] Although none of these changes has seriously harmed future retirees, neither have the financial circumstances been such as to require large responses in these cases. In contrast, in the recent Argentine crisis, individual social security accounts were tapped to help close the government budget deficit. To be sure, the likely political outcomes may vary with the basic structure of the system. But the point is that Social Security is not alone in being subject to political risk, and the extent of any difference in the exposure to such risk between Social Security and alternative retirement systems is unclear.

Replacement Rates at Retirement

One partial measure of the strength of Social Security's social insurance is its replacement rate, or the share of a worker's previous earnings replaced by Social Security benefits in retirement. Under existing legislation, replacement rates are already scheduled to fall between now and 2025, because of the scheduled rise in the full benefit age, for any given age at retirement, as noted in chapter 2. Table 3-1 shows the replacement rate for medium earners retiring at age 65 in different years. (Medium earners are those with career-average earnings about equal to the average wage in the economy.)

Table 3-1 does not take into account other factors affecting the adequacy of Social Security benefits, including the changing income taxation

Table 3-1. *Replacement Rates under Current Law for Medium Earners Retiring at Age 65*
Percent of previous earnings

Worker's age in 2004[a]	Year worker reaches age 65	Replacement rate
55	2014	39.0
45	2024	36.7
35	2034	36.2
25	2044	36.2
15	2054	36.3
5	2064	36.3
0	2069	36.3

Source: *2003 Annual Report of the Board of Trustees of the Federal Old-Age and Survivors Insurance and Disability Insurance Trust Funds,* March 2003, table VI.F11.
a. The worker reaches the indicated age sometime during 2004.

of benefits over time or the rising projected premiums for Medicare part B, which are subtracted from the Social Security checks paid to beneficiaries who are also covered by Medicare.[22] As a calculation for a hypothetical single worker, table 3-1 also does not reflect the evolving diversity in earnings histories or in marriage and divorce patterns. Finally, because the calculation is done for workers of a single age at retirement (65), it does not reflect the possibility of an increase in average replacement rates as a result of longer careers. The table does, however, give a sense of where the system is heading.

Providing more revenue for Social Security beyond the existing 12.4 percent payroll tax (and the existing income taxation of benefits) would allow replacement rates to be raised. An important link thus exists between providing resources to Social Security and ensuring that the program meets its social purpose of providing an adequate core level of financial security in time of need.

Given the projected imbalance in Social Security, one perspective on this link is provided by asking what fraction of the actuarial deficit should be closed through additional revenue and what fraction should be closed by reducing benefits.[23] There is no hard and fast rule for striking this balance; any successful reform will have to forge a compromise among the widely diverse views on this topic. Indeed, the need for a suitable compromise is one of the lessons from the success of the balanced 1983 reform of Social Security that we think important to bear in mind. In our view, a successful reform must involve both benefit reductions and revenue increases in restoring long-term balance to Social Security. Relying exclusively on one or the other would be misguided.

Protecting the Most Vulnerable

Social Security has many features that provide relatively larger benefits to those with particular needs. Yet even with this progressive benefit structure, some groups continue to have significantly greater financial difficulties in retirement or at other times of potential financial danger than does the general population of beneficiaries. Analysts have identified several such groups.

Despite Social Security's protections, surviving spouses tend to have significantly greater financial needs (and higher poverty rates) than they experienced when still part of a couple.[24] Disabled workers and their families also have higher poverty rates than nondisabled retirees.[25] Some workers have had long careers with low earnings in jobs covered by Social Security yet live in poverty during retirement. Some people, particularly women, have short careers because of time spent caring for children or because they enter the labor force late after a divorce; as a result, they, too, tend to have high poverty rates.[26]

A number of reform proposals would bolster benefits for each of these groups. Helping the needy in this way has costs, however, and so requires either revenue increases or benefit reductions in the rest of the program. Social Security reform thus should include protections for the most needy, but any such protections should be targeted as efficiently as possible to relieve hardship at the least cost.[27]

Improving Macroeconomic Performance

A final set of objectives for Social Security reform is to improve the overall performance of the American economy. That typically involves two dimensions: encouraging more work effort and raising national saving.

Labor Market Incentives

Any system of social security will affect the work effort ("labor supply" in economists' terms) of workers both young and old. Indeed, the goal of Social Security should not be to avoid influencing labor supply at all, but rather to strike a good balance between these effects on labor supply and the adequate provision of social insurance. Beyond a minimal level, it is usually possible to provide more social insurance only at the cost of weakened work incentives.[28] In other words, any real-world system of social insurance distorts work incentives; the key question is whether the benefits of additional social insurance are worth the additional costs of distorted incentives. Currently, Social Security does a reasonably good job of striking this balance, especially in comparison with some European systems.

The current Social Security system affects both the incentives of younger workers to work and the choice of older workers of when to retire (see box 3-4).[29] The labor supply of younger workers is influenced by the obligation to pay payroll taxes and the anticipation of future benefits. Retirement timing incentives are affected by several factors: the age at which retirement benefits can first be claimed, the rules for adjusting monthly benefits for the age at which they begin, the link from additional work to possibly higher benefits, the presence of auxiliary benefits (such as the spousal benefit), and the rule that a beneficiary receives the largest of any benefit to which he or she is entitled.

The evidence suggests that the effects of Social Security on work effort are real, but they do not involve substantial losses in economic efficiency. In particular, empirical studies of the impact of Social Security on labor supply have generally found an effect on retirement timing decisions, but the overall labor supply distortions are generally small.[30] These costs seem worth bearing in order to preserve the social insurance protections available under the current system.

In summary, the effects of a Social Security reform on work incentives are an important criterion to be used in evaluating reforms, but they must be weighed against the effects of any changes in the social insurance the system provides. In designing reforms, it is particularly important to preserve a structure in which the system is roughly actuarially fair, so that delayed retirement does not impose significant financial penalties.

National Saving

Social Security reform also affects macroeconomic performance through its effect on national saving. The issue of how generous a Social Security system the nation can afford in the future comes down in part to the nation's ability to produce more goods and services in the future. A Social Security burden that appears onerous under one projection for future national income will appear less so if national income is projected to be, say, 10 or 20 percent higher. The future size of the economy depends on many factors, but one of the most crucial is how much Americans save and invest between now and then. Higher national saving increases the size of the capital stock owned by Americans, and that larger capital stock increases future national income. There are many ways in which the federal government can increase national saving; Social Security is just one of these.[31]

Increasing national saving, however, requires a reduction in aggregate consumption in a full-employment economy. Aggregate consumption, in turn, can be lowered by reducing Social Security benefits or by increasing Social Security taxes, provided these legislated changes are not fully offset by changes in the rest of the budget or elsewhere. Since restoring actuarial balance to Social Security is bound to include some degree of revenue increases or benefit reductions, any reform that legitimately restores balance to the program will also add to national saving. Proposed reforms will differ in how much they would contribute to national saving through higher taxes and how much they would contribute through reduced benefits, and in when these actions would take effect.

Many proposed Social Security reforms appear to raise national saving by far more than they actually would. To understand why, we must first deal with some confusing semantics. Many reformers talk of "prefunding" Social Security benefits, but prefunding can mean either of two different things.[32] In its narrow sense, prefunding means that a pension system is accumulating assets against future projected payments. In a broader sense, however, prefunding means increasing national saving.

The difficulty is that prefunding in the narrow sense need not imply prefunding in the broader sense, and vice versa. For example, consider a system of individual accounts that is prefunded in the narrow sense. In such a system, individuals would hold assets in their retirement accounts

Box 3-4. *Social Security, Reform, and Labor Supply*

Social Security affects work incentives only to the extent that it induces participants to do things they would not have done in the absence of the program. For example, if Social Security merely collected taxes from workers during their careers and then returned all of the taxes paid, plus a market rate of return, when the workers retired, the system would not necessarily have any effect on the behavior of workers if they would have saved the same amounts (or more) in the absence of Social Security. Such a system could, however, affect work effort if the program mandated saving more than workers would have saved in the program's absence.* Indeed, the goal of Social Security is to ensure a foundation for income after the retirement, death, or disability of a worker, especially for those who would not have saved enough for a reasonably comfortable retirement and would not have purchased sufficient life and disability insurance to protect themselves and their families. Thus a social security system that addresses the real world, in which such people do exist, must inevitably affect labor supply.

The actual Social Security system is more complex than this simple hypothetical model, for four reasons. First, it provides higher replacement rates for low earners than for high earners. As discussed in chapter 2, such progressive benefits are a form of insurance, and insurance provided in this form generally affects labor decisions. In particular, one cannot generally insure in the private insurance market against the risk that one's career will not turn out as well as expected; such insurance is typically available only from government programs like Social Security.† And just as auto insurance or home insurance may somewhat attenuate one's incentive to exercise caution while driving or in taking care of one's home, so, too, the existence of social insurance may attenuate incentives to work somewhat harder or longer. The key question, however, is whether society is better off with more insurance or less. As long as the adverse incentive effects are modest enough and the risks being insured against important enough—both of which conditions Social Security appears to meet—society is ultimately better off because of the insurance it provides; the issue then becomes just how much insurance is optimal.

Second, financing the legacy debt stemming from Social Security's early history reduces the rate of return on worker contributions below the mar-

*Workers may not value the benefits received from this system as highly as the income they are required to pay in taxes; the worker's discount rate may exceed the interest rate paid on the contributed taxes. The prevalence of high discount rates, or a general tendency to pay too little attention to the future, suggests that some workers may be in this situation even if Social Security paid a market rate of return.

†A progressive tax system also provides some insurance of this form, since it cushions the adverse effects on after-tax income of a career that turns out to be less financially rewarding than one had hoped. And a progressive tax system distorts work incentives, just as the Social Security system does. A key point is thus that one cannot provide this kind of insurance without distorting incentives.

ket rate of return. The simple example above assumed that the system paid a market rate of return and therefore implicitly assumed away this legacy cost. In the real world, this assumption is simply false: the legacy debt exists, and the costs associated with it are unavoidable. Furthermore, the manner in which the legacy debt is reduced can itself affect work effort; comparisons between the current system and a "reform" in which the legacy debt is ignored or assumed away are misleading.

Third, Social Security benefits are paid as inflation-adjusted annuities with spousal protections. That is, under Social Security, a worker and his or her spouse will receive an inflation-adjusted payment for as long as either is alive. This type of product simply does not exist in private markets in the United States; even remotely similar products come at a high price for the typical worker. The fact that Social Security provides a form of benefit unavailable in the private sector affects work incentives. Indeed, some workers may work *more* in order to raise their Social Security benefits, because they realize that Social Security is the only source of inflation-adjusted benefits they cannot outlive.[‡]

Fourth, Social Security also differs from the simple example above because of its "earnings test," which requires that workers below the full benefit age retire, or at least have low earnings, as a condition for receiving benefits. Once a worker has reached the full benefit age, the earnings test does not apply; benefits may start regardless of whether the worker is retired. Any delay in benefits because of the earnings test triggers an increase in monthly benefits later, as a consequence of the delay in receiving benefits. For workers aware of this connection and for whom the delayed benefit adjustment is actuarially fair, the disincentive to work created by the earnings test is minimal.[§]

In summary, Social Security has a variety of effects on work incentives. The most important trade-off to remember is that improved social insurance is generally available only at the cost of distorting work incentives; improving work incentives, conversely, may mean a less effective social insurance system.

[‡]Some people who are eligible for retirement benefits (older than 62 and not earning) choose to delay claiming benefits in order to have larger benefits that start later. See Courtney Coile, Peter Diamond, Jonathan Gruber, and Alain Jousten, "Delays in Claiming Social Security Benefits," *Journal of Public Economics,* vol. 84 (2002), pp. 357–85.

[§]Two factors are important to take into account in evaluating the underlying incentives of the earnings test. First, the increased monthly benefits triggered by the earnings test provide a form of insurance; the increased benefits are paid as an annuity, which has valuable insurance properties. Second, even if the system is actuarially fair on average, different workers have different life expectancies. The uniform rules of Social Security thus mean that a delayed start offers some people an increase in expected lifetime benefits but imposes a reduction on others.

with which to finance their retirement. The contributions to these accounts, by themselves, would amount to an increase in private saving and would appear to raise national saving. But individuals or the government could offset that increased saving by reducing saving elsewhere, thereby reducing or even eliminating the net contribution to national saving. For example, if the government diverted Social Security revenue into individual accounts and then borrowed to offset the loss of revenue from the diversion, the reduction in government saving represented by the borrowing would offset the increase in private saving achieved through the individual accounts. Or individuals might offset their contributions to the individual accounts by reducing their contributions to Individual Retirement Accounts, 401(k)s, or other savings vehicles, leaving total private saving unaffected. In other words, in the absence of the individual accounts system, individuals might have saved an equivalent amount in some other form. (Since many workers do little saving for retirement, however, one would not expect to see a full offset from reduced individual saving.)

One of the central issues in the debate over Social Security reform is whether increased surpluses within Social Security (narrow prefunding through the trust fund) will contribute to national saving (broad prefunding). This debate often focuses on whether *past* Social Security surpluses have contributed to national saving, since that history may be informative about what might happen if Social Security surpluses were increased in the near future. As we explain in appendix A and in box 3-5, the view that past Social Security surpluses have contributed nothing to national saving is, in our opinion, implausible. Similarly, our interpretation of how policymakers behave suggests that increased Social Security surpluses in the future would raise national saving to some degree. Furthermore, and despite frequent claims by others to the contrary, we see no reason to believe that narrow prefunding through individual accounts is likely to lead to a significantly larger increase in national saving than the same narrow prefunding accomplished through the Social Security system, unless the accounts are funded through additional dedicated taxes that would not be present if the prefunding were done through the Social Security system.

Box 3-5. *The Social Security Trust Fund and National Saving*

The Social Security trust fund currently holds $1.5 trillion in special-purpose Treasury securities. These holdings and their significance, or lack thereof, have been the subject of much heated debate. In evaluating the economic effects of the Social Security trust fund, it is important not to conflate two issues. The first is whether the bonds held by the trust fund represent assets to the Social Security system; the second is whether the trust fund has caused the publicly held debt to be lower than it otherwise would have been.

The answer to the first question is unambiguous: the bonds held by the trust fund are an asset to the Social Security system because they earn interest income and, when the time comes, can be redeemed to pay benefits. The fact that these bonds are "paper" assets does not in any way reduce their value. *All* pension funds hold paper IOUs; so would the individual accounts that some reformers favor. The value of any paper asset depends on the willingness of someone to honor it. The bonds held by the trust fund are, if anything, more secure than other paper assets, given their U.S. government backing.

The second issue is by how much the accumulation of the trust fund assets has reduced the publicly held debt.˙ This is precisely the same as asking to what extent the Social Security surpluses have generated offsetting increases in non–Social Security deficits, an issue that is discussed in appendix A. To the extent that Social Security surpluses have resulted in smaller unified budget deficits than would otherwise have been the case, the trust fund accumulation has reduced publicly held debt and contributed to national saving. (It is theoretically possible that improvements in the federal budget would not translate into improvements in national saving, but the empirical evidence suggests that they do.) As we argue in appendix A, our reading of history is that the Social Security program *has* contributed to national saving, to some substantial degree, by accumulating reserves.

˙It is important to recognize that the impact of a trust fund buildup on both the Treasury and the economy depends on how the trust fund was built up. The fact that, since 1983, payroll tax revenue has been greater than what was needed to just cover expenditure means, in our view, that the buildup in the trust fund has affected consumption and national saving. In contrast, a trust fund of the same size could have been achieved by having the Treasury simply issue additional bonds, with no increase in payroll tax revenue, but this would not have had the same effect on either debt outstanding in the hands of the public or the level of investment and growth.

(Box continues on the following page.)

Box 3-5 *(continued)*

Such increased saving will make it easier for the government to meet its future obligations.

This issue is related to the relevance of 2018 as a "crisis" date for Social Security and the budget. It is projected that, in 2018, Social Security tax revenue (which does not include the interest earned by the trust fund on the bonds it holds) will fall short of projected benefits and administrative costs. Because of the reserves it will have accumulated by 2018, however, the trust fund will be able to pay full scheduled benefits until 2042. We therefore fail to see the significance that others attach to 2018. In particular, the argument that the trust fund does not affect the government's ability to pay Social Security benefits in the future assumes that the Social Security surpluses have not increased national saving at all. Our reading of the history, however, suggests that the Social Security surpluses *have* raised national saving, at least to some substantial degree.

A number of observers similarly claim that the buildup of the trust fund is irrelevant when the time comes to cash in the bonds.[†] For example, one

---

[†]For example, Sylvester Schieber and John Shoven have written, "It may be interesting to review what will happen when the contributions to Social Security begin to fall short of benefit payments in about 2012 [now 2018]. At some point slightly later than that, Social Security will need to turn in its bonds to the rest of the federal government and ask for payment. Money will be transferred from the rest of the government to the Social Security system in return for the bonds. Where will the money come from? Presumably from taxes or government borrowing. But these are the same choices that the government would face if the system didn't have the bonds and simply asked for a bailout. The point is that the bonds have helped save the system only if they have resulted in greater investment in the economy and hence higher productivity and higher wages for those who are going to have to either pay the taxes or buy the bonds. Selling the bonds to the rest of the government doesn't really generate money by itself, because in a very real sense, we are selling them to ourselves. Both the accumulation of these bonds and their liquidation are accounting transactions—they don't guarantee real saving during the accumulation phase

---

Two further points are worth emphasizing. First, although higher national saving is an important goal for Social Security reform, it requires, as already noted, lower current consumption if the economy is at full employment. Social Security reform must thus strike a balance between lowering consumption today and raising it tomorrow. At some point, additional national saving would *not* be socially beneficial. We

hears arguments like the following: "Where will the money come from? Presumably from taxes, reductions in other spending programs, or government borrowing. But these are the same choices that the government would face if Social Security didn't have the bonds and simply asked for a bailout." In one quite uninteresting sense, the argument is factually accurate: unless it simply prints money, the government finances all of its activities through increasing taxes, cutting spending for other purposes, or borrowing. But this is not a particularly interesting insight. To the extent that the trust fund buildup has decreased the publicly held debt, those same choices are occurring in a different context than if it had not. In other words, to the extent the Social Security surpluses did contribute something to reducing overall budget deficits, they have reduced interest costs and increased the government's ability to borrow, and so made it easier for the government to operate. The same logic holds when one shifts the focus from the government budget to the economy as a whole. Building up the trust fund has added to national saving, thereby making more resources available in the future, and so enlarging the set of possible alternative actions.

As an analogy, consider two individuals who want to purchase a new car. The first saves additional funds to help pay for the car; the second does not. It is true that when each of them goes to the car dealer, each has the same three options: cash, check, or credit. Just as the saving undertaken by the first person does not change the choices available to pay for the car, so, too, the existence of the trust fund does not change the choices available to pay for future Social Security benefits. But in both cases, any saving done ahead of time substantially affects the burden associated with the transaction.

---

and real dissaving during the spend-down phase. All in all, the trust fund balances do not offer much reason to be sanguine about the burden we are passing on to future generations." Sylvester J. Schieber and John B. Shoven, *The Real Deal* (Yale University Press, 1999), p. 207.

believe, however, that the nation has not reached that point yet, and therefore designing Social Security reforms to increase national saving still makes sense.

Second, as mentioned above, any sensible plan that restores actuarial balance to Social Security is likely to contribute to national saving beyond what would occur with a system that continues to be out of balance. It is therefore important to remember that reform itself is difficult, and that, as far as boosting national saving is concerned, a successful reform is better than no reform. It seems to us far more important to enact a reasonable reform that eliminates the long-term deficit in Social Security, and thereby is likely to raise national saving, than to risk further delays in the quest for a plan that would maximize the increase in national saving. It is a case of not allowing the perfect to be the enemy of the good.

Conclusion

We have identified five criteria to be used in evaluating a reform plan for Social Security. Any such plan should
  —restore actuarial balance while addressing the terminal-year problem
  —avoid imposing a fiscal burden on the rest of the federal budget
  —distribute the burden of financing the legacy debt fairly, both within and across generations
  —preserve and improve the social insurance character of Social Security, and
  —improve the functioning of the economy as a whole.
  Most reform proposals that have been advanced to date do not, in our opinion, address all these objectives adequately. In chapters 5 and 6 we put forward a reform plan that we believe does. First, however, we review in chapter 4 the existing long-term deficit of Social Security and how it came about.

4 | Social Security's Long-Term Deficit

S ocial Security faces a significant long-term deficit, requiring some type of reform to put the system on a sounder financial footing. This chapter discusses alternative ways of accounting for the projected long-term deficit and three of the principal factors that contribute to it.

Ultimately, delineating the causes of the long-term deficit is somewhat arbitrary, since the accounting can be done in many different ways. For example, box 4-1 focuses on changes in the deficit since 1983. From that perspective the terminal-year effect, discussed in chapter 3, looms large: more than half of the net deterioration in the seventy-five-year actuarial deficit since 1983 reflects the fact that the seventy-five-year window, which then extended from 1983 through 2057, has now shifted forward to include twenty more years of large deficits. Other ways of doing the accounting would bring other factors to the fore. Thus, relying solely on any one accounting is problematic.

Rather than attempt a literal accounting of the contribution to the long-term deficit from all these different factors,

Box 4-1. *The Change in the Actuarial Deficit since 1983*

In 1983, following the bipartisan reforms recommended by the National Commission on Social Security Reform (the Greenspan Commission), Social Security was projected to be in seventy-five-year balance. Now, however, it faces a deficit equal to 1.9 percent of payroll over the next seventy-five years. One perspective on the long-term deficit in Social Security is therefore to trace the factors that have changed since 1983; since the system was projected to be in long-term balance at that time, the entire projected deficit must reflect factors that have changed since 1983. Indeed, various factors have contributed to the change in the seventy-five-year projected balance since 1983. Some of these have raised the deficit, whereas others have lowered it, so that the 1.9 percent change is a net figure.

More than half of the net deterioration in the seventy-five-year actuarial deficit since 1983 reflects the terminal-year effect (see table). As described in chapter 3, this effect arises because, as each year passes, that year's actual outcome is reflected in the trust fund balance, and an additional year is included in the seventy-five-year projection window. Because retirees in the future are expected to live longer than today's retirees, and because the system is still absorbing the effects of a lower fertility rate, adding 2058 to the projection period caused a deterioration in the seventy-five-year projected deficit calculated in 1984 compared with the calculation in 1983. This process has been repeated each year since then, causing a cumulative deterioration in the seventy-five-year projected deficit equal to 1.15 percent of payroll.

As Social Security is currently designed, the terminal-year problem will continue. In 2004, for example, whatever else changes in the new seventy-five-year projection, the addition of 2078 to the projection period will worsen the actuarial balance by roughly 0.07 percent of payroll. Attenuating the terminal-year problem would require changing the structure of Social Security to alter the net cash flow in distant years in a way that tends to offset one or more of the causes of the problem. One way to do this would be to adjust the Social Security payroll tax or the benefit formulas to recognize the impact of increasing longevity, which is predicted to continue. We discuss longevity in the next section and use it as a basis for the first component of our Social Security reform proposal, described in chapter 5. In addition to helping with the terminal-year problem, this specific reform was selected because it seems to us to improve overall intergenerational fairness.

Sources of Change in the Actuarial Balance since 1983
Percent of taxable payroll

Source	Change
Changes in economic assumptions	−0.17
Changes in demographic assumptions	0.68
Changes in actuarial projection methods	−0.75
Change in terminal year	−1.15
Changes in legislation	0.16
Other	−0.01
Changes in disability assumptions	−0.69
Total change in balance, 1983–2003	−1.91

Source: John Hambor, personal communication to the authors, using data from annual Trustees' Reports.

Many of the other factors that have caused changes in the actuarial balance since 1983 are more obscure. For example, certain changes in the details of how the actuarial projections are undertaken caused a decline in the balance by 0.75 percent of payroll. These include changes in the assumed age distribution of immigrants and a change in the definition of actuarial balance itself.

It is not our goal to track down every development that has affected Social Security since the 1983 reform and propose a change to offset that effect. Such an approach would be particularly difficult since some changes—such as those in actuarial projection methods—do not lend themselves to obvious policy responses. Nonetheless, some of the developments since 1983 would warrant a policy response even if they did not worsen Social Security's financing; any contribution they make to the deterioration in Social Security's projected deficit just makes the case for the policy response all the stronger. In our opinion, the increase in inequality in incomes and the increase in inequality in mortality rates by earnings level are two such developments, which, interestingly, the Greenspan Commission seems to have made no mention of. We discuss these below, and the second component of our reform proposal is intended to respond to these changes.

we simply focus on three important contributing factors: improvements in life expectancy, increases in earnings inequality, and the burden of the legacy debt resulting from Social Security's early history. These factors interact with one another, further underscoring the problems involved in making a precise accounting, as well as revealing the arbitrary nature of such classifications. Nonetheless, each of these three factors, examined by itself, has an adverse effect on Social Security's financing—and motivates a component of our reform plan.

Increasing Life Expectancy

Life expectancy at age 65 has increased greatly since the creation of Social Security (figure 4-1). It has risen by four years for men and five years for women since 1940 and is expected to continue rising in the future. Increasing life expectancy contributes to Social Security's long-term deficit. Because Social Security pays a benefit that continues as long as the beneficiary is alive, any increase in life expectancy at the age at which benefits start increases the cost of Social Security, unless there is an offsetting decrease in the monthly benefit level. The last major reform of the program, in 1983, increased the full benefit age gradually over two six-year periods (2000–05 and 2017–22), in anticipation of increased life expectancy, thus effectively reducing benefits for those affected by the change. But the 1983 reform did not include any ongoing adjustment for life expectancy after 2022. So, as time goes on and life expectancy continues its steady increase, the projected cost of Social Security steadily rises.

The life expectancy projections in figure 4-1 are averages and thus do not by themselves provide a sense of the variation in age at death. In fact, they are consistent with any of an infinite number of distributions. For example, a life expectancy of 75 years could, in principle, arise because the entire population is expected to die at precisely age 75, or because half the population is expected to die at age 50 and the other half at age 100. Yet for many purposes, including the adequacy of Social Security benefits in protecting against poverty in very old age, these two cases would have very different implications. Thus, in considering how to respond to longer expected lives, we need to recognize as well that there is a wide distribution of ages at death.

Figure 4-1. *Projected Life Expectancy at Age 65*[a]

Years

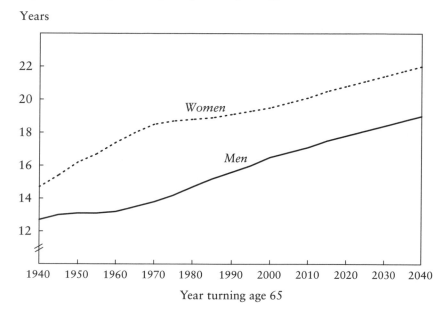

Year turning age 65

Source: *2003 Annual Report of the Board of Trustees of the Federal Old-Age and Survivors Insurance and Disability Insurance Trust Funds,* March 2003, table V.A4.
a. Projections are based on the Social Security trustees' intermediate cost assumptions and are for cohort rather than period life expectancies.

Figure 4-2 shows, for a single cohort (those born in 1943), the substantial variation in age at death implied by the mortality rates that generated the average life expectancy shown in figure 4-1. (The mortality rate is the probability of dying at a given age, assuming that one has lived to that age. For example, the mortality rate for 65-year-olds is defined as the share of those age 65 who die within one year.)[1] Among those born in 1943 who live until 2005 (that is, to age 62, the earliest age of eligibility for retirement benefits), 46 percent of men and 62 percent of women are projected to live at least another twenty years, and 12 percent of men and 27 percent of women are projected to live at least another thirty years. Figure 4-3 takes the projected distribution of ages at death for men for the cohort shown in figure 4-2 and compares it with the same distribution for men born in 1983 (who had therefore reached age 20 in 2003 and will

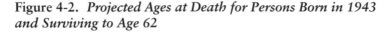

Figure 4-2. *Projected Ages at Death for Persons Born in 1943 and Surviving to Age 62*

Percent

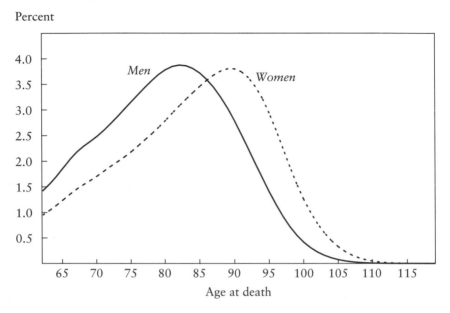

Age at death

Source: Authors' calculations based on cohort mortality projections by the Office of the Chief Actuary, Social Security Administration.

reach age 62 in 2045). As the figure shows, those born in 1983 and surviving to 62 are expected to die at later ages than those born in 1943 and surviving to 62. Whereas, as noted above, 46 percent of the group born in 1943 are expected to live at least another twenty years, 53 percent of the group born in 1983 are expected to do so. Figure 4-4 makes the same comparison for women born in the same two years. Of those born in 1943 and surviving to age 62, 12 percent are expected to live at least another thirty years, whereas 18 percent of those born in 1983 and surviving to age 62 are expected to live at least thirty more years.

Figures 4-2 through 4-4 underscore that a large and growing number of Americans will live for many years after they first become eligible for Social Security benefits. Thus benefits paid after retirement should be designed in a way that makes sense for someone expecting to live a long time. One aspect of this is how benefits are structured to deal with inflation. Over

Figure 4-3. *Projected Ages at Death for Men Born in 1943 and 1983 and Surviving to Age 62*

Percent

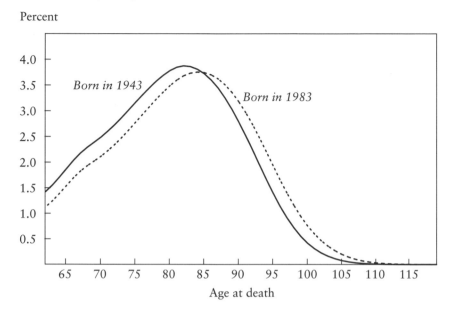

Age at death

Source: Authors' calculations based on cohort mortality projections by the Office of the Chief Actuary, Social Security Administration.

long periods, even moderate levels of inflation can significantly reduce the real value of an income that is fixed in nominal terms. For example, with 2 percent inflation, a given nominal benefit loses one-third of its real value in twenty years and half its real value in thirty-five years. Yet many private pension plans pay monthly benefits that are fixed in nominal dollars. Inflation steadily erodes the purchasing power of these benefits, which disproportionately reduces their lifetime value for those who expect to live a long time. By contrast, a retired worker's Social Security benefits are automatically adjusted each year for inflation, so that their purchasing power does not erode over time. As chapter 2 emphasized, this indexing of benefits to inflation is an important source of protection against unexpectedly high inflation late in life.[2]

This point is further emphasized when disabled workers are taken into consideration. Life expectancy for disabled workers is well below that

Figure 4-4. *Projected Ages at Death for Women Born in 1943 and 1983 and Surviving to Age 62*

Percent

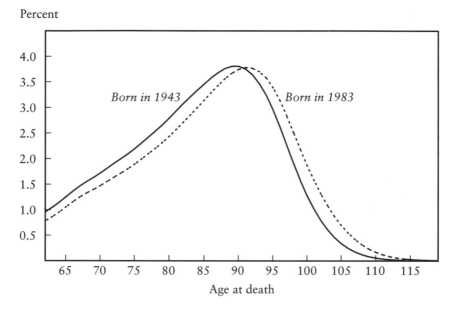

Age at death

Source: Authors' calculations based on cohort mortality projections by the Office of the Chief Actuary, Social Security Administration.

for their nondisabled contemporaries, but some of the disabled will live a very long time after the start of their Social Security disability benefits.

Although demographers, actuaries, and other experts agree that mortality rates will continue to decline well into the future, there is heated debate in academic and actuarial circles about how rapid an improvement to expect.[3] This is not the appropriate place to assess that dispute, but the debate underscores the fact that projections of mortality improvements are subject to considerable uncertainty. Indeed, this uncertainty is one of our motivations for proposing (in chapter 5) that Social Security benefits and taxes be indexed to future mortality levels, so that rather than try to make adjustments today based on today's mortality projections, such adjustments will be made automatically as time goes on and actual improvements in mortality become known. Such improvements have historically varied from year to year, and indeed even from decade

Table 4-1. *Mortality Rates among the Elderly, 1950–2000*[a]

Year	Deaths per 100 people	Change from 10 years earlier (percent)
1950	7.36	−16.3
1960	6.97	−5.3
1970	6.28	−9.9
1980	5.47	−12.9
1990	4.99	−8.9
2000	4.84	−2.9

Source: *Annual Report of the Board of Trustees of the Federal Old-Age and Survivors Insurance and Disability Insurance Trust Funds,* March 2003, table V.A1.

a. Data are for persons age 65 and over and are adjusted for age and sex.

to decade (see table 4-1). Thus one should expect to see significant deviations from current mortality projections even if those projections are accurate on average over long periods.

Increasing life expectancy raises the value of Social Security benefits to workers, because benefits last as long as the recipient is alive. By the same token, however, improving life expectancy adversely affects Social Security's financial condition, because beneficiaries then collect benefits over a longer period.[4]

One might think that any adverse financial effect on Social Security from increased life expectancy would be substantially diminished by longer careers, as people choose to spend part of their longer expected lives continuing to work. But as appendix B explains, that is not the case, for two reasons. First, it seems unlikely that longer life expectancy will be associated with significant increases in career lengths. Second, even if people did extend their careers, the effect on Social Security would be relatively modest because, as chapter 2 explained, the system is roughly actuarially fair. Working longer and claiming benefits later does not have much effect on Social Security's financing because annual benefits are increased when the initial benefit claim is postponed. The bottom line is that increased life expectancy, whether or not it is accompanied by longer careers, imposes financial costs on Social Security.

The steady increases in life expectancy that have occurred since the 1983 reform of Social Security are not a total surprise. Indeed, the actuarial projections done at the time of the reform assumed steadily improving life expectancy. But the target in 1983 was to restore actuarial balance for the next seventy-five years, not forever. Now we are twenty years into that seventy-five-year projection period, and with the projection period now including an additional twenty years, financing difficulties are again on the horizon. Ongoing increases in life expectancy are therefore one cause of the long-term deficit in Social Security.

Increasing Earnings Inequality

A second factor affecting Social Security's financing is earnings inequality. Here we examine two such effects: the increase in the share of earnings that is untaxed because earnings are above the maximum taxable earnings base, and the widening difference in life expectancy between lower earners and higher earners.

These changes, by themselves, have made Social Security less progressive on a lifetime basis over the past twenty years. But many factors affect the overall progressivity of Social Security, and it is not our intent to address all of them. For example, the increased tendency of women to have substantial careers outside the home has diminished the relative importance of the spousal benefit. The spousal benefit has tended historically to reduce Social Security's progressivity, because it has accrued disproportionately to spouses in high-income families; the decline in the relative importance of the spousal benefit therefore makes Social Security more progressive as a whole.[5] Although some of these other factors are also important, we focus on just one—the effect of earnings inequality— that we believe particularly warrants a policy response.

Increases in Earnings Inequality in Recent Decades

Over the past two decades, earnings have risen most rapidly at the top of the earnings distribution, that is, among those workers who already were receiving the highest earnings. Economists have explored a variety of explanations for this increase in earnings inequality. The leading explanation involves technological changes that have increased the return to skill, although social norms also seem to play an important role.[6]

Figure 4-5. *Share of Aggregate Earnings above the Maximum Taxable Earnings Base, 1977–2003*

Percent

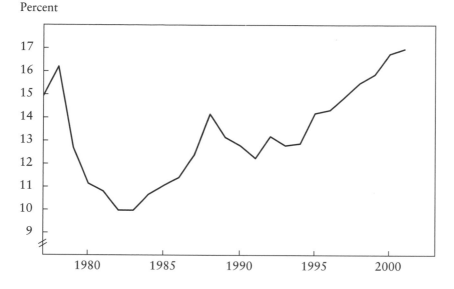

Source: Social Security Administration, *Annual Statistical Supplement*, table 4.B1.

The increase in the share of earnings accruing to the top of the income distribution affects Social Security's financing because, as noted in chapter 2, the Social Security payroll tax is imposed only up to a maximum taxable level ($87,000 in 2003). The increasing inequality in earnings in recent years implies that a much larger fraction of aggregate earnings is not subject to the payroll tax than in the past. In other words, when the earnings distribution changes so that more of total earnings goes to those earning more than the taxable maximum, the fraction of total earnings subject to Social Security tax decreases.

Figure 4-5 shows the fraction of aggregate earnings that was above the maximum taxable earnings base in each year since 1977. This fraction has risen substantially since the early 1980s, from 10 percent in 1983 to 15 percent in 2002. The decline in the late 1970s and early 1980s shown in the figure reflects legislation passed in 1977, which raised the maximum taxable earnings base from $17,700 in 1978 to $29,700 in 1981.

Figure 4-6. *Share of Workers with Earnings at or above the Maximum Taxable Earnings Base, 1977–1999*

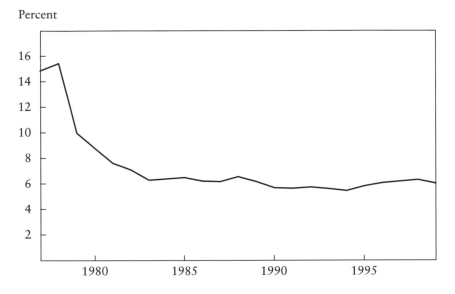

Percent

Source: Social Security Administration, *Annual Statistical Supplement*, table 4.B4.

Since 1982 this base has increased automatically in line with average wage growth. Thus the increase in the fraction of earnings not subject to tax reflects the fact that earnings growth at the top of the income distribution has been much more rapid than the growth of average earnings.[7]

Surprisingly, given figure 4-5, the fraction of workers with earnings at or above the maximum taxable earnings base has remained roughly constant since the early 1980s. As figure 4-6 shows, this fraction declined rapidly in the late 1970s and early 1980s as the 1977 legislation raised the maximum taxable earnings base: as it increased, a smaller fraction of workers had earnings at or above it. In each year since the early 1980s, however, an approximately constant 6 percent of workers have had earnings at or above the taxable maximum. Thus the increase in earnings that escape the payroll tax does not reflect an increase in the fraction of workers with earnings above the maximum, but rather an increase in the average earnings of those workers relative to other workers. For example, in

1983 the average earnings of workers with earnings more than the taxable maximum were five times the average earnings of all other workers; by 2001 that ratio had risen to more than seven.

In contrast to this increase in inequality below versus above the maximum taxable earnings base, the increase in inequality *within* the taxable earnings base has been relatively modest. Interestingly, increases in earnings inequality here can have the effect of improving Social Security's financing. As explained in chapter 2, Social Security's benefit formula is progressive. One implication of the progressive benefit formula is that benefits for those with higher earnings have a lower replacement rate, effectively helping finance benefits for those with lower earnings, whose replacement rate is higher. Another implication of the progressive formula, however, is that increases in earnings inequality within the taxable wage base reduce Social Security's total benefit obligations. To see this, imagine that a dollar of lifetime earnings is transferred from a lower earner to a higher earner. The resultant reduction in benefits for the lower earner would exceed the increase in benefits for the higher earner, so that total benefits would decline.[8]

Another reflection of increased earnings inequality across workers generally is the fact that the payroll taxes collected by Medicare have grown significantly relative to those collected by Social Security. In contrast to the payroll tax for Social Security, the payroll tax for the Hospital Insurance component (part A) of Medicare now applies to all earnings. Until 1990 the maximum taxable earnings base for Hospital Insurance was identical to that for Social Security. In that year both Social Security and Hospital Insurance taxes applied only to the first $51,300 of earnings (a level indexed to the rate of wage growth). Legislation in 1990, however, roughly doubled the level of earnings subject to the Hospital Insurance tax, and the Omnibus Budget Reconciliation Act of 1993 removed the cap altogether. As a result, whereas in 1990 Medicare payroll tax revenue amounted to 24 percent of Social Security payroll tax revenue, by 2000 that ratio had increased to 29 percent, without any change in tax rates.

Earnings Inequality and Improving Mortality

The trend to longer life expectancy and its impact on Social Security, examined above, are widely known. Somewhat less well known, but also

Figure 4-7. *Relative Mortality Rates for White 65- to 75-Year-Olds of Differing Educational Attainment, Selected Periods*

Relative index of inequality (percent)[a]

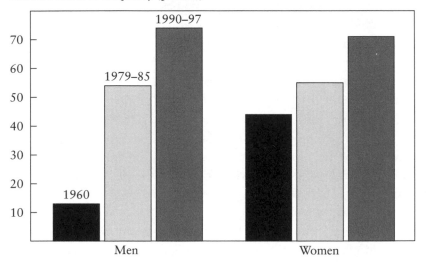

Source: Irma Elo and Kirsten P. Smith, "Trends in Educational Differentials in Mortality in the United States," paper presented at the Annual Meeting of the Population Association of America, Minneapolis, May 2003.

a. Mean proportionate decrease in mortality as educational attainment increases from the bottom of the education distribution to the top.

bearing implications for the program, is the fact that people with higher earnings and more education tend to live longer than those with lower earnings and less education.[9] Even less well known is that these mortality differences by earnings and education have been expanding over time.[10]

Figure 4-7 shows the percentage difference in mortality rates from the bottom to the top of the education distribution, for white men and women between 65 and 75 years old, in three periods over the last forty-five years: 1960, 1979–85, and 1990–97.[11] In 1960 mortality rates for men at the very top of the education distribution were approximately 10 percent lower than those for white men at the very bottom. By the 1990s this differential had grown to over 70 percent. Relative differences in mortality rates have thus increased markedly for older men since the 1960s; the increase for older women is much smaller but still considerable.[12]

This increasing gap in mortality rates by level of education has two implications for Social Security. First, to the extent that projected improvements in life expectancy reflect disproportionate improvements for higher earners (a reasonable supposition since higher earners tend to have more education than lower earners), the adverse effect on Social Security's financing is larger than if the projected improvement occurred equally across the earnings distribution. The reason is that higher earners receive larger annual benefits in retirement; a disproportionate increase in their life expectancy therefore imposes a larger burden on Social Security than an equivalent increase in life expectancy for other beneficiaries. Second, when one thinks of the progressivity of Social Security on a lifetime basis, rather than an annual basis, the changing pattern of mortality tends to make Social Security less progressive than it would be without such a change, since it means that higher earners will collect benefits for an increasingly larger number of years, and thus enjoy larger lifetime benefits, relative to lower earners.

The Legacy Debt Burden

A third important influence on the future financing of Social Security reflects, somewhat ironically, the past. That is the fact, already discussed in chapter 3, that the benefits paid to almost all current and past cohorts of beneficiaries exceeded what could have been financed with the revenue they contributed. This history imposes a legacy debt on the Social Security system. That is, if earlier cohorts had received only the benefits that could be financed by their contributions plus interest, the trust fund's assets today would be much greater. Those assets would earn interest, which could be used to finance benefits. The legacy debt reflects the absence of those assets and thus directly relates to Social Security's funding level. In this section we use the legacy debt as an alternative lens through which to view Social Security's financing challenges.

The decision, made early in the history of Social Security, to provide the first generations of beneficiaries benefits disproportionate to their contributions represented sound policy. It was a humane response to the suffering imposed by World War I, the Great Depression, and World War II on Americans who came of age during those years, and it helped to reduce unacceptably high rates of poverty among them in old age. Moreover, the higher benefits not only helped the recipients themselves but also relieved part of the burden on their families and friends, and on the taxpayers of that era, who would otherwise have contributed more to their support. Benefits paid by Social Security reduced the cost of transfers to the elderly poor from other programs and reduced the need for children to provide financial and other support to their parents.[13] Thus the decision to grant generous Social Security benefits to workers who had contributed little or nothing to Social Security during their careers provided crucial assistance to more people than just those workers themselves.

But whatever the rationales for and positive effects of those decisions, all workers covered by Social Security now face the burden of financing them. To measure that burden and explore in detail how it accumulated, one can examine how much each cohort paid and is projected to pay in Social Security taxes (in present value) and how much that cohort received and is projected to receive in benefits (again in present value). To include projected future taxes and benefits in the calculation, however, one must make some assumption regarding how the projected actuarial imbalance will be addressed; different assumptions about future benefits and taxes affect both the size of the legacy debt and how it is borne by future generations.

Figure 4-8 shows, for each cohort born from 1876 to 2046, the difference between what that cohort paid or will pay in taxes to Social Security, and what it received or is projected to receive in benefits, in present value. This particular calculation assumes that taxes will increase in the future to finance in full the benefits currently scheduled under Social Security. Specifically, it is assumed that the payroll tax rate for Social Security rises linearly beginning in 2020 and continuing until 2099, when it reaches 14.74 percent, and remains constant afterward. This assumption thus does not reflect the reform we propose in chapter 5, but instead is merely one of many ways of illustrating the buildup of the legacy debt and how it could be financed in the future. One could instead assume that actuarial balance is achieved entirely through a reduction in benefits, or through some combination of tax increases and benefit reductions; such an analysis would show a similar picture, but with some differences in the detail.

Figure 4-8. *Actual and Projected Net Intercohort Transfers under Social Security*

Billions of 2002 dollars   Trillions of 2002 dollars

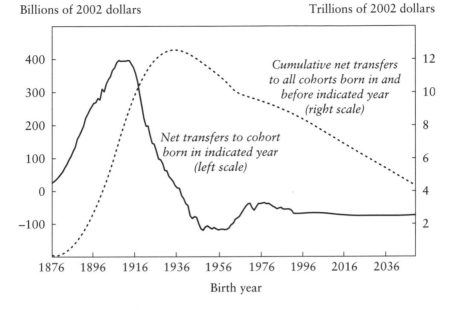

Birth year

Source: Dean R. Leimer, "Cohort-Specific Measures of Lifetime Net Social Security Transfers," Social Security Administration, Office of Research and Statistics Working Paper 59, February 1994.

The solid line in figure 4-8 shows clearly that the earliest cohorts received more from Social Security than they paid into it. Because the program as a whole was small in those early years, however, the total net transfer was not very large, either for each cohort individually or for all the early cohorts cumulatively (depicted by the dotted line). As the program grew, however, it continued to provide more generous benefits than could have been financed by previous contributions (plus a market rate of interest), and the cumulative transfer grew rapidly. Following the 1983 reforms, all cohorts starting with that born in 1936 are now scheduled to pay in more than they receive in present value, thereby reducing the legacy debt that is passed on to the future. In other words, the "rate of return" received on contributions is lower than a market interest rate, and a legacy cost is borne because of this difference between the return on contributions under Social Security and the market interest rate. Without the assumed tax increase (or a benefit reduction) in the future, however, the picture would not show such a continuing decline in cumulative transfers. We discuss this issue in more detail in appendix C.

Implications of the Legacy Debt

Nothing anyone can do today can take back the benefits that were given to Social Security's early beneficiaries, and most Americans would be unwilling to reduce benefits for those now receiving them or soon to receive them. Those two facts largely determine the size of the legacy debt. For example, on one reasonable assumption, namely, that benefits will not be reduced for anyone age 55 or over in 2004, the legacy debt amounts to approximately $11.6 trillion.[14]

Because the size of the legacy debt is mostly already determined, the only remaining issue is how to finance it across different generations, and different people within generations, in the future. To be sure, the legacy debt does not have to be paid off immediately. Indeed, some of it need never be paid off, just as there is no need ever to pay off the entire public debt. But any ongoing legacy debt, like other outstanding public debt, incurs a cost for continuing to finance it, which, if not paid as it accrues, increases the debt. And just as a continuously rising public debt-to-GDP ratio would eventually become unsustainable, as holders of the debt come to doubt whether they will be repaid in full, so, too, the legacy debt cannot grow faster than taxable payroll indefinitely without disrupting the functioning of Social Security.

That workers today bear a cost of financing the legacy debt does not necessarily mean that Social Security is a bad deal for those workers. Many workers, no doubt, are pleased that their parents and grandparents received higher benefits than their contributions would have paid for. And, just as in the past, some current workers benefit from the fact that Social Security reduces the need for them to support their parents directly. Also, as discussed in chapter 2, Social Security provides today's workers with life insurance, disability insurance, and an inflation-indexed annuity, and does so at a remarkably low administrative cost—far lower than the private financial market could match. Moreover, the mandatory nature of Social Security avoids the problem of adverse selection that can arise in private insurance markets. (Adverse selection stems from the fact that those who expect to benefit more from insurance are more likely to buy it; this raises the average cost of insurance to the insurer, leading to price increases and possibly a vicious cycle of ever-fewer participants and ever-higher prices.) Finally, Social Security's mandatory character also protects individuals and their families from myopically undersaving and underinsuring themselves. Thus, although younger workers will receive less in benefits from Social Security than they would have in the absence of the legacy debt, they still stand to inherit a system that will provide them with valuable benefits, some of which cannot be duplicated in the market.

The Legacy Debt and the Projected Long-Term Deficit as Alternative Perspectives

There is no necessary relationship between the projected actuarial long-term deficit in Social Security and the legacy debt. The projected deficit derives from how the program works each year: taxes are collected from workers, and benefits are paid to retirees, disabled workers, and their families and survivors. It thus reflects the difference between projected tax revenue and projected expenditure, year by year, over the next seventy-five years.

The legacy debt, on the other hand, derives from how Social Security works over the lifetime of each worker. From this perspective, each worker pays into Social Security while working and then receives benefits (possibly along with other family members). Given this lifetime perspective, one can calculate whether the government expects to collect more in taxes from a given worker than it expects to pay out to the worker and his or her family over their lifetime in present value. This calculation of the net transfer—taxes less benefits—captures the financial impact on the government from that worker's participation in Social Security.[15] The sum of these net transfers, over many workers and cohorts of workers, is what determines how the legacy debt has built up and how it will be financed in the future.

The connection between the legacy debt and the projected long-term deficit is complicated by these different perspectives: the first is based on cohorts and the second on years. Even if benefit payments were exactly equal to incoming revenue in each year in the future, and there were thus no deficit in Social Security, a legacy debt could still exist. It would manifest itself in the fact that future beneficiaries would be receiving lower benefits than could be financed by their contributions plus interest.

The bottom line is that the legacy debt and the projected long-term deficit both offer insightful, albeit somewhat different, perspectives on the financing difficulties facing Social Security. The legacy debt calculation is backward looking by cohort; the projected deficit calculation is forward looking by year. The two have no necessary relationship with each other. However, under current law, cohorts that today are 15 years old and younger on average are projected to enjoy benefits that are equal to their taxes paid plus interest.[16] That fact implies that the legacy debt and the long-term actuarial imbalance are not too far apart. The concepts of legacy debt and legacy cost permit us to ask whether the burden from the program's history is being borne fairly by different generations, and to allocate the burden of restoring actuarial balance in a way that makes that allocation fairer. Current projections for those 15 and under imply that they are not bearing their share of the legacy cost, which would require them to receive less back than their taxes with interest.

Effects of Fertility and Immigration Rates on the Legacy Debt and Its Financing

The legacy debt will remain at a constant ratio to taxable payroll over time if the amount financed each year equals the difference between the interest rate and the growth rate of taxable earnings, multiplied by the level of the legacy debt at the end of the previous year.[17] The growth rate of taxable earnings is a key part of this calculation; that growth is in turn equal to growth in the labor force plus growth in productivity, adjusted for any changes in the relationship between taxable earnings and productivity (which arise mostly from the nontaxation of health benefits). Figure 4-9 shows the projected annual, inflation-adjusted rate of growth in taxable payroll under the 2003 intermediate cost projections of the Social Security actuaries.

The rapid decline in the growth rate of taxable payroll in the near term reflects the retirement of the baby-boomers. In the long term, the slower

Figure 4-9. *Projected Annual Real Growth in Taxable Payroll, 2004–80*

Percent

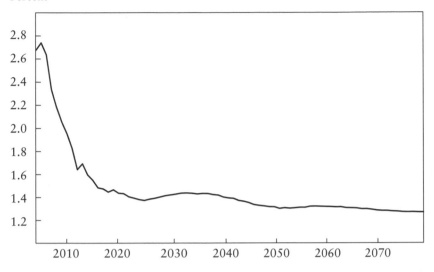

Source: *2003 Annual Report of the Board of Trustees of the Federal Old-Age and Survivors Insurance and Disability Insurance Trust Funds*, March 2003, table VI.F7.

ongoing declines reflect a variety of forces. In particular, the long-term growth of the labor force depends on fertility rates, immigration rates, and changes in work patterns over a long period.

Figure 4-10 shows the actual and projected path of the nation's fertility rate from 1940 to 2080.[18] The fertility rate rose sharply after the end of World War II, increasing from 2.42 children per woman of childbearing age in 1945 to 3.18 in 1947. It continued to increase throughout the 1950s, reaching 3.64 in 1959, before declining in the 1960s and 1970s. It has since fluctuated near 2.0 and is projected to decline to 1.95 by 2027 under the intermediate cost assumptions.

Lower fertility rates affect Social Security with a lag. A reduction in the fertility rate today, for example, does not immediately affect the number of workers or retirees. Instead, the lower fertility rate gradually affects Social Security's financing, as smaller cohorts of young people enter the work force. The decline in the fertility rate over the past several decades

Figure 4-10. *Actual and Projected Fertility Rates, 1940–2080*[a]

Births per woman

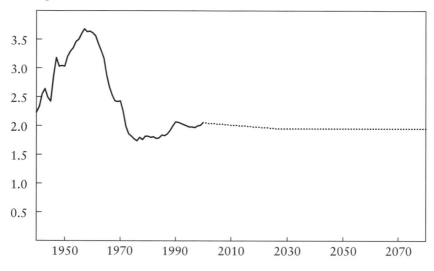

Source: *2003 Annual Report of the Board of Trustees of the Federal Old-Age and Survivors Insurance and Disability Insurance Trust Funds,* March 2003, table V.A1.
a. The total fertility rate is the average number of children who would be born to a woman in her lifetime if she were to experience the birth rate by age for that year, assuming she survives her childbearing years.

is therefore still affecting the financing of Social Security and will do so for decades to come.

The transition to lower fertility rates, like the trend to lower mortality rates, makes the future financing of Social Security more costly.[19] Relative to a world in which fertility does not decline, the decline in the fertility rate means that the legacy debt from the system's history will be higher on a per capita basis in the future: if the fertility rate had not declined, the legacy debt would be spread over more people.

The same point holds with regard to immigration rates, which are projected to decline under the intermediate cost estimates, since the projection assumes a constant absolute level of net immigration yet the population continues to grow. Figure 4-11 shows projected immigration as a share of the population.

Figure 4-11. *Projected Immigration Rates, 2003–80*

Percent

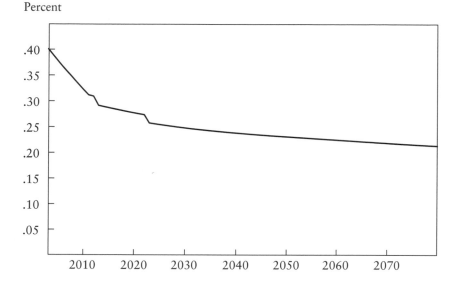

Source: *2003 Annual Report of the Board of Trustees of the Federal Old-Age and Survivors Insurance and Disability Insurance Trust Funds,* March 2003, table V.A1 and table V.A2.

The basic point is that the lagged effects of both the decline in the fertility rate and a projected decline in the immigration rate contribute to the long-term slowdown in the growth of taxable payroll shown in figure 4-9. In turn, this slowdown increases the amount that must be financed per year in order to maintain a constant ratio of legacy debt to payroll.

Conclusion

Social Security's long-term financing problems reflect a variety of factors. We have chosen three important ones to highlight: improvements in life expectancy, earnings inequality, and allocation of the cost of financing the implicit debt that arises from the program's past generosity. A wide variety of other factors affect Social Security's financial condition, including marriage and divorce patterns and productivity growth. The relative importance of these factors can be seen from the data in the annual report of the chief actuary, which accompanies the annual report of the Social Security trustees. All these factors affect the program's projected imbalance. One important objective of reform is to eliminate the projected imbalance in Social Security. In the next chapter we describe our plan for doing so. That plan takes as its point of departure the factors we have highlighted in this chapter.

5 | A Three-Part Plan to Shore Up Social Security

This chapter presents our three-part proposal to restore actuarial balance to Social Security. Like the successful Social Security reforms of the past, our plan involves a combination of changes in the determination of both benefits and revenue. Each element of our plan is intended to address one of the three sources of the program's long-term deficit discussed in chapter 4: increasing life expectancy, increased earnings inequality, and the legacy debt arising from the program's history. Together these three components of our plan would not only restore actuarial balance but also provide revenue for several improvements in Social Security's social insurance protections to be described in chapter 6.

Our proposal in each area combines revenue increases and benefit adjustments. This reliance on both benefit and tax changes is important to the plan's potential viability. Some analysts argue that Social Security reform should rely entirely on payroll tax rate increases. They note the projected increase in health care costs paid for by the elderly and the already-legislated future increases in the full benefit age and expansion in the income taxation of benefits.[1] The Bush administration's principles for reform, by contrast, explicitly rule out payroll tax increases.[2]

In our opinion, the competing demands of ensuring adequate retirement income for all Americans, restoring long-term balance to Social Security, protecting the program's core social insurance functions, avoiding massive increases in payroll tax rates, and balancing burdens fairly across future workers and retirees require a combination of benefit and tax changes. This approach also builds on the tradition established in the 1983 reform, in which benefit reductions were combined with revenue increases in a bipartisan agreement that improved Social Security's long-term prospects.

Adjustments for Increasing Life Expectancy

As the previous chapter showed, the projected increase in the life expectancy of retirees is an important contributor to both the actuarial imbalance and the terminal-year problem in Social Security. That is, if life expectancy were not expected to continue to increase, the actuarial deficit would be considerably smaller, and the balance in the seventy-sixth year of the projection would be closer to the average balance over the preceding seventy-five years.

In thinking about how Social Security should be modified to deal with increases in life expectancy, it is helpful to examine how a worker would sensibly react to a change in life expectancy, if that worker could rely only on his or her own resources, and how different types of pension systems would adjust to such a change. On learning that he or she will live longer than previously expected, an individual worker could adjust in any of three ways to the resulting need to finance consumption over a longer life: by consuming less before retirement (that is, saving more), consuming less during retirement, or working longer. A sensible approach would likely involve all three.[3]

As we have seen, Social Security benefits are higher for those who start them at a later age, and are higher for each additional year of work that raises the worker's average indexed monthly earnings. The current system thus already allows for one response to increases in life expectancy: working longer in order to enjoy higher annual benefits.

The other two elements of the adjustment can be thought of as corresponding to an increase in the payroll tax rate (consuming less and saving more before retirement) and a reduction in benefits for any given age at retirement (consuming less during retirement). Both responses thus involve reductions in consumption.[4] Our approach, described below, reflects a balance between these two responses, given that Social Security already provides the opportunity for higher benefits from more work.

As noted in chapter 4, Social Security does not presently include an automatic adjustment for changes in life expectancy. As life expectancy increases, benefits just get paid for more years. So even if Social Security were in long-term balance under current law, it would eventually go out of balance as successive cohorts live longer.

In contrast, consider an individual accounts system in which the accumulated balance in the account upon retirement is used to purchase an annuity in the market. As life expectancy increases, the price of such an annuity will rise, reflecting the market's changing expectations about life expectancy. Thus, for any accumulated balance that a retiring worker might wish to convert to an annuity, any increase in life expectancy will translate into a decrease in the monthly benefit that one could purchase with that sum, sufficient to fully offset the effect of the change in life expectancy. To be sure, workers could choose to respond to the increase in life expectancy by working longer, thus accumulating more in their accounts as well as having a shorter remaining life expectancy to finance.

The question thus becomes how to change the current structure of Social Security to make it respond in a flexible way to changes in life expectancy. Again a balance seems appropriate. Our view is that the system should neither rely solely on additional work as the response to a longer life, nor rely solely on reduced monthly benefits to adapt to the higher cost of a longer retirement, nor rely solely on reduced consumption and increased revenue during one's career. Instead, since the system already allows the option of a longer career in exchange for higher monthly benefits, the necessary adjustment should come partly through increased revenue and partly through reduced benefits.

A separate question is what life expectancy projections to use. Two approaches are possible. An adjustment for anticipated increases in life expectancy could be set at the time the reform is enacted, based on the increases in life expectancy projected at that time. Or the adjustment could be left to be determined over time, based on the actual increases in life expectancy that occur (in other words, benefits or revenue, or both, could be indexed to life expectancy). The first approach was used in the 1983 reform legislation, which gradually increased the full benefit age from 65 to 67 (see chapter 2). Given the role of the full benefit age in determining benefits, increasing that age was tantamount to a reduction in benefits (while also changing how monthly benefits are increased in response to a delay in claiming at different ages).[5] The pattern of benefit reductions across cohorts loosely reflected the change in life expectancies that was projected when the legislation was enacted. In other words, the increase in the full benefit age was intended in part to respond to the projected increase in life expectancy that was anticipated at the time of the 1983 reform.[6]

The second approach, and the one that we prefer, would automatically adjust Social Security each year based on contemporaneous projections of life expectancy, rather than on life expectancy projections calculated today. Just as benefits and earnings subject to tax currently vary with changes in prices and wages, respectively, so, too, benefits and tax rates could vary with changing life expectancy. This approach responds to the great uncertainty about how rapidly life expectancy will increase in the coming decades.

As discussed in chapter 3, mortality rates adjusted for age and sex, which are key to determining life expectancy, have declined historically at varying rates across years and decades. Since such variations in the rate of decline are difficult to predict, it seems preferable to allow the adjustments to be based on the latest data, instead of relying solely on today's projection of future declines in mortality rates. This kind of ongoing approach to life expectancy adjustments has been followed in several countries, including Sweden under its system of notional accounts. Such an approach was also included in one of the plans presented in the final report of President Bush's Commission to Strengthen Social Security. Adapting to life expectancy projections as they are revised over time seems much more sensible than relying only on current projections.

Automatic adjustment of benefits and taxes for ongoing increases in life expectancy would enhance the financial soundness of Social Security, but it still leaves open a key question, namely, the extent to which the adjustment should be divided between taxes and benefits. Both Sweden's approach and the proposal from President Bush's commission allocate all of the adjustment for longer life expectancy to benefit cuts. We consider that an extreme approach, and instead we propose a balanced combination of benefit and tax adjustments.

Specifically, under our proposal, in each year the Office of the Chief Actuary would calculate the net cost to Social Security from the improvement in life expectancy observed in the past year for a typical worker at the full benefit age. This would be done by comparing the cost of benefits for different cohorts, using successive mortality tables.[7] Half of this "net cost of increased life expectancy" would be offset by a reduction in the PIA, which would apply to all covered workers age 59 and younger.[8] (Once a worker reaches age 60, the rules for his or her benefits would be finalized and would not change further in response to ongoing life expectancy changes.) The tax change is intended to balance the actuarial effects of the benefit reductions over a seventy-five-year period. Since the seventy-five-year cost of benefits to all newly eligible beneficiaries is roughly 85 percent of the seventy-five-year cost of benefits in total, the percentage increase in the tax rate would be 85 percent of the percentage decrease in the PIA.[9]

The first benefit adjustment would occur for those first eligible to receive benefits in 2012, and the first adjustment to the payroll tax rate would also occur in 2012, with further changes each year thereafter. (As a result, benefits for those age 55 and older in 2004 would be unaffected.) Each tax rate change would affect all earnings below the maximum taxable earnings base from then on. Since the already-legislated increases in the full benefit age are supposed to reflect improvements in life expectancy, the adjustment of benefits called for above would be decreased to the extent that these increases in the full benefit age already reduce benefits in the relevant years.[10] To do otherwise would be to adjust twice for the same change in life expectancy. Since this already-legislated change is likely to exceed our life expectancy adjustment to benefits, this is tantamount to skipping the benefit decrease for life expectancy in those years when the age for full benefits changes.

It is worth emphasizing that our proposal would *not* change either the full benefit age or the earliest eligibility age. Indeed, we do not support any simple principle for adjusting Social Security based on an expectation regarding how much longer people should work in response to lower mortality rates. The reason is that the age at which it is sensible for a worker to retire depends on more than just life expectancy. It depends as well on how a worker's ability to work, interest in work, and the availability of jobs vary as mortality decreases. It also depends on the extent to which, because of higher earnings, workers are more interested in retiring earlier. Furthermore, the diversity in the labor force and the appropriateness (in some cases the need) for some workers to take early retirement also underscore the importance of preserving early retirement options. And future declines in mortality will widen the variance in ages at death, which is also exacerbated by the income-related difference in the rate of decline in mortality rates. These factors, if anything, *increase* the importance of providing an option of early retirement for those with shorter life expectancy.

Implementing this proposal would reduce the seventy-five-year actuarial deficit by 0.55 percent of taxable payroll, or slightly less than a third of the currently projected deficit. Moreover, the change would attenuate the terminal-year effect of moving from one seventy-five-year projection period to the next.

Adjustments for Increased Earnings Inequality

As explained in chapter 4, the increasing inequality in earnings of recent years means that a much larger fraction of aggregate earnings is not subject to payroll tax than in the past. In 1983, when the last major Social Security reform was enacted, 10 percent of earnings were untaxed because they were above the taxable maximum. In 2002, in contrast, the share of earnings above the maximum was about 15 percent. For Social Security this increase has meant less revenue relative to expenditure, contributing to the program's long-term deficit. That is, if the earnings distribution were more equal, a larger share of earnings would be subject to tax.

In addition to having more of their earnings above the taxable maximum, higher earners have enjoyed increasing life expectancy relative to lower earners. As shown in chapter 4, the decline in mortality rates for more highly educated (and on average higher-earning) men has been more rapid than for less educated men. (Among women, mortality declines have not varied as much by education, at least through the mid-1980s.) As a result, the system has become less progressive on a lifetime basis: the gap between higher and lower earners in how long they collect benefits has been growing.

The life expectancy adjustment included in the first component of our proposal does not vary with income but instead is based on average changes in life expectancy. It therefore does not adjust for the faster-than-average life expectancy gains among higher earners. To the extent that higher earners have experienced and continue to experience more rapid increases in life expectancy than the average earner, their expected lifetime benefits have increased and will continue to rise relative to other workers.

As also noted in chapter 4, the substantial growth in earnings above the taxable maximum has not been accompanied by similar growth in the number of workers with earnings above the maximum. The growth in untaxed earnings thus reflects higher earnings among a roughly constant fraction of highest earners (6 percent of covered workers), relative to the other 94 percent of earners whose earnings are below the maximum. The result has been a reduction in the extent to which higher earners bear the cost of Social Security's progressivity, relative to their total earnings. At the same time, the growth in earnings above the taxable maximum has reduced the replacement rate of Social Security benefits relative to total earnings (as opposed to taxable earnings) for those with earnings above the maximum.

We propose two changes to offset these effects. First, we would raise the maximum taxable earnings base so that the percentage of aggregate earnings covered is closer to that which prevailed in 1983. The large increase since 1983 in the share of earnings that is untaxed because those earnings are above the taxable maximum does not reflect a policy decision, but rather the outcome of changes in earnings patterns in the economy over the past two decades. One could argue that policymakers implicitly agreed in 1983 that only about 10 percent of earnings should escape taxation by virtue of being above the maximum. Thus one reasonable approach would gradually increase the maximum until the 1983 share is restored. But this would generate so much revenue as to result in a large imbalance between our proposed revenue and benefits adjustments in this category. Therefore, in order to achieve a closer balance between the two, we adopt instead the more moderate approach of returning the share of earnings above the taxable maximum about halfway to its 1983 level, that is, to 13 percent, which is approximately its average over the past two decades. We also phase in this reform over an extended period to allow workers time to adjust to the change. In particular, starting in 2005, the maximum taxable earnings base would increase by 0.5 percentage point more than the percentage increase in average wages each year, until 87 percent of covered earnings are subject to payroll taxation in 2063 and later.[11]

Increasing the maximum taxable earnings base would affect only the 6 percent of workers in each year with earnings at or above the current maximum. Moreover, although it would raise their payroll tax payments, it would raise their subsequent benefits as well. (The increase in benefits associated with earnings in the relevant range would, however, only partly offset the increase in revenue, because of the progressivity of Social Security's benefit formula.)[12] Gradually returning the share of untaxed earnings to 13 percent would reduce the seventy-five-year actuarial imbalance by 0.25 percent of payroll, or about one-eighth of the existing deficit.

Second, in response to the increase in earnings inequality and the growing spread in life expectancies between higher earners and lower earners, our plan would increase the progressivity of the Social Security system through changes to the benefit formula. To gain some insight into the effects of this widening disparity in life expectancies, some illustrative calculations may be helpful. In particular, consider benefits received over an entire lifetime rather than in a single year.[13] The increasing difference in life expectancies manifests itself primarily in the relatively longer time that higher earners would be expected to collect benefits. To examine the effect of the growth in this gap, we calculate the expected present discounted value of lifetime benefits. This is the amount today that, with interest, would just pay for the flow of benefits in the future, taking into account the probability that a typical member of the group we are analyzing is alive in each year.[14]

For these types of illustrative calculations, economists commonly use a set of hypothetical workers, data for which are computed by the Office of the Chief Actuary at Social Security. We consider the "low earning" worker and the "maximum earning" worker. In 2003 the low earner (with career average annual earnings of approximately $15,600) claiming benefits at age 65 would receive an annual Social Security benefit of $8,380.[15] The maximum earner (with career average annual earnings of approximately $87,000) claiming benefits at age 65 would receive an annual Social Security benefit of $20,692.

Although precise comparisons are impossible given the imperfect correlation between education and income, the shifts in relative mortality rates for workers of differing educational attainment, documented in chapter 4, provide at least some guidance. For simplicity, we assume that the relative difference in mortality rates does not vary by age, and we assume a simple "composite" worker by taking the average of the male and female mortality rates in each year.[16] Based on rough extrapolations from the available evidence, we assume that, over the past thirty years, the mortality rate for the low earner has increased from 15 percent above the average mortality rate to 30 percent above that rate. We further assume that, over the same period, the mortality rate for the maximum earner has declined from 15 percent below the average mortality rate to 30 percent below it.

Table 5-1 shows the effect of the widening disparity in mortality rates on expected lifetime benefits for the low earner and the maximum earner. The figures are shown as discounted present values assuming a 3 percent real discount rate. The change in mortality rates raises the ratio of lifetime benefits for the maximum earner from 2.75 times the lower earner to 3.10.

As explained in chapter 2, a worker's monthly Social Security benefits are based on a primary insurance amount, which is itself computed by applying a three-tiered formula to the worker's average indexed monthly earnings. In the highest tier of the PIA calculation, which is relevant only for relatively high earners, benefits are increased by 15 cents for every extra dollar in AIME. To respond to the effect of increasing differences in mortality rates illustrated in table 5-1, we would gradually reduce this 15 cents in benefits on each dollar in the top tier by 0.25 cent a year for newly eligible beneficiaries in 2012 and thereafter, until it reaches

10 cents in 2031. This benefit adjustment, which was also adopted by one of the three plans proposed in 2001 by the President's Commission to Strengthen Social Security, reduces the seventy-five-year deficit by 0.18 percent of payroll.

This reduction would affect approximately the highest-earning 15 percent of all workers. If the change had been fully in effect in 2003, for example, it would have affected only those whose AIME exceeds $3,653, or almost $44,000 a year. Social Security data suggest that only about 15 percent of newly retired and disabled workers have consistently had earnings at or above this level over their lifetime. Furthermore, the change would have larger effects on higher earners than on those whose earnings just barely put them in the 15-cent tier. For example, reducing the 15-cent rate to 10 cents would ultimately reduce benefits by 1.6 percent for those with an AIME of $4,167 (and therefore career-average annual earnings of $50,000), but would reduce benefits by 8.7 percent for those with the maximum AIME of $7,250 (and therefore career-average annual earnings of $87,000).

Table 5-1 shows the effect of the reduction in annual benefits for the maximum earner if our proposed change took effect immediately; in fact, we are proposing that the change be phased in gradually and not take full effect until 2031. On a lifetime-benefit basis, the change would roughly offset the increase in the lifetime benefit received by the maximum earner because of the increased spread in mortality rates assumed in constructing the table. Instead of rising from 2.75 to 3.10, the ratio of lifetime benefits for the maximum earner compared to the lower earner only rises to 2.83.

Adjustments for Legacy Costs

As discussed in chapters 3 and 4, Social Security paid far more in benefits to early cohorts than their contributions could have financed. As a result, later cohorts must receive less in benefits than could otherwise be financed from their contributions, unless some additional sources of revenue are provided. The iron logic of this accounting means that current workers, particularly young workers, will not do as well under Social Security as earlier cohorts. This is not a shortcoming in the design of

Table 5-1. *Expected Lifetime Social Security Benefits for Low and High Earners under Alternative Assumptions about Differences in Mortality Rates*

Dollars in present value as of 2003 except where stated otherwise[a]

		Difference in mortality rate between indicated earners and the average earner[c]	
		30 percent	
Type of earner[b]	15 percent	Under current benefit formula	Under authors' proposal[d]
Low earner	101,183	96,323	96,323
Maximum earner	279,532	298, 588	272, 610
Ratio of lifetime benefits, maximum earner to low earner	2.76	3.10	2.83

Source: Authors' calculations based on mortality data provided by the Office of the Chief Actuary, Social Security Administration.

a. Calculations assume a 3 percent real discount rate.

b. Earners are standard hypothetical workers constructed by Social Security from historical data. Low earners are defined as those with career average annual earnings of approximately $15,600 in 2003; maximum earners are those who consistently earn the maximum earnings taxable under Social Security ($87,000 in 2003).

c. The assumed mortality rate of the low earner is the indicated percentage above the average, and that of the maximum earner the same percentage below the average.

d. In this proposal, the primary insurance amount calculation would be changed so that benefits are increased by 10 cents for every extra dollar in AIME within the top tier, rather than 15 cents as under the current formula.

Social Security, but rather a legacy of the relative generosity of benefits provided to earlier cohorts. Estimates suggest that, in an actuarially balanced system, roughly 3 to 4 percentage points of the 12.4 percent payroll tax would be devoted to financing the program's legacy debt.[17]

As we underscored in chapter 3, a crucial question is how to spread the cost arising from the legacy debt fairly across different workers. In our view, several groups do not presently bear their fair share of that cost. First, those state and local government workers who are not covered by Social Security bear none of the legacy cost. We think they should. Second, the limit on taxable earnings reduces the share of the legacy cost borne by higher earners. Because earnings above the taxable maximum are not taxed, those with earnings considerably above the maximum do not bear more of the legacy cost than those at or just above the maximum. We think they should. Third, the legacy debt needs to be spread fairly across cohorts and not allowed to slide indefinitely into the future. For all cohorts not currently close to retirement, benefits should be reduced and the payroll tax increased so as to recognize the cost of financing the legacy debt from Social Security's history. We propose setting as a target that the ratio of the legacy debt to fully taxable payroll be roughly stabilized over time.

Thus we propose changing the way in which the program's legacy debt is financed, in three ways: through universal coverage under Social Security; through a legacy tax on earnings above the maximum taxable earnings base, with the tax rate beginning at 3 percent and gradually increasing over time; and through a universal legacy charge that would apply to workers and beneficiaries in the future.

Universal Coverage

About 4 million state and local government employees are not covered by Social Security.[18] It is unfair to workers who are covered by Social Security (including the great majority of state and local government workers) that many state and local government workers are not included in the program and so do not bear their fair share of the cost of the system's past generosity. On average, state and local government workers are well paid. It therefore seems appropriate that they pay their fair share, along with other higher earners, of Social Security's redistributive cost (the cost of relatively more generous benefits for low earners) as well as the cost of more generous benefits to earlier cohorts.

Pension systems for state and local government workers are generous, on average, compared with those available to privately employed workers. Such generosity can be maintained for current workers while revising the system's parameters for newly hired workers. Of course, state and local governments would need several years to design suitable changes in their systems, and so any requirement that newly hired workers be included in Social Security should only begin some time after legislation is enacted requiring such inclusion. We propose 2008, which is about the phase-in period adopted in 1983 for inclusion of newly hired federal workers in Social Security.

Moreover, inclusion in Social Security would result in a net benefit to some state and local government workers and their families. The clearest beneficiaries are some of those workers who leave state and local government employment before retirement to take jobs in the private sector that are covered by Social Security. Eligibility for Social Security disability benefits does not begin until a worker has held Social Security-covered employment for a given number of years. For example, a worker who has been in uncovered work for ten years would not have Social Security disability coverage for at least five years after beginning covered work. Since many employers do not provide such coverage, many of these workers would thus find themselves without any disability coverage. This gap in coverage can be a source of great financial hardship in the event of disability during the early years of a new job.

Coverage under Social Security would also help workers who leave state and local government jobs before their retirement benefits vest. Even those with vested benefits who leave early in their careers may benefit from being covered under Social Security, since the real value of their state or local government pension typically declines with any inflation that occurs until they reach retirement age; such a decline does not occur under Social Security. After retirement, many (but not all) state and local government plans do provide automatic adjustment of benefits for inflation, but in many cases these increases are capped at 3 percent, whereas Social Security has no such cap.

In addition, the retirement and survivor provisions of some state and local government pension plans do not offer all the protections, to workers and their spouses, provided by Social Security. For example, in the event of death before retirement, some systems offer only a lump sum that reflects the employee's past contributions plus a modest return, and some only refund the contributions, without any return. Instead, Social Security provides annuitized benefits to the deceased worker's young children and, upon retirement, to his or her spouse. After retirement, workers in state and local government plans can choose between single life and joint life annuities, implying that some surviving spouses (those whose spouse chose the single life annuity) will no longer receive benefits once the worker dies. Thus Social Security coverage offers elements of real value to state and local government workers, over and above what their current pension plan offers.

We therefore propose that all state and local government workers hired in and after 2008 be required by law to be included in Social Security.[19] This change would reduce the seventy-five-year actuarial deficit by 0.19 percent of taxable payroll, or roughly 10 percent of the deficit itself.

A Legacy Tax on Earnings above the Maximum Taxable Earnings Base

As previously noted, in an actuarially balanced system, approximately 3 to 4 percentage points of the current payroll tax would generate revenue sufficient to keep the legacy debt from growing faster than taxable payroll. Those with earnings above the maximum taxable earnings base do not bear a share of this legacy cost proportional to their total earnings. Thus we propose a tax on earnings above the taxable maximum; the tax rate would begin at 3 percent.[20] (A similar tax on earnings above the maximum has been proposed by Robert Pozen, a member of the President's Commission to Strengthen Social Security.)[21] This "legacy charge" would reduce the seventy-five-year actuarial deficit by an estimated 0.55 percent of taxable payroll.

How onerous would this legacy tax be? It is worth noting that the 2.9 percent payroll tax for the Hospital Insurance component of Medicare already applies to all earnings. The tax we propose is approximately equal to this tax. Furthermore, the legacy tax would be smaller than the 4.6 percentage point reduction in the top marginal income tax rate since the beginning of 2001. Both these considerations suggest that the tax would not have substantial adverse effects on either the higher earners to whom it would apply or the economy as a whole.[22]

A Universal Legacy Charge on Payroll Taxes and Benefits

The legacy debt arises from decisions that we as a society made decades ago, and it is fitting that future workers and beneficiaries should contribute a fair share toward financing that debt. The final element of our proposal therefore involves a universal legacy charge on both benefits and tax rates, which would apply to all workers from 2023 forward. We select this starting date because the increases in the full benefit age continue until 2022. After 2023 we smoothly increase the legacy charge, since the growth rate in taxable payroll declines thereafter, requiring an offsetting increase in the legacy cost.

The benefit adjustment would reduce initial benefits for newly eligible beneficiaries by 0.31 percent for each year after 2022. (The benefit reduction would be calculated as $1 - 0.9969^{\,t-2022}$, where t is the year in which the worker becomes eligible for benefits.) The benefit reduction for newly eligible beneficiaries in 2024 would be 0.62 percent relative to current law, and so on. This benefit reduction spreads part of the legacy cost over all retirees thereafter.

The revenue adjustment would raise the payroll tax rate by 85 percent of the benefit reduction percentage from this component of our plan. The logic for this 85 percent factor is the same as that for the life expectancy component of the plan; that is, benefits for newly eligible beneficiaries equal 85 percent of total benefits over a seventy-five-year horizon, whereas all earnings within that horizon are subject to the higher tax rate. To balance the seventy-five-year actuarial effect of the benefit reduction, the tax rate must therefore increase by roughly 85 percent of the percentage reduction in benefits. The result is that the tax rate would increase by 0.26 percentage point, or 85 percent of 0.31, each year starting in 2023. (These tax changes would be combined with those called for under the life expectancy component in evaluating a de minimis threshold for tax changes.) Both the benefit and the revenue changes would be adjusted at the end of the seventy-five-year projection horizon to ensure a stable ratio of legacy cost to taxable payroll thereafter.

The legacy charge above the maximum taxable earnings base would also increase over time. Since earnings above the maximum taxable level do not contribute to benefits, the increase in the legacy tax on these earnings would be twice the increase in the legacy charge below the maximum taxable level.

The universal legacy changes combined with the *increase* in the legacy charge above the maximum taxable level would reduce the seventy-five-year deficit by an estimated 0.97 percent of payroll.

The Estate Tax as an Alternative Revenue Source

Throughout its history, all Social Security tax revenue has been linked to benefits in some way, either through the payroll tax (with earnings subject to tax being the basis for benefits) or through the taxation of benefits. The third component of our proposal would set a precedent in that earnings above the taxable maximum would be subjected to partial taxation but would not affect the calculation of benefits.[23] An alternative deviation from the historical pattern could come from dedicating some other source of revenue to Social Security. Given that unified federal budget deficits are projected for the foreseeable future, however, any reform proposal should devote only dedicated revenue to Social Security rather than an unspecified source of general revenue. Moreover, as discussed in chapter 3, any such dedicated revenue that makes use of existing revenue sources should have a strong likelihood of being eliminated otherwise, so that it does not make the problem of reducing the federal deficit even more difficult. One possible source of dedicated revenue for Social Security is a reformed estate tax.[24] Such revenue could substitute for one or more of the specific revenue proposals in our plan.

Under the Economic Growth and Tax Relief Reconciliation Act of 2001, the estate tax is scheduled to be gradually eliminated. The legislation increases the assets exempt from the estate tax to $3.5 million per person by 2009, reduces the top estate tax rate to 45 percent by 2007, and abolishes the estate tax altogether in 2010. At the end of that year, however, the estate tax would be reimposed in exactly the same form it had in 2001. Virtually no one expects that to happen. Indeed, there is a considerable push to have the estate tax repeal continued in full past 2010. We note that the 2001 legislation did not address the loopholes in estate taxation that have been the focus of many analyses and that weaken the role of the estate tax in both raising revenue and affecting the inequality in income distribution.[25]

The Center on Budget and Policy Priorities estimates that retaining the estate tax in its 2009 form (that is, with a $3.5 million per person exemption and a 45 percent rate) rather than allowing it to be repealed altogether would result in only 0.5 percent of estates—the largest 5 of every 1,000—being subject to taxation in 2010. The total number of estates taxed at all in a given year would be approximately 10,000, and these estates would enjoy lower estate tax rates and a higher exemption than today. More important for our purposes, the revenue raised by retaining the estate tax in its 2009 form rather than repealing it would address about 20 percent of the seventy-five-year actuarial deficit in Social

Security. A reform that closed loopholes in the estate tax would add to its revenue potential at any given tax rate and could be used to replace one or more of our proposed reforms. Alternatively, the estate tax could be transformed into an inheritance tax and the revenue dedicated to Social Security. (Under an inheritance tax, the tax would legally be borne by the recipient of the bequest rather than by the estate.)

Relative to unspecified general revenue transfers to Social Security, an estate tax or inheritance tax is attractive because it could be used as a dedicated source of funds. The revenue collected under the tax is explicit; no estimation or projection is necessary. Moreover, dedicating estate or inheritance tax revenue to Social Security would support the important tradition of keeping Social Security out of the annual budget discussion. Given that so many Americans rely so much on Social Security, its provisions should be adjusted only from time to time, not every year, and with lead times to help workers adapt. The idea of using an estate tax to finance benefits for elderly persons and disabled workers is not new. Indeed, it is over 200 years old, Thomas Paine having proposed it in 1797.[26]

Like many other economists, we consider the estate tax a good source of revenue: it is progressive and seems likely to distort the economy less than other, similarly progressive revenue sources. Several considerations suggest that an estate or inheritance tax makes sense as part of the nation's overall tax structure (although the case for earmarking this revenue source particularly for Social Security rather than other government services is ambiguous).

One element of the logic for an estate tax is that people would tend to prefer paying a tax at death rather than an equivalent amount in tax while living.[27] A second is that, as a measure of ability to pay, bequests may be preferable to income. Indeed, more generally, a measure reflecting both wealth and income would better reflect ability to pay than income alone, and some other industrial countries already impose an annual tax on wealth, something that has not been done in the United States. The estate tax provides a substitute.[28] Third, estate and inheritance taxes are typically imposed in conjunction with gift taxes; such gift taxes are crucial to avoiding gaming of the income tax system.[29]

Given the highly progressive nature of an estate or inheritance tax, we think that part of its revenue could, if policymakers prefer, be dedicated to Social Security in place of one or more of our other proposals that likewise affect high earners disproportionately. For example, estate or inheritance tax revenue could substitute for the partial taxation of earnings above the maximum taxable earnings base, or to limit the increase in the taxable maximum or the decrease in the benefit rate for those with the highest earnings.

Summary and Conclusions

Our three-part proposal would restore seventy-five-year actuarial balance to Social Security, as summarized in table 5-2. These proposals were designed to achieve actuarial balance while also achieving "sustainable solvency" by ensuring a stable Social Security trust fund ratio at the end of the projection period. The proposal also addresses the terminal-year problem described in chapters 3 and 4, by adjusting the system to increases in life expectancy and phasing in a universal legacy charge. (One of the causes of the terminal-year effect is that the system is still adjusting to the reduction in fertility rates that has occurred since the 1960s. The universal legacy charge facilitates that adjustment.) In combination with the mortality adjustments and the other elements of our proposal, the terminal-year effect basically disappears under our proposal (short-run factors may nonetheless generate some minimal changes in the projection from one year to the next, even if the long-run assumptions do not change).

Other proposed reform packages have contained elements similar to some of our provision (table 5-3). Unlike many other recent reform proposals, however, ours combines reductions in benefits and increases in revenue while preserving the critical social insurance function of the Social Security program. In the next chapter, we turn to four proposals that would improve the functioning of the system in providing this insurance.

Table 5-2. *Impact of Proposed Reforms on Social Security's Seventy-Five-Year Actuarial Balance*

Percent

Proposed reform[a]	Effect on actuarial balance	
	As share of taxable payroll	As share of actuarial deficit[b]
Adjustments for increasing life expectancy		
Adjust benefits	0.26	13
Adjust revenue	0.29	15
Subtotal	0.55	29
Adjustments for increased earnings inequality		
Increase maximum taxable earnings base	0.25	13
Reduce benefits for higher earners	0.18	9
Subtotal	0.43	22
Adjustments for fairer sharing of legacy cost		
Make Social Security coverage universal	0.19	10
Impose legacy tax on earnings over maximum	0.55	29
Impose legacy charge on benefits and revenue	0.97	51
Subtotal	1.71	89
Reforms to strengthen social insurance functions[c]	−0.43	−22
Interactions of above reforms	−0.26	−14
Total effect	2.00	104
Alternative: reform existing estate tax[d]	0.60	31

Source: Authors' calculations based on memorandum from the Office of the Chief Actuary.

a. See the text for details of specific proposed reforms.

b. The seventy-five-year deficit is currently estimated to be 1.92 percent of taxable payroll over that period. Numbers may not sum to totals because of rounding.

c. These reforms and their separate impacts on actuarial balance are described in chapter 6.

d. This reform could be enacted in place of one of the other proposed reforms that affect primarily higher earners.

Table 5-3. *Elements of Proposed Actuarial Balance-Improving Reforms Also Included in Other Recent Plans*

Proposed reform[a]	Plans including similar or related proposals
Adjustments for increasing life expectancy	
Adjust benefits	President's Commission (Model 3), Pozen, Aaron-Reischauer, Kolbe-Stenholm, Breaux-Gregg, Personal Security Accounts, Gramlich
Adjust revenue	None
Adjustments for increased earnings inequality	
Increase maximum taxable earnings base	Ball, Kolbe-Stenholm, some members of President's Commission
Reduce benefits for higher earners	President's Commission (Model 3), Pozen, Kolbe-Stenholm, Breaux-Gregg, Gramlich
Adjustments for fairer sharing of legacy cost	
Make Social Security coverage universal	Personal Security Accounts, Maintain Benefits, Aaron-Reischauer, Breaux-Gregg, Ball, Gramlich
Impose legacy tax on earnings over maximum	Pozen
Impose legacy charge on benefits and revenue	Maintain Benefits (included future payroll tax increase not explicitly linked to legacy cost)

Sources: Alternative proposals listed in the table, as follows:

Aaron-Reischauer: plan proposed by Henry Aaron of the Brookings Institution and Robert Reischauer of the Urban Institute in *Countdown to Reform: The Great Social Security Debate* (New York: Century Foundation Press, 2001).

Ball: plan proposed by Robert Ball, former commissioner of Social Security, in Ball and Thomas N. Bethell, *Straight Talk about Social Security* (New York: Century Foundation Press, 1998).

Breaux-Gregg: plan proposed by Senators John Breaux (D-LA) and Judd Gregg (R-NH) and introduced in Congress as the Bipartisan Social Security Reform Act of 1999 (S. 1383); this plan shares many elements with the more recent Kolbe-Stenholm plan.

Gramlich: plan proposed by Edward Gramlich, chairman of the 1994–1996 Advisory Council on Social Security, in Advisory Commission on Social Security, *Report of the 1994–1996 Advisory Commission on Social Security* (Government Printing Office, 1997).

Kolbe-Stenholm: plan proposed by Reps. Jim Kolbe (R-AZ) and Charlie Stenholm (D-TX) and introduced in Congress in August 2001 as part of the 21st Century Retirement Security Act (H.R. 2771).

Maintain Benefits and Personal Security Accounts: plans proposed by different factions of the Advisory Commission on Social Security, *Report of the 1994–1996 Advisory Commission on Social Security* (GPO, 1997).

Pozen: plan proposed by Robert Pozen, formerly a member of the President's Commission to Strengthen Social Security, in "Arm Yourself for the Coming Battle over Social Security," *Harvard Business Review* (November 2002), pp. 52–62.

President's Commission (Model 3): proposal included in *Strengthening Social Security and Creating Personal Wealth for All Americans: Final Report of the President's Commission to Strengthen Social Security*, December 2001, p. 131.

6 Strengthening Social Security's Effectiveness as Social Insurance

The previous chapter described our plan for restoring long-term balance to Social Security. This chapter describes the provisions of our plan that would buttress Social Security's protections for the most vulnerable beneficiaries while still maintaining long-term financial balance in the program. Our goal is to ensure that Social Security continues to provide an adequate base of inflation-protected income in time of need and to cushion family incomes against the possibility of disability, death of a family wage earner, or having one's career not turn out as well as expected. That is one of the reasons that our plan combines benefit reductions and revenue increases, rather than relying excessively on benefit reductions. By limiting the benefit reductions required to achieve long-term balance in the program, our approach preserves a basic level of progressive benefits that are protected against inflation and downturns in financial markets.

Even the relatively modest benefit reductions that workers would experience under our plan, however, would be too much for Social Security's most vulnerable beneficiaries to bear. Three groups that would be particularly affected are workers with low lifetime earnings over a long career, widows and widowers, and disabled workers and young survivors. This chapter therefore proposes ways to mitigate or in some cases eliminate any adverse consequences for these groups from the benefit cuts needed to restore long-term balance. In addition, we propose augmenting the program's protection against unexpected inflation, to shelter all beneficiaries from its potentially serious effects.

Selectively strengthening Social Security in these areas would significantly improve its ability to provide cost-effective social insurance. We explore changes in each area that would better meet the program's social insurance objectives while preserving long-term actuarial balance. Some of these changes use revenue made available by the changes proposed in chapter 5; others do not.

Provisions for Workers with Low Lifetime Earnings

Workers with low lifetime earnings receive meager benefits under Social Security despite the progressive benefit formula. For example, a worker claiming retirement benefits at age 62 in 2003 who has had steadily growing earnings ending at about $15,500 a year would receive an annual benefit of under $7,000. (By "steadily growing," we mean that the worker's wage grew each year at the same rate as average wages in the economy.) That is about 25 percent below the official poverty threshold for a single elderly person.[1] A worker who works 2,000 hours a year at the current minimum wage of $5.15 has annual earnings of $10,300. Such a worker who has had steadily increasing earnings over his or her career and claims Social Security benefits at age 62 in 2003 would receive an annual benefit of less than $6,000.

Low lifetime earnings can arise from a variety of causes. Some people labor at full-time, low-paying jobs over an entire career. Others are in and out of the formal work force at different points in their lives, and therefore their average lifetime earnings (counting the years they are not in the paid work force as zero earnings) are relatively low. Finally, some workers have relatively low lifetime earnings as counted by Social Security simply because most of their career is spent in jobs currently not covered by

Table 6-1. *Retired Beneficiaries Living in Poverty, by Years of Covered Work in 1993*[a]

Percent

Years of covered work	Share living in poverty
20 or less	47.8
21–30	22.9
31–40	18.8
41 or more	10.4

Source: Kelly Olsen and Don Hoffmeyer, "Social Security's Special Minimum Benefit," *Social Security Bulletin,* vol. 64, no. 2 (September 2002), table 6.

a. Table excludes dually entitled beneficiaries.

the program. In designing reforms to improve Social Security's protections against poverty, it is important to distinguish among these various reasons for having low lifetime earnings; in particular, we should avoid giving windfalls to workers whose lifetime earnings are understated by Social Security simply because they worked outside Social Security for some extended period.

In 1993, taking into account all sources of income, 9 percent of retired Social Security beneficiaries lived in poverty. Of these poor beneficiaries, 10 percent had worked for forty-one or more years in employment covered by Social Security, and more than 40 percent had worked between twenty and forty years (table 6-1). Many policymakers remain concerned, as do we, that workers who have had such substantial connections to the work force throughout their careers nonetheless face poverty in retirement.[2]

Before 1982, Social Security included a minimum benefit for low earners, which supplemented what they received under the regular benefit formula. This benefit, however, was not well targeted to workers with low-paying employment over a career: it also provided significant benefits to workers with higher wages who had not worked many years in jobs covered by Social Security. That minimum benefit was therefore eliminated for beneficiaries becoming entitled in 1982 and thereafter. A more targeted special minimum benefit, created in 1972, still exists but is automatically phasing itself out because the value of regular Social Security benefits, which are indexed to wages, is increasing more rapidly than the special minimum benefit, which is indexed to prices. Indeed, under the intermediate cost assumptions of the 2000 Trustees' Report, the special minimum benefit will no longer be payable to any retired workers becoming eligible in 2013 or later.[3]

In light of the declining role of the special minimum benefit under current law, various reforms have proposed strengthening the minimum benefit within Social Security. For example, the reform plan proposed in 2001 by Representatives Jim Kolbe (R-AZ) and Charlie Stenholm (D-TX) included a minimum benefit proposal.[4] The plans proposed by the President's Commission to Strengthen Social Security also incorporated proposals to boost benefits for lower earners that were somewhat similar to the Kolbe-Stenholm approach.[5] Wendell Primus, now on the staff of the Joint Economic Committee, has proposed another version of a new minimum benefit.[6]

Analysis undertaken at the Social Security Administration suggests that a minimum benefit would provide some benefit to a substantial fraction of workers, even though only a modest number of workers would receive the full minimum benefit. Researchers studied the effect of a minimum benefit that would provide 60 percent of the poverty level for workers with twenty years of covered earnings and 100 percent of the poverty level for workers with forty or more years.[7] For workers reaching age 62 between 2008 and 2017, this minimum benefit would provide at least some benefit supplement to 21 percent of men and 49 percent of women (table 6-2). The full minimum benefit would be provided to only a small fraction of these beneficiaries: 3 percent of retired men and 6 percent of retired women. The effect is more pronounced among lower earners, however. More than two-thirds of both men and women with average indexed monthly earnings of less than $1,200 (in 1998 dollars) would receive some benefit from the proposal. Roughly one-tenth of low-income retired workers would receive the full minimum benefit.

We propose a benefit enhancement for low earners that is quite similar to the Kolbe-Stenholm proposal and the approach adopted by the President's Commission to Strengthen Social Security. Our low-earner enhanced benefit would apply to workers with at least twenty years of covered earnings at retirement; for such workers with steadily rising earnings that amount to $10,300 in 2003, the benefit at the full benefit age would be

Table 6-2. *Shares of Retired Beneficiaries Receiving Supplemental Benefits*[a]

Percent

Supplemental benefit received	All retired beneficiaries		Low-earning retired beneficiaries[b]	
	Men	Women	Men	Women
Partial or full minimum benefit	21	49	70	72
Full minimum benefit	3	6	11	8

Source: Steven H. Sandell, Howard M. Iams, and Daniel Fanaras, "The Distributional Effects of Changing the Averaging Period and Minimum Benefit Provisions," *Social Security Bulletin,* vol. 62, no. 2 (1999), charts 2 and 3.

a. Data are projections for workers reaching eligibility between 2008 and 2017.

b. Those with AIMEs less than $1,200 in 1998 dollars.

increased, to equal 60 percent of the poverty threshold in 2012. The benefit enhancement would increase with each additional year of covered earnings, so that benefits would equal 100 percent of the poverty threshold in 2012 for newly eligible workers with at least thirty-five years of covered and steadily rising earnings that amount to $10,300 in 2003.[8] For such workers, the benefit increase would amount to almost 12 percent.[9]

After 2012, the benefit enhancement would increase in line with retirement benefits for an average earner under our plan. (That is, the minimum benefit level would increase by average wage growth minus the mortality and legacy adjustments that would apply to average benefits under our plan, as described in chapter 5.) Because the official poverty threshold increases in line with prices, whereas retirement benefits for the average worker tend to grow faster than prices under our plan, the minimum benefit would tend to increase relative to the official poverty threshold over time. As a result, Social Security would become increasingly effective at ensuring that people who have worked their entire careers will not live in poverty in old age. This proposal would cost 0.14 percent of payroll over the next seventy-five years.

Provisions for Widows and Widowers

A second area in which Social Security should be strengthened is its financial protection of widows and widowers. Widows typically suffer a

30 percent drop in living standards around the time they lose their husband.[10] This decline represents a challenge for a wide variety of widows, pushing some into poverty. Indeed, whereas the poverty rate for elderly married couples is only about 5 percent, that for elderly widows is more than three times as high.[11]

Social Security's spousal and survivor benefits were designed decades ago, when work and family patterns were very different from what they are now. With increasing female labor force participation and evolving family structures, many have come to question this basic structure of benefits. A number of panels and commissions have reviewed this basic structure but failed to come up with an overall reform that attracted wide support.[12] The reason is that all of the proposed reforms would have helped some groups but, because any improvements must be paid for, would have hurt others. And the fact that most of the affected groups include both high-income and low-income individuals made it almost impossible to do good for some without also harming many vulnerable beneficiaries. Rather than tackle the full array of issues involved in reforming Social Security's benefit structure for families, we propose only a partial adjustment in the area where the most agreement exists and where the need for reform may be the most urgent: improving survivor benefits.

Consider a retired husband and wife covered by Social Security. Should either die, the survivor will receive a benefit that is some fraction of the total benefits the couple was receiving while both were alive. In the current system, this "survivor replacement rate" varies with the couple's earnings history. In the case of a one-earner couple, the survivor receives two-thirds of what the couple was receiving, apart from any changes as a result of actuarial reductions and delayed retirement credits. In contrast, for married earners both of whom have identical earnings histories, the replacement is only one-half.[13]

Several reforms have suggested raising the survivor benefit so that it equals at least three-quarters of the couple's combined benefits. The goal would be to increase the benefits of widows, who are generally recognized as making up the majority of survivors. One approach, proposed by Richard Burkhauser and Timothy Smeeding of Syracuse University, would finance this increase in the survivor replacement rate by reducing the spousal benefit.[14] Such a reduction would have little or no effect on two-earner couples, since both members qualify for their own retirement benefit and therefore rely little, if at all, on the spousal benefit. But the reduction in the spousal benefit would have significant effects on one-earner couples, who do rely heavily on that benefit. In other words, the increase in the survivor benefit would benefit all couples, but the method of financing that increase would place a burden on one-earner couples. The package as a whole thus would redistribute from single-earner couples to two-earner couples. Such an approach would also reduce benefits for divorced spouses, a group with a high poverty rate. To avoid increasing their poverty rate, benefits for divorced spouses could be made larger than benefits for still-married spouses, but that seems unlikely to be politically acceptable. Another approach, implicitly followed by the President's Commission to Strengthen Social Security, would finance the increase in the survivor replacement rate (for those with low benefits) out of the program's general resources.

Our alternative proposal makes use of two approaches. For survivors with low benefits, we rely on resources from the reform described in chapter 5. For survivors with higher benefits, we take a different approach.

We propose that the survivor benefit for couples with modest benefits be raised to 75 percent of the combined couple's benefit. To limit the cost of the proposal and target its benefits toward reducing poverty, this enhancement would be capped at what the survivor would receive as a worker with the average primary insurance amount for all retired workers. (President Bush's Commission to Strengthen Social Security also would have imposed this limit.) This targeted proposal would cost 0.08 percent of payroll and be financed by the program as a whole.

For higher-benefit couples we endorse a survivor replacement rate of 75 percent, financed by reducing the couple's own combined benefits while both are alive and using the funds to raise the benefit for the survivor. (Here and below, we use the word "endorse" to indicate changes that we support but are not officially scored in our plan.) In other words, for survivors who would receive the average PIA or more, and therefore would have received a capped benefit or would not be affected by the above proposal, we support a redistribution of the couple's expected benefits toward the survivor and away from the time when both members of the couple are alive. For these couples, the goal is to produce no expected effect on the couple's combined lifetime benefits.[15] Such an approach would merely involve redistribution across time for the couple. (To the extent that the couple's expected mortality experience differed from the population's, there would also be some redistribution toward or away from the couple.) Since the actuarial valuation of our plan is based on a seventy-five-year horizon, and the benefit reductions for the couple would precede the benefit increases for the survivor, this proposal would improve the system's seventy-five-year actuarial balance. However, we did not request that the implied increase be included in the official actuarial evaluation of our plan, since we would prefer that this change not be seen as contributing toward restoring seventy-five-year actuarial balance.

A related issue involves Supplemental Security Income and Medicaid. Increasing survivor benefits or other Social Security benefits could disqualify some people from the SSI program, by increasing their income above the threshold for eligibility in the program. In most states, access for the elderly to Medicaid is tied to SSI eligibility; disqualification from the SSI program could thus result in the loss of Medicaid benefits.[16] Reforms to the SSI eligibility rules are required to avoid this steep implicit tax on increased Social Security benefits.

Provisions for Disabled Workers and Young Survivors

Another group of vulnerable beneficiaries deserves protection from the adverse effects of restoring long-term solvency to Social Security: disabled workers and the young survivors of deceased workers.[17] Despite Social Security's protections, disabled workers and their families have higher poverty rates and are more financially vulnerable than the general population.[18] For example, those who become disabled at young ages typically have substantially less in assets than retired workers—and less than workers who become disabled later in their careers (table 6-3). But even workers who become disabled late in their careers tend to have less in assets than retired workers; how much this differential reflects smaller accumulations of assets while working and how much the adverse financial effects of disability is unknown.[19]

Given the financial vulnerabilities of disabled workers despite Social Security's benefits, various reforms to the disability program seem worthy

Table 6-3. *Median Assets of Married New Beneficiaries in 1982*
Dollars

	Disabled		
Excluding or including home	*Age under 55*	*Age 55–64*	*Retired*
Excluding home	300	3,600	20,000
Including home	23,000	41,000	68,300

Source: Social Security Administration, "SSA's 1982 New Beneficiary Survey: Compilation of Reports" (Washington: Government Printing Office, September 1993), table 7, as reproduced in Peter A. Diamond, Stephen C. Goss, and Virginia P. Reno, "Shifting from Defined Benefit (DB) to Defined Contribution (DC) Benefits: Implications for Workers' Disability and Survivor Benefits," National Academy of Social Insurance, October 1998.

of further examination. An extensive study of these issues should be undertaken by a nonpartisan group, either appointed by Congress or formed by the National Academy of Social Insurance, perhaps upon congressional request. In the absence of a more exhaustive study, we merely propose that, in the aggregate, disabled workers as a group be held harmless from the benefit reductions that would otherwise apply under our plan over the next seventy-five years. Our reform plan thus imposes no net reduction in benefits for the disabled beneficiary population as a whole relative to the scheduled benefit baseline over the next seventy-five years.

We do not propose simply maintaining the current benefit formula for disabled workers, however, for two reasons. The first is that workers who become disabled at younger ages should not be locked into lower real benefits than workers who become disabled at older ages to the degree that occurs under the current system. Imagine disability benefits as replacing the retirement benefits that would have occurred had one not become disabled, as well as providing a bridge to retirement. Then one can see how the current rules leave those who became disabled at young ages far behind where they might have been if the disability had not occurred or had occurred later. In calculating the PIA for a retired worker, past earnings are indexed to the average wage up to the year when the worker turns 60. Then the PIA formula is applied to this indexed earnings level. After disability benefits start, however, benefits only keep pace with prices, as they do for retired workers after age 62. Thus, for a given cohort of workers, the continued growth of productivity in the economy raises retirement benefits for workers who are not disabled, but workers who have been disabled do not share in these productivity gains. From the perspective of social insurance, the result is an inadequate benefit for workers who become disabled at a young age.

A second reason not to simply maintain the current benefit formula for the disabled is that it would add to the tensions already associated with application for disability benefits for those nearing or passing the earliest eligibility age for retirement benefits; the incentive to claim disability benefits arises because, unlike retirement benefits, disability benefits are not actuarially reduced at those ages. For example, consider a worker age 62. If such a worker claims retirement benefits, those benefits are reduced because the worker is claiming before the full benefit age. If the worker succeeds in qualifying for disability benefits, however, his or her benefits are not reduced. Under the current system, there is thus an incentive for workers to claim disability benefits rather than early retirement benefits. If retirement benefits were further reduced but disability benefits were not, this incentive would be strengthened, and concerns about gaming of the system would be more worrisome. To avoid exacerbating that tension and to better target disability benefits to the most needy disabled workers, we propose redistributing benefits toward workers who become disabled very young and therefore are deprived of the opportunity to enjoy the rising earnings that are typical of American workers.

Table 6-4 shows benefit levels for a 25-year-old average-earning worker in 2003 who continues to earn the average wage until becoming disabled. If this worker becomes permanently disabled at age 30, he or she will receive an inflation-adjusted benefit of less than $16,000 for the rest of his or her life. (Most disability beneficiaries do in fact remain permanently eligible for benefits once they have begun receiving them.) Had the same worker become disabled at age 55 instead, he or she would have enjoyed twenty-five years of additional real wage growth and would therefore receive slightly more than $20,000 a year in benefits.

In other words, workers who become disabled while relatively young find themselves locked into a benefit level that does not reflect ongoing productivity growth in the economy, in which they would likely have shared had they not become disabled. Moreover, workers typically experience more rapid earnings growth earlier in their career followed by a decline in relative earnings toward the end of their career (figure 6-1).

Table 6-4. *Disability Benefits for Average-Earning Workers Age 25 in 2003, by Age at Disability*[a]

Age at disability	Year in which worker becomes entitled to disability benefits	Real benefit level (2003 dollars)
30	2008	15,408
35	2013	16,326
40	2018	17,203
45	2023	18,089
50	2028	19,062
55	2033	20,104

Source: *2003 Annual Report of the Board of Trustees of the Federal Old-Age and Survivors Insurance and Disability Insurance Trust Funds,* March 2003, table VI.F11.

a. Data are estimates based on retirement benefits for medium earners turning 62 in the indicated year and subsequently claiming benefits at the full benefit age.

Thus the current benefit formula causes those who become disabled at young ages to miss out not only on economy-wide average wage growth, but also on the above-average wage growth that they would likely have experienced as they advanced in their career.

To allow workers who become disabled at younger ages to share partially in the benefits of aggregate productivity growth that occurs after their disability, we propose indexing disability benefits *after* they have been initially claimed to a combination of wage and price growth rather than to price increases alone. The determination of initial disability benefits would continue to rely on wage indexation, as under current law.

Specifically, to raise real benefit levels over time for workers who become disabled earlier in their careers, our plan includes a "super" cost-of-living adjustment for disability benefits.[20] The super-COLA would have the effect, relative to the current structure of disability benefits, of increasing benefits for those who become disabled at younger ages compared with those who become disabled at older ages. The size of the super-COLA is chosen so that disabled workers as a whole would be held harmless from the benefit reductions in our plan over the next seventy-five years.[21] In particular, the super-COLA would increase disability benefits by 0.9 percentage point a year more than the overall inflation rate. (Although the actuarial evaluation was based on using this figure each year, the actual super-COLA in each year would be an average of wage

Figure 6-1. *Earnings of Medium Earners, by Age*

Percent of average wage index

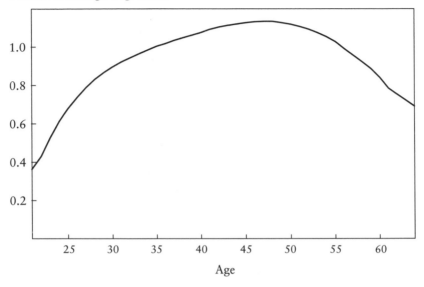

Age

Source: Orlo R. Nichols, Michael D. Clingman, and Milton P. Glanz, "Internal Real Rates of Return under the OASDI Program for Hypothetical Workers," Actuarial Note 144, June 2001, Office of the Chief Actuary, Social Security Administration.

and price growth. The expected value of the super-COLA given current projections for wages and prices is inflation plus 0.9 percentage point.) The excess of the super-COLA over the normal COLA would be treated as an increase in PIA.

This approach has several advantages relative to the alternative of not applying any benefit changes to disabled beneficiaries. First, it retains the close connection between disability benefits and retirement benefits; as under current law, disabled beneficiaries would transfer seamlessly to retired worker status at the full benefit age. Second, as noted above, making no changes whatsoever to disability benefits while reducing retired worker benefits would create even stronger incentives for workers to apply for disability rather than retirement benefits before the full benefit age. Our approach attenuates this problem by redistributing lifetime benefits within the disabled population toward workers who become eligible for disability benefits at younger ages, even while holding disabled workers as a whole harmless from our changes. It strikes us as implausible that younger workers would apply for disability benefits, and thereby forgo substantial future labor earnings, just to offset part or all of the reductions that would otherwise apply to their retirement benefits. Finally, the redistribution seems to us valuable even in the absence of other changes, since workers who become disabled at younger ages seem more needy and are locked into lower real annual benefits than workers who become disabled at later ages.

Two other implications of our approach should be noted. First, workers who become disabled in the near future would receive higher lifetime benefits than under current law, since they would experience little reduction in their initial benefit level and then receive a super-COLA. Second, workers who become disabled at older ages in the distant future would receive lower lifetime benefits than under the scheduled benefit baseline. In other words, this approach holds the disabled worker beneficiary population as a whole harmless from the benefit reductions we would impose over the next seventy-five years, but it does not hold each cohort of disabled workers harmless.

We would apply the same system of super-COLAs to benefits for young survivors. Again, the effect would be, roughly, to hold the young survivor population as a whole harmless from the benefit reductions that would otherwise apply over the next seventy-five years. Together with the super-COLAs for disabled workers, this change would cost 0.21 percent of payroll over the next seventy-five years. That is precisely the effect over the same period of the other provisions of our plan on benefits that apply to all disabled workers and young survivors.

The result is that our proposal to restore long-term balance to Social Security over the next seventy-five years does not rely on any net reduction in benefits for these vulnerable beneficiary groups. Rather, we hold both disabled workers and young survivors as a whole harmless from the benefit reductions that would otherwise apply over the next seventy-five years.

Closing Gaps in the Protection of Benefits against Inflation

This chapter's fourth reform to strengthen the social insurance provided by Social Security differs somewhat from the previous three: we endorse enhancing Social Security's protections against unexpected inflation, thus providing improved insurance to all beneficiaries. (Again, we "endorse" rather than "propose" this reform because this element of our plan was not officially scored by the Social Security actuaries. It should have de minimis actuarial effects, however.)

Social Security benefits were first indexed for inflation in 1972; legislation enacted in 1977 introduced some changes in the system of indexation.[22] The result is that moderate inflation now has little effect on either real benefits or the fiscal position of Social Security. However, a gap remains in the indexing of Social Security, such that a return to very high inflation would have adverse effects on some generations, while saving money for Social Security. We propose to fill this gap in a revenue-neutral way.

The gap in indexing comes about from the way in which benefits are adjusted for inflation after the determination of the AIME. For any year after the year a worker turns 62, benefits are increased by the inflation rate from the year of turning 62 until that year.[23] But the AIME is based on indexing career earnings until the year a worker turns 60, and key components of the benefit formula are indexed in the same way. Thus there is a two-year gap, between ages 60 and 62, in the protection against inflation.

If inflation happened to be particularly severe in some two-year period, workers age 60 at the start of that period would experience a significant decline in their inflation-adjusted benefits. For example, a repeat of the inflation rates of 1980 and 1981 (which resulted in Social Security cost-of-living adjustments of 14.3 percent and 11.2 percent, respectively) would reduce real benefits for that unfortunate cohort by almost 25 percent. Although inflation above the level used in the actuarial projection would reduce real costs for Social Security, there is no reason to subject workers to the risk of an unknown level of inflation during those two years. Thus we propose that the indexing of benefits for inflation start from the year in which a worker turns 60 rather than the year in which a worker turns 62.

By itself, such a change would increase benefits and thus the actuarial imbalance. To preserve projected revenue neutrality, we combine this change in indexing with an across-the-board percentage reduction in benefits meant to leave all workers in the same position relative to expected inflation. The goal is neither to make nor to lose money for

Social Security, and neither to increase nor to decrease lifetime projected benefits, but rather to remove an element of risk that arises from the lack of indexing during these years.[24] This rule applies to disabled workers as well as retirees, since the gap is present in both cases.

To address this gap in indexing, one would ideally use the average earnings index. The problem is that it takes time for the data used to calculate this index to become available, which is why the gap exists in the first place. It is nonetheless feasible to use the consumer price index (CPI) to index benefits starting at age 60. (The CPI is used to adjust benefits after age 62 and is reported with minimal delay.) Thus we propose that all earnings be indexed using the average earnings index for the years before turning age 60, as at present, and that the CPI then be applied to benefits for all years after age 60.

We would also better insulate the Social Security system itself, as opposed to its beneficiaries, against unexpected inflation. The Social Security trust fund currently holds special-issue Treasury bonds that pay an interest rate indexed to the average interest rate the Treasury pays on its long-term bonds. Thus, although Social Security liabilities are indexed to inflation, its assets are not.

Since 1997, the Treasury has made available to the public bonds whose value is protected against inflation. Investing some trust fund revenue in such bonds would better balance Social Security's assets with its liabilities. These inflation-indexed bonds are still relatively new, however, and are sold in a relatively thin market. Hence it is not clear that the trust fund should be tied exclusively to the interest rate on such bonds. Instead we propose that the Treasury make available to Social Security, should the trustees choose to invest in them, special-issue bonds that are indexed to interest rates on long-term inflation-indexed bonds outstanding.

Conclusion

Social Security reform should do more than merely restore long-term financial balance to the program. It should also improve Social Security's protection of some of the most vulnerable beneficiaries: low earners, widows and widowers, and disabled workers and survivors. Because restoring long-term financial solvency to the program is likely to require

Table 6-5. *Impact of Proposed Social Insurance Reforms on Social Security's Seventy-Five-Year Actuarial Balance*

Percent

	Effect on actuarial balance	
Proposed reform	*As share of taxable payroll*	*As share of actuarial deficit*
Enhance benefits for lifetime low earners	−0.14	−7
Increase benefits for widows and widowers	−0.08	−4
Protect disabled workers and young survivors	−0.21	−11
Complete indexation of benefits to inflation	0	0
Total	−0.43	−22

Source: Authors' calculations.

Table 6-6. *Elements of Proposed Social Insurance Reforms Also Included in Other Recent Plans*

Proposed reform	*Plans including similar or related proposals*
Enhance benefits for workers with low lifetime earnings	President's Commission (Models 2 and 3), Kolbe-Stenholm, Breaux-Gregg, Pozen
Enhance benefits for widows and widowers with low benefits	President's Commission (Models 2 and 3), Aaron-Reischauer, Pozen, Kolbe-Stenholm, Breaux-Gregg, Gramlich, Personal Security Accounts
Shift part of couple's benefits to survivor after death of spouse	None
Protect disabled workers and young survivors from effects of other proposed reforms	Aaron-Reischauer, Kolbe-Stenholm
Fill gaps in protection of benefits against inflation	None

Source: Alternative proposals listed in the table, described in table 5-3.

some benefit reductions, balancing those reductions with selective improvements in critical areas seems essential, to cushion the impact of these reductions on the most vulnerable. Our plan therefore not only achieves long-term solvency, but also strengthens Social Security's social insurance protections for these beneficiaries. Table 6-5 shows the cost of these provisions, and table 6-6 shows the use of similar provisions in other reform plans. Finally, it makes sense to eliminate the existing gaps in inflation indexing in Social Security, to improve the program's social insurance function and thus make it more valuable for all workers and their families.

7 Implications for Benefits and Revenue

Our Social Security reform plan would restore long-term balance to the program, update it for developments since the last major reform in 1983, and strengthen some of its most important social insurance features. This chapter traces out some of the implications of our proposed reforms for Social Security benefits and revenue.

In evaluating reform plans, it is important to be clear about the baseline against which the proposed benefits and revenue are compared. In presenting our proposals in previous chapters, we compared all our proposed benefit changes against the scheduled benefit baseline, which reflects what would be paid in the future under the current benefit formula and current projections. The proposed tax changes were described relative to the current tax structure, even though that structure is insufficient to finance scheduled benefits. This combination seemed the most straightforward way to explain the proposed changes to ensure that they were properly understood. For the more detailed comparisons in this chapter, however, we must explicitly

Figure 7-1. *Projected Trust Fund Ratio under Alternative Scenarios, 2004–80*[a]

Percent

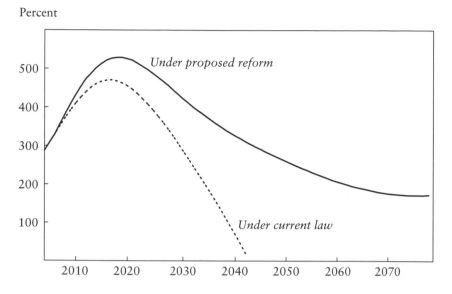

Source: Office of the Chief Actuary, Social Security Administration.
a. Ratio of the trust fund balance to total program expenditure in the indicated year.

recognize the ambiguity involved in how benefits under the scheduled benefit baseline would be financed. The gap between benefits scheduled under the current benefit formula and the revenue that would be raised by the current tax structure could be closed with either general revenue or payroll tax increases. We do not adopt one assumption or the other in the comparisons that follow, but instead report enough information to allow either interpretation.[1]

Actuarial Effects

Figure 7-1 shows the projected path of the trust fund ratio under current law and under our reform plan. (The trust fund ratio is the ratio of the assets of the Social Security trust fund to the program's expenditure in a given year.) As the figure illustrates, our plan achieves a positive trust fund ratio throughout the next seventy-five years and leaves the trust

Figure 7-2. *Projected Cost and Income Rates under Alternative Scenarios, 2004–80*[a]

Percent of taxable payroll

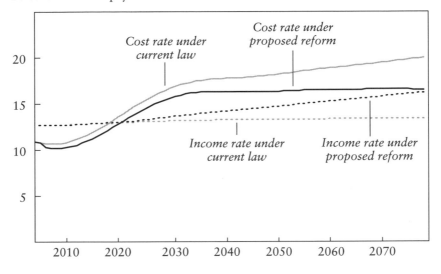

Source: *2003 Annual Report of the Board of Trustees of the Federal Old-Age and Survivors Insurance and Disability Insurance Trust Funds,* March 2003; and Office of the Chief Actuary, Social Security Administration.
a. Projections are based on the Social Security trustees' intermediate cost assumptions.

fund ratio stable at the end of that period, under the intermediate cost projections used by the Office of the Chief Actuary. Note that under our plan the trust fund ratio peaks somewhat higher and somewhat later than under current law and then begins a steady decline. This decline is relatively rapid at first, as the continued financing of benefits to baby-boomer retirees draws the trust fund down. Over time, however, as the baby-boomers die and our changes to both taxes and benefits are slowly phased in, the decline in the ratio slows. By the end of the projection period, the trust fund ratio is again beginning to rise.

Figure 7-2 shows Social Security income and cost rates (see chapter 3 for definitions) under our plan and under current law, as estimated by the Office of the Chief Actuary. As the figure shows, our plan both raises the income rate and reduces the cost rate relative to current law. Note also

Table 7-1. *Changes in Benefits Resulting from Life Expectancy Adjustments under the Proposed Reform, by Age of Beneficiary*
Percent

Age at end of 2004	Change in benefits[a]
55	0.0
45	−0.6
35	−1.8
25	−3.1
15	−4.2

Source: Authors' calculations.
a. Change from benefits provided under current law.

that the two curves converge under our plan, whereas they diverge under the current benefit formula and tax structure.

Effects of Specific Provisions

In this section we report the effects of each of the specific provisions in our plan separately, as if it were the only change from current law. In the next section we report the combined effects of all our proposed changes, which sum the effects of the individual changes and then adjust for the interactions among them. For example, if two separate provisions both multiply the tax rate, the combined effect reflects the product of the two adjustments, which differs from the sum of the two adjustments by the amount of the interaction between them.

Provisions Addressing Increasing Life Expectancy

The first component of our plan adjusts the system to account for continuing increases in life expectancy, through changes to both benefits and revenue. As table 7-1 shows, our proposed life expectancy adjustment would reduce future benefits by only 0.6 percent for those who are 45 years old in 2004 (who become eligible for retirement benefits in 2021) and by 1.8 percent for those who are 35 years old in 2004 (who become eligible for retirement benefits in 2031). As we noted in table 5-3 in chapter 5, many proposed reform plans include automatic adjustments for life expectancy. The other plans, however, make the entire life

Table 7-2. *Payroll Tax Rates Resulting from Life Expectancy Adjustments under the Proposed Reform, 2005–55*

Percent

Year	Employee tax	Combined employer and employee tax
2005	6.20	12.40
2015	6.22	12.45
2025	6.30	12.60
2035	6.37	12.74
2045	6.44	12.87
2055	6.50	13.00

Source: Authors' calculations.

expectancy adjustment on the benefit side. Since we apply only one-half the adjustment to benefits, and the other half to taxes, the decline in benefits due to life expectancy adjustments under our plan is smaller than that in other plans.[2]

Table 7-2 shows that the payroll tax rate would rise slightly over time under this component of our proposal. The employee share of the payroll tax would rise from 6.2 percent today to 6.5 percent by 2055, and the combined employer-employee payroll tax rate would rise from 12.4 percent today to 13.0 percent by 2055.[3]

Provisions Addressing Increased Earnings Inequality

The component of our plan that deals with increased earnings inequality includes two changes: a reduction in the 15 percent factor in the top tier of the PIA formula to 10 percent, and an increase in the maximum taxable earnings base. These changes affect relatively high earners only. As noted in chapter 4, only about 6 percent of workers in any given year have earnings at or above the current taxable maximum. Moreover, only about 15 percent of newly eligible retired workers have sufficiently high earnings to be affected by the top tier of the benefit formula.

The reduction in the 15 percent PIA factor would ultimately reduce monthly benefits for high-income workers in proportion to the amount of their earnings that is within that top tier. Table 7-3 shows the reduction in benefits relative to the scheduled benefit baseline after the reduction in the top tier of the PIA formula is fully phased in. This reduction in monthly

Table 7-3. *Changes in Benefits Resulting from Earnings Inequality Adjustments under the Proposed Reform, by Lifetime Earnings*[a]

Lifetime average annual earnings (2003 dollars)	Change in benefits (percent)
10,000	0.0
20,000	0.0
30,000	0.0
40,000	0.0
50,000	−1.6
60,000	−3.9
70,000	−5.9
87,000	−8.7

Source: Authors' calculations.

a. Data are results of immediately implementing the full change in 2003, even though 2031 is the first year in which the reduction in the top tier of the primary insurance amount formula is fully phased in.

benefits for higher earners, as discussed in chapter 5, is intended roughly to offset the relatively greater life expectancy increases experienced by high-income workers over the past two to three decades.

The second component of the earnings inequality adjustment, the gradual increase in the maximum taxable earnings base, is phased in over time and does not take full effect until 2063. Nonetheless, to illustrate its effects, table 7-4 shows distributional analyses for 2012, using the Urban-Brookings Tax Policy Center tax model, under the assumption that different percentages of this adjustment were already in place by then.[4] We provide the analysis for 2012 because some of our other changes, such as the life expectancy adjustments, do not begin until then.

The top panel of table 7-4 assumes that one-third of the ultimate increase in the maximum taxable earnings base is in effect by 2012 (even though, under the proposal, one-third of the increase would not take effect until 2024); similarly, the middle panel assumes that two-thirds of the ultimate increase is in effect by 2012 (rather than 2043 as under the proposal), and the bottom panel assumes that the full increase is in effect in 2012 (rather than 2063). As the table shows, the overall change in federal taxes is somewhat more modest than the change in payroll taxes alone, because the higher employer share of the payroll tax would reduce taxable wages and therefore reduce income tax payments.[5] The table also

Table 7-4. *Changes in Taxes Resulting from Proposed Increase in the Maximum Taxable Earnings Base, by Income, in 2012*

				Changes in taxes due			
				Payroll tax		Total tax	
Adjusted gross	Tax units[b]		Change in after-tax income		Class share		Class share
(thousands of 2002 dollars)[a]	Thousands	Percent of total	(percent)[c]	Dollars[d]	(percent)[c]	Dollars[d]	(percent)[c]
Assuming one-third of eventual increase in effect by 2012							
Less than 10	37,984	23.8	0.0	0	0.1	0	0.1
10–20	25,364	15.9	0.0	0	0.1	0	0.1
20–30	19,598	12.3	0.0	0	0.1	0	0.1
30–40	14,790	9.3	0.0	0	0.1	0	0.1
40–50	10,860	6.8	0.0	1	0.2	1	0.2
50–75	18,773	11.8	0.0	2	0.4	2	0.4
75–100	12,054	7.6	0.0	15	2.2	15	2.1
100–200	14,612	9.2	–0.3	333	56.6	330	56.7
200–500	3,609	2.3	–0.3	733	30.8	722	30.7
500–1,000	563	0.4	–0.2	896	5.9	882	5.8
More than 1,000	290	0.2	0.0	1,007	3.4	996	3.4
All	159,440	100.0	–0.1	54	100.0	53	100.0
Assuming two-thirds of eventual increase in effect by 2012							
Less than 10	37,984	23.8	0.0	0	0.1	0	0.1
10–20	25,364	15.9	0.0	1	0.1	1	0.1
20–30	19,598	12.3	0.0	1	0.1	1	0.1
30–40	14,790	9.3	0.0	1	0.1	1	0.1
40–50	10,860	6.8	0.0	2	0.2	2	0.1
50–75	18,773	11.8	0.0	3	0.4	3	0.4
75–100	12,054	7.6	0.0	22	1.6	21	1.6
100–200	14,612	9.2	–0.5	608	55.4	602	55.5
200–500	3,609	2.3	–0.6	1,424	32.1	1,406	32.0
500–1,000	563	0.4	–0.3	1,745	6.1	1,725	6.1
More than 1,000	290	0.2	–0.1	1,979	3.6	1,964	3.6
All	159,440	100.0	–0.2	101	100.0	99	100.0

shows that the revenue increases are concentrated among higher earners, as would be expected given the nature of the provision. Even if the provision went fully into effect in 2012, rather than fifty-one years later as under our plan, households with adjusted gross income below $100,000 would face almost no tax increase on average, and the average tax

Table 7-4 *(continued)*

Adjusted gross (thousands of 2002 dollars)[a]	Tax units[b] Thousands	Tax units[b] Percent of total	Change in after-tax income (percent)[c]	Changes in taxes due Payroll tax Dollars[d]	Changes in taxes due Payroll tax Class share (percent)[c]	Changes in taxes due Total tax Dollars[d]	Changes in taxes due Total tax Class share (percent)[c]
Assuming full increase in effect by 2012							
Less than 10	37,984	23.8	0.0	0	0.1	0	0.1
10–20	25,364	15.9	0.0	1	0.1	1	0.1
20–30	19,598	12.3	0.0	1	0.1	1	0.1
30–40	14,790	9.3	0.0	1	0.1	1	0.1
40–50	10,860	6.8	0.0	3	0.1	3	0.1
50–75	18,773	11.8	0.0	5	0.4	4	0.4
75–100	12,054	7.6	0.0	25	1.4	25	1.3
100–200	14,612	9.2	−0.7	829	54.0	822	54.0
200–500	3,609	2.3	−0.8	2,072	33.3	2,049	33.3
500–1,000	563	0.4	−0.4	2,565	6.4	2,540	6.4
More than 1,000	290	0.2	−0.1	2,924	3.8	2,906	3.8
All	159,440	100.0	−0.3	141	100.0	139	100.0

Source: Authors' calculations using the Urban-Brookings Tax Policy Center Micro-simulation Model.

a. Returns reporting negative adjusted gross income are excluded from the lowest income class but included in the totals.

b. Includes nonfilers but excludes dependent filers.

c. After-tax income is adjusted gross income less the employee and employer payroll tax shares and individual income tax net of refundable credits.

d. Change in taxes due for the average tax unit in the indicated income class.

e. Share of the total change in taxes due that is paid by the indicated income class.

increase among households with between $100,000 and $200,000 in income would amount to under $70 a month, or less than $850 a year. Well under 5 percent of the tax increase would be borne by the 87 percent of tax units with adjusted gross incomes of $100,000 or less.

Provisions Addressing the Legacy Cost

The third component of our plan consists of the legacy cost provisions. These have three elements: universal coverage for state and local government workers, the legacy tax on earnings above the maximum taxable earnings base, and the universal legacy charge on both benefits and taxes.

Table 7-5. *Changes in Taxes Resulting from Proposed Legacy Tax on High Earners, by Income, in 2012*[a]

Adjusted gross (thousands of 2002 dollars)	Tax units		Change in after-tax income (percent)	Changes in taxes due			
				Payroll tax		Total tax	
	Thousands	Percent of total		Dollars[b]	Class share (percent)[c]	Dollars[b]	Class share (percent)[c]
Less than 10	37,984	23.8	0.0	0	0.0	0	0.0
10–20	25,364	15.9	0.0	0	0.0	0	0.0
20–30	19,598	12.3	0.0	0	0.0	0	0.0
30–40	14,790	9.3	0.0	1	0.0	1	0.0
40–50	10,860	6.8	0.0	1	0.0	1	0.0
50–75	18,773	11.8	0.0	3	0.1	3	0.1
75–100	12,054	7.6	0.0	6	0.1	6	0.1
100–200	14,612	9.2	–0.4	431	10.2	428	10.2
200–500	3,609	2.3	–2.2	5,543	32.5	5,522	32.4
500–1,000	563	0.4	–3.3	19,188	17.5	19,155	17.5
More than 1,000	290	0.2	–3.3	83,231	39.2	83,195	39.2
All	159,440	100.0	–0.8	387	100.0	386	100.0

Source: Authors' calculations using the Urban-Brookings Tax Policy Center Microsimulation Model.

a. The proposal would apply a 3 percent surcharge on earnings above the maximum taxable earnings base (increasing above 3 percent after 2023). Treatment of returns with negative adjusted gross income and of nonfilers and dependent filers is the same as in table 7-4.

b. Change in taxes due for the average tax unit in the indicated income class.

c. Share of the total change in taxes due that is paid by the indicated income class.

The legacy tax on earnings above the taxable maximum is intended to ensure that higher earners share in the financing of Social Security's legacy debt in proportion to their full earnings, not just their earnings below the maximum. Table 7-5 shows the distributional effects of the 3 percent legacy tax on earnings above the maximum, which under our plan would apply at that rate until 2023. After 2023, when the universal legacy charge would also take effect, the legacy tax rate would slowly increase over time, reaching 3.5 percent in 2080.

As the table shows, the vast majority of the 3 percent legacy tax is borne by households with very high incomes. (The table assumes that the ultimate increase in the maximum taxable earnings base under our proposal has occurred—this is an exception to our general approach of considering each provision on its own at this stage.) For example, tax units

Table 7-6. *Changes in Taxes Resulting from Repeal of Sunsets on 2001 and 2003 Tax Cuts, by Income, in 2012*[a]

Adjusted gross (thousands of 2002 dollars)	Tax units		Change in after-tax income (percent)[c]	Changes in income tax due		Average effective income tax rate[b]	
	Thousands	Percent of total		Dollars[d]	Class share (percent)[c]	Under current law	As proposed
Less than 10	37,984	23.8	0.2	−8	0.1	−10.8	−11.1
10–20	25,364	15.9	2.3	-443	3.8	−2.6	-4.9
20–30	19,598	12.3	2.7	−814	5.5	5.8	3.2
30–40	14,790	9.3	2.4	−957	4.8	9.2	7.0
40–50	10,860	6.8	2.4	−1,218	4.5	10.9	8.8
50–75	18,773	11.8	2.9	−1,997	12.8	12.5	9.9
75–100	12,054	7.6	3.7	−3,470	14.3	14.6	11.4
100–200	14,612	9.2	3.0	−4,106	20.5	18.0	15.5
200–500	3,609	2.3	2.7	−7,282	9.0	24.4	22.4
500–1,000	563	0.4	5.9	−35,771	6.9	29.0	24.8
More than 1,000	290	0.2	6.9	−177,501	17.6	30.0	25.2
All	159,440	100.0	3.3	−1,833	100.0	16.5	13.7

Source: Authors' calculations using the Urban-Brookings Tax Policy Center Microsimulation Model.

a. Repeal of sunsets would extend all income tax provisions scheduled under current law to expire in 2010; baseline for changes is current law. Treatment of returns with negative adjusted gross income and of nonfilers and dependent filers is the same as in table 7-4.

b. Average income tax, net of refundable credits, as a percentage of average adjusted gross income, for the indicated class.

c. Share of the total change in taxes due that is paid by the indicated income class.

d. Change in taxes due for the average tax unit in the indicated income class.

with incomes of between $100,000 and $200,000 would pay an average of $428 a year under this 3 percent tax in 2012. The 0.6 percent of tax units with incomes of $500,000 or more would pay more than half the total tax, and the roughly 3 percent of tax units with incomes of $200,000 or more would pay almost 90 percent. The top 0.2 percent of tax units—those with incomes of $1 million or more—would pay almost 40 percent of the total for this provision.

To put these figures in context, consider the tax *cut* that high-income households will enjoy in 2012 from the 2001 and 2003 tax cuts if those cuts are kept in force through that year, as the Bush administration has proposed. As table 7-6 shows, tax units with incomes of $1 million or more

Table 7-7. *Changes in Benefits Resulting from Proposed Universal Legacy Charge Starting in 2023, by Worker Age in 2004*
Percent

Age at end of 2004	Change from benefits scheduled under current law
55	0.0
45	0.0
35	−2.8
25	−5.7
15	−8.6

Source: Authors' calculations.

would receive an average tax cut of more than $177,000 in 2012 from the 2001 and 2003 laws, more than offsetting the changes proposed here.

The final element in the legacy cost component of our plan, the universal legacy charge, applies to all workers in 2023 and thereafter. As noted in chapter 5, this charge would be roughly evenly split between reductions in benefits and increases in revenue. Table 7-7 shows the resultant pattern of benefit reductions under the benefit component of the universal legacy charge. The tax component of the universal legacy charge would increase the payroll tax rate by 0.26 percent in 2023 and by an additional 0.26 percent each year thereafter. Table 7-8 shows the effect on the payroll tax rate from this effect alone. The combined employer-employee payroll tax rate would rise from 12.4 percent of payroll today to 12.8 percent in 2035 and 13.5 percent in 2055.

Table 7-8. *Payroll Tax Rates with Imposition of Universal Legacy Charge under Proposed Reform, 2005–55*
Percent

Year	Employee tax	Combined employer and employee tax
2005	6.20	12.40
2015	6.20	12.40
2025	6.25	12.50
2035	6.42	12.83
2045	6.59	13.17
2055	6.76	13.52

Source: Authors' calculations.

Table 7-9. *Overall Effect of Proposed Reform on Future Benefits for Workers with Average Earnings, by Age in 2004*

Age at end of 2004	Change in benefits from scheduled benefit baseline (percent)	Benefit at full benefit age (2003 dollars)[a]
55	0.0	15,408
45	−0.6	17,100
35	−4.5	18,200
25	−8.6	19,400
15	−12.4	20,716

Source: Authors' calculations.

a. For a retired worker with scaled medium preretirement earnings pattern. This scaled earnings pattern allows wages to vary with the age of the worker but ensures that lifetime earnings are approximately equal to those of a worker with the average wage in every year of his or her career.

Combined Effects

As we emphasize throughout this volume, our plan combines benefit reductions and tax changes to restore long-term solvency to Social Security. Having analyzed the benefit and revenue effects of each of the individual components of our plan, we now examine the overall implications of our plan, first for benefits and then for the payroll tax rate.

Table 7-9 shows the overall benefit reductions that our plan would impose on a worker with average earnings. For lower earners the reductions in annual benefits would be smaller than shown because of the low-earner benefit enhancement. For higher earners the reductions would be larger than shown, because the income inequality adjustment to the top PIA factor would apply to them and not to lower earners.

As the table also shows, real benefits under our plan would continue to rise from one generation to the next, despite the reductions from baseline, because benefit increases due to ongoing productivity gains are projected to more than offset our modest benefit reductions. An average-earning worker age 55 today, for example, would receive an annual benefit at the full benefit age of $15,408 (in 2003 dollars). An average-earning worker age 25 today would receive an annual benefit at the full benefit age of $19,400 (in 2003 dollars), or more than 25 percent more than the 55-year-old.[6]

Table 7-10. *Overall Effect of Proposed Reform on Future Benefits for Workers Earning the Minimum Wage, by Age in 2004*
Percent

| Age at end of 2004 | Change in benefits from scheduled benefit baseline | | Benefit for minimum wage worker as fraction of poverty threshold[a] |
	For average earner	For minimum wage worker	
55	0.0	0.0	89.4
45	−0.6	11.2	107.3
35	−4.5	6.8	109.0
25	−8.6	2.2	116.2
15	−12.4	−2.1	124.1

Source: Authors' calculations.
a. For retired workers claiming benefits at full benefit age.

Table 7-10 shows the benefit change for long-career, full-time workers earning the minimum wage, defined as those with steadily increasing earnings over their lifetime who earned about $10,000 in 2003. As the table shows, these workers are cushioned from most or all of the modest benefit reductions that apply to the average worker. For example, a 15-year-old in 2004 who earns the average wage over his or her career would experience a 12 percent future benefit reduction under our plan, but a 15-year-old in 2004 who earns the wage-indexed equivalent of the minimum wage would experience only a 2 percent future benefit reduction. Older workers who have low career earnings would experience an *increase* in benefits relative to the current benefit formula, because our low-earner enhancement more than offsets the benefit reductions that would otherwise apply under our plan.

The final column of table 7-10 shows the benefit under our plan for minimum wage workers who retire at full benefit age, as a share of the official poverty threshold. As that column shows, the low-earner enhancement does an increasingly good job at raising long-career minimum wage workers above the poverty threshold: benefits for minimum wage workers of different cohorts rise over time as a fraction of the poverty threshold. For example, the future retirement benefit for a minimum wage worker who is 45 years old in 2004 would be 107 percent of

Table 7-11. *Overall Effect of Proposed Reform on Future Benefits for High-Earning Workers, by Age in 2004*[a]

Percent

Age at end of 2004	Change in benefits from scheduled benefit baseline		Total change in benefit for high-earning workers including interactions
	For average earner	*Applying only to high-earning workers*	
55	0.0	0.0	0.0
45	−0.6	−4.1	−4.7
35	−4.5	−8.7	−12.8
25	−8.6	−8.7	−16.6
15	−12.4	−8.7	−20.1

Source: Authors' calculations.

a. Data are for workers earning, throughout their careers, the wage-indexed equivalent of $87,000 in 2003.

the poverty threshold, whereas the benefit for a minimum wage worker age 25 in 2004 would be 116 percent of the poverty threshold.

Higher earners would experience larger benefit reductions than the average. Table 7-11 shows the benefit reductions for workers who earned $87,000 in 2003 (equal to the current maximum earnings subject to tax; this is approximately the 94th percentile of earners) and whose wages rise with average earnings thereafter. A high earner who is 35 years old in 2004 would experience a 13 percent benefit reduction under our plan, and a high earner age 15 in 2004 would experience a 20 percent reduction; the reductions for average-earning workers of those ages are 4.5 and 12 percent, respectively. As emphasized in chapter 5, the additional benefit reductions for higher earners are intended to offset the relative increases in life expectancies for such workers. In the absence of this or an equivalent change, lifetime benefits under Social Security would become less progressive as higher earners received benefits over an increasing number of years, on average, relative to the rest of the population.

The effect of the plan on disabled workers depends on the year in which the worker becomes disabled and the worker's age at that time. Table 7-12 shows the benefit change for workers who become disabled at different ages in different years. For example, an average-earning worker

Table 7-12. *Overall Effect of Proposed Reform on Future Disability Benefits for Average Earners, by Year of Disability*

Percent

Year disability benefits begin	Benefit change upon receipt of disability benefits	Benefit change when disabled worker reaches full benefit age		
		Disabled at age 25	Disabled at age 45	Disabled at age 55
2015	−0.5	43.7	20.1	9.8
2025	−1.9	42.9	19.4	9.2
2035	−6.2	36.7	14.2	4.5
2045	−10.2	30.9	9.4	0.0
2055	−13.9	25.4	4.9	−4.1

Source: Authors' calculations.

who becomes disabled in 2025 at the age of 45 would experience a 2 percent benefit reduction upon initial receipt of disability benefits. But because of the super-COLA provision that we propose for disabled workers, benefits would exceed current-law levels after three years of benefit receipt for workers who become disabled in that year. If the worker in this example survives to the full benefit age, his or her inflation-adjusted benefits would be almost 20 percent *higher* at that point than under the current benefit formula. These benefit increases for some disabled workers are balanced by benefit reductions for others, particularly those who become disabled later and at older ages, as also shown in table 7-12. Over the seventy-five-year projection period as a whole, the benefit increases for some disabled workers offset the benefit reductions for others, such that aggregate benefits for disabled workers as a whole are thus equal to those for disabled workers under the current benefit formula.

The combined revenue effects of our plan give rise to a gradual increase in the payroll tax. As table 7-13 shows, the employee payroll tax rate under our plan slowly increases from 6.2 percent in 2005 to 7.1 percent in 2055. The combined employer-employee payroll tax increases from 12.4 percent today to 12.45 percent in 2015, 13.2 percent in 2035, and 14.2 percent in 2055.

By 2055 the tax rate is thus 14 percent higher than under the current tax structure (14.18/12.40 = 1.14). For an average worker becoming

Table 7-13. *Payroll Tax Rates under Proposed Reform and Assuming No Reform*

Percent

Year	Current payroll tax rate		Proposed reform		No reform[a]	
	Employee rate	Combined employer-employee rate	Employee rate	Combined employer-employee rate	Employee rate	Combined employer-employee rate
2005	6.20	12.40	6.20	12.40	6.20	12.40
2015	6.20	12.40	6.22	12.45	6.20	12.40
2025	6.20	12.40	6.35	12.69	6.20	12.40
2035	6.20	12.40	6.59	13.18	6.20	12.40
2045	6.20	12.40	6.84	13.68	8.52	17.04
2055	6.20	12.40	7.09	14.18	8.83	17.65

Source: Authors' calculations.

a. Payroll tax rates that would be required to finance scheduled benefits under intermediate cost projections.

eligible for retirement benefits in that year, the PIA is also 14 percent lower than under the current benefit formula. This reflects the rough balance between benefit and revenue changes that we have pursued in our plan.

The overall results for benefit reductions (table 7-9) and tax increases (table 7-13) underscore that it is possible to restore long-term balance to Social Security while retaining the program's core social insurance role and spreading the legacy costs from the program's history fairly across generations. For the vast majority of workers, the provisions included in our plan would involve quite modest changes. The payroll tax rate would rise slowly in response to increasing life expectancy and to adjusting the ratio of legacy costs to taxable payroll; by 2035, the combined employer-employee payroll tax rate under our plan, at 13.2 percent, would be less than a percentage point higher than today's 12.4 percent. The benefit reductions would also be modest and gradual: today's average-earning 35-year-olds, for example, would experience less than a 5 percent reduction in annual benefits compared with the current benefit formula. To be sure, the required adjustments for higher earners would be larger, but so is their ability to absorb those adjustments.

Given how modest the required changes are for most workers when we approach Social Security reform in a balanced manner, a natural question to ask is why reform seems so difficult. In our concluding chapter, we briefly discuss that question. But first we explain, in chapter 8, why we did not include individual accounts in our plan, and in chapter 9 we answer some other possible questions about our plan.

8 | *Individual Accounts*

U nlike many other proposals for Social Security reform, our plan does not call for the creation of individual accounts within Social Security. Individual accounts, which include tax-favored private sector accounts such as 401(k)s and Keoghs, already provide an extremely useful supplement to Social Security, and they can be improved and expanded. But they are simply inappropriate for a social insurance system intended to provide for the basic tier of income during retirement, disability, and other times of need.

Furthermore, individual accounts would help address the actuarial deficit in Social Security only if they are linked to reductions in traditional benefits in some way, either explicitly or implicitly. They would not by themselves improve the ability of the Social Security system to finance its traditional benefits, and they might actually undermine that ability. In particular, if individual accounts were financed by diverting payroll tax revenue away from the Social Security trust fund, the immediate effect would be to *increase* the deficit within Social Security. In that case, individual accounts could help reduce the projected deficit only if they more than compensated for the diverted revenue either by directly returning sufficient funds to Social Security or by being linked in some less direct way to benefit reductions within the traditional system.

However, reducing traditional Social Security benefits to make room for individual accounts would be, in our opinion, a very bad deal for society as a whole. The reason is that the benefits that could be financed from a system of individual accounts would differ from the benefits that Social Security provides today in several important ways, including the following:

—Retirement benefits under Social Security provide an assured level of income that does not depend on what happens in financial markets.[1] Instead, benefits are related to the beneficiary's average lifetime earnings and when the beneficiary chooses to retire. With an individual account, by contrast, benefits during retirement depend on the value of the assets accumulated in the account, which likewise depends in part on lifetime earnings and retirement timing, but also depends on how well one has invested and on how financial markets happened to perform during one's career.[2] It is entirely appropriate and indeed beneficial in some settings for individuals to accept the risks of investing in financial markets; it does not, however, make sense to incur such risks as a way of providing for a base level of income during retirement, disability, or other times of need. This observation is particularly important for those workers who expect to rely heavily or exclusively on Social Security in retirement; recall from chapter 2 that Social Security represents the *only* source of income for one-fifth of elderly beneficiaries.

—Retirement benefits under Social Security are protected from inflation and last as long as the beneficiary lives. A retirement system based on individual accounts could, in principle, achieve similar protection by requiring accountholders, upon retiring, to convert their account balances into a lifelong series of inflation-adjusted payments (that is, an inflation-indexed annuity), but many proposals for individual accounts do not include such a requirement. Furthermore, any such requirement might not be politically sustainable. Individual accounts have been promoted on the grounds that they would enhance "personal wealth" and "ownership" of one's retirement assets; this seems inconsistent with maintaining substantial restrictions on how accountholders may access and use their accounts. And the goal of "bequeathable wealth," an explicit selling point of some proposals, is in direct conflict with the financing of benefits that last as long as the beneficiary lives. One cannot use the same assets to both maximize benefits during one's own lifetime and leave something for one's heirs. Not all retirement income need be protected against inflation and last for the life of the beneficiary, but some base level of income during retirement, disability, or other times of need should be so protected. Again, this observation is particularly important for workers with little or no retirement savings other than Social Security.

—The Social Security benefit formula is progressive: it replaces a larger share of previous earnings for lower earners than for higher earners. It is difficult to incorporate this type of progressivity into individual accounts plans, and most such plans do not. For the nation, the progressivity of Social Security helps reduce poverty and narrow income inequalities; for the individual, it can cushion the blow from a career that turns out to be less rewarding than one hoped. These protections would be strengthened under our plan, which includes provisions to improve Social Security benefits for the most vulnerable members of society. Individual accounts generally do not provide these protections.[3]

—Social Security provides other benefits in addition to basic retirement income. Some of these, such as disability benefits, would be difficult to integrate into an individual accounts system. Under some individual accounts proposals, disabled workers would not have access to the accumulated assets in their accounts before they reach retirement age; thus the accounts would be of no help to them when needed most. Even with such access, workers who become disabled before retirement age will have had less time than other workers to accumulate a balance in their accounts. Thus, even though disabled workers are on average in worse financial condition than retirees, a movement to individual accounts is likely to treat them even worse than retirees.

—A system of individual accounts would require certain administrative costs to maintain those accounts—costs that the present structure of Social Security avoids. The higher these costs, the less generous the benefits that a given history of contributions can finance. Also, inevitably, some workers managing their own individual accounts will make poor investment choices that will leave them stranded in time of need, even if financial markets have performed well. Although some individual accounts proposals have rules that would limit administrative costs and restrict the opportunities for workers to make very poor investment choices, other proposals leave scope for very high administrative charges and misguided investment decisions. There is thus great uncertainty about the types of protective rules that may or may not accompany any individual accounts plan that is actually implemented.

To explore further why it may not make sense to divert revenue away from Social Security into individual accounts, we first review the broader system of retirement income in the United States. Next we examine a generic example of individual accounts in which the Social Security system is held harmless over the lifetime of a worker for the diversion of revenue into the accounts. We then compare that generic example against some recent proposals for individual accounts, showing that some do *not* hold the Social Security system harmless for the diverted revenue. Finally, we examine the broader macroeconomic effects of partly replacing the existing Social Security structure with individual accounts.

The Role of Social Security and Individual Accounts in Retirement Security

Social Security provides the foundation of retirement income for most households. Other sources of income can be thought of as building on this primary tier. As described in chapter 2, Social Security provides the majority of income for almost two-thirds of beneficiaries over age 65, and it accounts for *all* income for 20 percent of beneficiaries over 65. This basic level of income should be protected from unnecessary risks, including financial market risks borne by the individual.

Employment-based pensions represent a second tier of retirement income. Especially in comparison with Social Security, however, pension coverage in the United States is relatively low: only about half of workers are covered by a pension plan at any point in time, and only about two-thirds are covered at some point in their career.[4] A third tier of retirement income consists of private saving outside the employer-based system.

Keogh accounts, created in 1962, and Individual Retirement Accounts (IRAs), created in 1974, allow workers to save for retirement on a tax-preferred basis. A variety of other tax-preferred savings accounts have also been introduced. Households can and do accumulate financial assets outside tax-preferred accounts as well.

Individual accounts appear in the second as well as in the third tier of the retirement income system. Many employers provide tax-favored individual defined-contribution accounts. Indeed, employer-provided pensions have shifted increasingly from traditional defined-benefit plans toward defined-contribution accounts, such as 401(k), 403(b), and 457 plans. In 1998, employer-provided defined-contribution plans received almost $170 billion in contributions and held more than $2 trillion in assets.[5] Individuals who do not have access to employer-provided pensions of either type, as well as an increasing number of individuals who do, enjoy access to tax-favored individual accounts in the third tier, such as traditional and Roth IRAs. Appendix D provides more details about the array of IRAs and other defined-contribution plans available, including the interactions in availability among them.

Although many workers today own individual accounts, whether provided by their employers or otherwise, higher earners are more likely than lower earners to have such accounts, and they tend to have larger balances as well. Table 8-1 shows the distribution of ownership in defined-contribution pension and IRA assets by level of income, using data from the 2001 Survey of Consumer Finances, conducted by the Federal Reserve. According to the table, roughly half (52 percent) of all households owned at least some assets in a defined-contribution pension or IRA in 2001, but such ownership was much more prevalent among higher earners than lower earners. The value of such accounts is even more skewed toward higher earners, with the top 10 percent of households ranked by income owning more than half of aggregate assets. The bottom 40 percent, in contrast, held only 5 percent of aggregate assets in defined-contribution plans and IRAs. Table 8-2 shows a similar breakdown for households headed by persons nearing retirement. Naturally, older workers tend to have accumulated more in their accounts, but the relative distribution of assets by income level is very similar to that for all workers.

Table 8-1. *Ownership of Defined-Contribution and IRA Assets by Household Income, 2001*

Income percentile	No. of households (thousands)	Median income (dollars)	Share with DC or IRA assets (percent)	All households in range	Households with DC plan or IRA	Share of total assets in DC plans and IRAs (percent)
				Median assets in DC plan or IRA (dollars)		
Below 20	21,296	10,300	13.3	0	4,500	1.1
20–39.9	21,295	24,400	33.3	0	8,000	3.5
40–59.9	21,300	39,900	53.4	800	13,500	8.8
60–79.9	21,298	64,800	74.4	16,000	31,000	18.9
80–89.9	10,645	98,700	84.9	36,000	52,000	17.3
90 and above	10,660	169,600	88.3	102,000	130,000	50.4
All	106,496	39,900	52.2	600	29,000	100

Source: Authors' calculations using data from the 2001 Survey of Consumer Finances and Ana M. Aizcorbe, Arthur B. Kennickell, and Kevin B. Moore, "Recent Changes in U.S. Family Finances: Evidence from the 1998 and 2001 Survey of Consumer Finances," *Federal Reserve Bulletin* (January 2003), pp. 1–32.

Although many workers have tax-preferred defined-contribution accounts, the vast majority of workers do not make the maximum allowed contributions to the accounts already available to them. For example, an unpublished Treasury study in 2000 found that only 4 percent of all taxpayers who were eligible for traditional IRAs in 1995 made the maximum allowable contribution, which was $2,000 at that time.[6] Likewise, the General Accounting Office has found that fewer than 3 percent of participants are constrained by the legal maximum on 401(k) contributions.[7] Other recent studies also find that the fraction of individuals constrained by the IRA or 401(k) limits is very small, on the order of 5 percent of those eligible to participate.[8] This is an important observation when considering the potential role of individual accounts in Social Security. If people do not make full use of the tax-favored individual accounts already available, it is natural to question the need to create new ones. In other words, unless an individual accounts system linked to Social Security is designed to be quite different from existing types of accounts, it is not clear what it would accomplish.

Table 8-2. *Ownership of Defined-Contribution and IRA Assets among Households Age 55–59, by Household Income, 2001*

Income percentile	No. of households (thousands)	Share with DC or IRA assets (percent)	Median assets in DC plan or IRA (dollars)		Share of total assets in DC plans and IRAs (percent)
			All households in range	Households with DC plan or IRA	
Below 20	1,665	25.0	0	8,000	1.1
20–39.9	1,560	49.6	0	12,000	4.2
40–59.9	1,661	61.6	7,200	28,000	8.6
60–79.9	1,507	91.0	50,000	54,000	16.7
80–89.9	825	95.4	148,000	190,000	18.8
90 and above	769	92.1	215,000	299,000	50.6
All	7,986	63.6	10,400	50,000	100

Source: Authors' calculations using data from the 2001 Survey of Consumer Finances.

An Overview of Individual Accounts Plans

Individual accounts could be included in a Social Security reform plan in any of several different ways. For example, participation in the accounts could be voluntary or mandatory; the contributions could be financed through additional tax revenue, on top of the existing payroll tax (the add-on approach; box 8-1), or through the diversion of existing payroll tax revenue into the accounts (the carve-out approach); and accumulations in or withdrawals from the accounts could be explicitly or implicitly linked to reductions in the traditional Social Security benefit. In reality, each of these features represents one dimension of a possible arrangement, along which various intermediate solutions lie as on a continuum. Accounts could have both mandatory and voluntary components, they could be financed by a combination of add-on and carve-out elements, and they could be partly or fully linked to reductions in traditional Social Security benefits, either on a worker-by-worker basis or on an overall system basis.

If Social Security revenue were diverted into individual accounts without any corresponding reduction in benefits, Social Security's financial standing would clearly be worsened. To avoid this, individual accounts financed by such revenue diversion must be linked in some way to a

Box 8-1. *Add-On Voluntary Individual Accounts*

Individual accounts must be linked in some way—either explicitly or implicitly—to benefit reductions within the traditional Social Security system in order for them to play any role in reducing the program's projected deficit. Voluntary add-on accounts seem the least likely to be linked to reductions in benefits. Because participation would be voluntary, and funding would not be connected with the existing payroll tax, it would seem illogical to link reductions in Social Security benefits to participation in such accounts. Instead, voluntary add-on accounts would mostly just mimic the current system of individual accounts in the private sector. One difference is that they might allow the government to compete with the current, private providers of such accounts, but it is unclear how much would be gained from such competition.*

In any case, if voluntary add-on accounts were not linked to reductions in Social Security benefits, they would not contribute in any way to restoring long-term balance to the program. Since this seems to be the most likely outcome if voluntary add-on accounts are established, we do not devote any time to considering such an option.

*To be sure, the existing system of individual accounts could be improved: there is room for simplification, unification, and stronger incentives for low-income workers to make contributions. For example, the 2001 tax act created a "saver's credit" for contributions of up to $2,000 made to IRAs and 401(k) plans by those with modest earnings. But the credit is likely to be of limited value to most low-income families, because it is not refundable and therefore provides no saving incentive to families with no income tax liability after other deductions and credits. For specific ideas regarding how to reform the private pension system, see William G. Gale and Peter R. Orszag, "Private Pensions," in Henry Aaron, James Lindsay, and Pietro Nivola, eds., *Agenda for the Nation* (Brookings, 2003)

reduction in traditional benefits sufficient to offset the cost of the diverted revenue. To examine the effects of individual accounts plans that are linked in this manner, we begin with a generic example of an account structure in which traditional benefits that would otherwise be paid to the individual accountholder are reduced in such a way that traditional Social Security finances are unaffected over the accountholder's lifetime. This holds the Social Security trust fund harmless over the lifetime of the average worker, but not necessarily in each year, from the diversion of revenue.

For our generic example, assume that a flow of revenue, such as payroll tax revenue, that otherwise would have flowed into the Social Security trust fund goes instead into a system of individual accounts. (It does not matter if the revenue is an existing flow or a new, additional flow, as long as it is assumed that it would have gone to the trust fund were it not being diverted to the individual accounts.) To ensure that the traditional Social Security system is held harmless from the diversion, a worker with an individual account in our generic example is considered to owe a "debt" to the Social Security trust fund. Upon retirement, the debt is repaid by reducing the worker's traditional Social Security benefits.[9] Those reductions in benefits must exactly equal the amounts diverted from the Social Security trust fund to the individual accounts, plus the interest the trust fund would have earned on the diverted funds had they remained in the trust fund, in order for the trust fund to be held harmless over the lifetime of the worker. Below we consider the implications of alternative ways of linking benefit reductions to the diversion of revenue.

This generic example raises several issues: the timing of cash flows, the differences between benefits provided by the current Social Security structure and benefits provided by the combined individual accounts–Social Security system, the likelihood that revenue available to the individual accounts would otherwise have been available to Social Security, and possible differences in policy actions due to the presence of the individual accounts.

Revenue Implications: The Cash-Flow Problem

In our generic example, a reduction in traditional benefits is what holds Social Security harmless over the lifetime of a worker for the flow of revenue into the individual account rather than into the Social Security trust fund. However, for each worker, the bulk of the flow of revenue into the individual accounts would precede by many years the offsetting reductions in traditional benefits.[10] For example, the benefit offset for a worker age 25 would occur over a period of several decades that does not begin until about four decades hence. Revenue would thus be diverted from the trust fund over many years before the corresponding "debt" would be repaid.

To analyze the implications of this difference in timing, we first examine the net effect on trust fund revenue of the diversion of revenue and the subsequent reduction of traditional benefits. Then we consider the implications of this pattern given the current financial position of Social Security, revealing a significant cash-flow problem. Currently, roughly 85 cents of every dollar in noninterest Social Security revenue is used to pay benefits during the same year. If revenue were diverted into individual accounts, the reduced cash flow would drive the trust fund balance to exhaustion sooner than currently projected, requiring either some source of additional revenue to continue paying benefits or a reduction in current benefits to offset the reduced revenue flow.

To examine our generic example in more detail, we assume that 2 percent of payroll is diverted to individual accounts, with an offsetting reduction in traditional benefits for accountholders upon retirement, as stipulated above.[11] Figure 8-1 shows the cash-flow effects. Over an infinite horizon, the individual accounts have no effect on the trust fund in present value terms—the trust fund is eventually paid back in full for the diverted revenue. However, the cash flow from the individual accounts is negative over a period of more than forty-five years, because the diverted revenue exceeds the benefit offsets until almost 2050.

The delay between the revenue flow and the corresponding benefit reductions thus poses a significant problem for the Social Security system. Figure 8-2 shows the time profile of the trust fund given the cash-flow changes in figure 8-1, illustrating that the net cash outflow causes the trust fund to be exhausted more than a decade earlier than in the absence of the generic accounts. To offset this negative cash flow, it would be necessary either to phase in benefit reductions more rapidly, to provide additional revenue to Social Security, or to allow Social Security to borrow from the rest of the budget. The problems with general revenue transfers and borrowing are discussed further later in the chapter.

Benefit Comparisons

Apart from the cash-flow problems it would generate, this generic individual accounts system might provide a different form of income during retirement or disability, or following the death of a family wage earner,

Figure 8-1. *Cash-Flow Effects of Generic Individual Accounts, 2005–75*[a]

Percent of taxable payroll

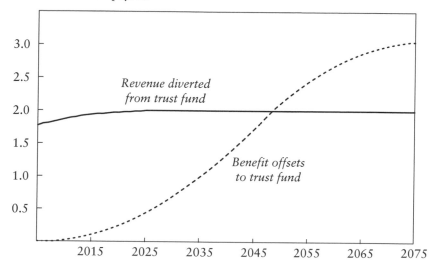

Source: Authors' calculations.

a. It is assumed that 2 percent of payroll for eligible workers is diverted into individual accounts each year and that the trust fund is repaid by reducing the benefits of account-holders over their retirement by the amount diverted plus the interest that the trust fund would have received absent the diversion.

than does the existing Social Security system. With generic individual accounts, workers can make deposits and purchase financial assets such as stocks and bonds today, in effect financing those deposits with decreases in their future traditional benefits. Because the benefit decreases, including interest, are calculated using a Treasury bond interest rate, workers would in effect be doing an "asset swap," substituting a mixed portfolio of stocks and bonds for an all-bond portfolio. Two effects follow from this swap. The first arises from the differences in risk and expected return between bonds and stocks. The second stems from any difference in the form of benefits if the accounts are not converted into annuities that are identical to the traditional Social Security benefits whose reduction ultimately finances the deposits into the individual accounts.

Figure 8-2. *Projected Trust Fund Balance under Generic Individual Accounts, 2002–37*

Trillions of 2002 dollars

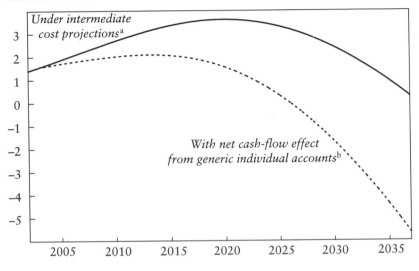

Source: Authors' calculations.

a. Trust fund projections are based on the 2001 intermediate cost assumptions, to facilitate use of the figures produced for the President's Commission to Strengthen Social Security.

b. The trust fund is assumed to be reduced by the difference between diverted revenue and benefit offsets as depicted in figure 8-1.

We divide the analysis of these differences into two components. First we contrast the two approaches on the assumption that the trust fund holds the same assets, on average, as individuals would hold in their individual accounts. Then we explore the implications of differences in the portfolios held by the trust fund and in individual accounts. Both components are needed for a complete analysis of the generic accounts plan.

Benefit Comparisons Assuming Identical Portfolios

Traditional Social Security benefits differ in many ways from the income that a system of individual accounts would generate, even assuming that Social Security and the individual accounts held identical portfolios:

—Social Security's defined benefits are paid as joint-and-survivor real annuities. That means that a worker and his or her spouse are protected against the risks of outliving their assets or seeing them eroded by inflation during retirement. A system of individual accounts could mandate that accountholders purchase such annuities. In the absence of mandatory annuitization, some individuals would likely make choices that are inconsistent with social insurance goals. For example, evidence from the market for private sector annuities indicates that, of the limited number of people who do purchase annuities, most do not select the type that seems most sensible according to basic insurance principles.[12] It appears that individuals do not adequately appreciate the insurance value inherent in annuities, do not adequately value the importance of protecting a survivor, and do not adequately recognize the importance of protection from inflation. Despite these benefits associated with annuitization, mandatory annuitization would be politically difficult, and many individual accounts proposals would not require full annuitization upon retirement. Thus it is entirely possible that an individual accounts plan would be enacted that does not mandate annuitization. Furthermore, one of the arguments put forth by some proponents of individual accounts is that the accounts can be bequeathed to heirs; that is not possible if the accounts are fully annuitized:[13] under the standard annuity arrangement, the pension dies with the annuitant.[14] In short, introducing the opportunity to avoid annuitization would undercut one of the basic principles of Social Security—to provide benefits that are protected against inflation and last as long as the beneficiary is alive.

—Although Social Security provides benefits to disabled workers and to survivors of workers who die before retiring, the individual accounts in our generic example allow workers no access to the funds before reaching retirement age. Instead the example assumes that funds intended for retirement are not spent earlier under any circumstance. In practice, earlier access to the funds in individual accounts could be legislated, either at the time of their enactment or later, just as many workers today may borrow from their 401(k) accounts. Indeed, because of their similarity to 401(k) and other existing accounts, the political pressure to allow preretirement withdrawals from individual accounts is likely to be much greater than the pressure to allow preretirement withdrawals from Social

Security. If earlier access were allowed, it would undercut another of the basic principles of Social Security—to preserve retirement funds until retirement. Earlier access to the funds would, of course, reduce the amounts available in this first tier of income during retirement, unless the funds were repaid in full, with interest, before retirement.

—Within a given generation, the pattern of benefits from individual accounts would likely differ from that under Social Security. The natural political outcome with individual accounts is for individuals to direct their contributions to their own accounts, and then to receive all of the benefits financed by those accounts.[15] The level of benefits financed by such accumulations would depend on interest rates and calculated life expectancies at the time the accumulations are annuitized (assuming that annuitization is made mandatory or that accountholders annuitize voluntarily). Any redistribution from higher to lower earners would have to be explicit, taking funds from one account and placing them in another. Thus, even if individuals with large balances had the same rate of return as those with small balances, benefits from the individual accounts would likely not be progressive within a generation.[16] In contrast, Social Security's defined-benefit structure has a progressive benefit formula. Although a system that *includes* individual accounts could retain overall progressivity, this would involve keeping the traditional system partly in place (and making it even more progressive than before) alongside the nonprogressive individual accounts. The increased progressivity required in the traditional system could be difficult to sustain in the face of adverse economic or demographic developments.

The pattern of benefits from individual accounts would likely differ from that under traditional Social Security *across* generations as well. Whereas the trust fund can be used to spread the risks associated with fluctuations in financial market returns across many generations, individual workers would bear these risks in a system of individual accounts. The inevitable variation in returns on portfolios means that some cohorts of workers will retire at a time when financial markets are depressed and asset values far less than they anticipated. If the individual accounts system mandated conversion to annuities, the pricing of those annuities would also vary significantly across cohorts because of fluctuations in interest rates.[17] In contrast, although traditional Social Security benefits must eventually adapt to the rates of return earned by assets in the trust fund, that adaptation can be spread out over time—indeed, Congress tends to spread Social Security changes widely across cohorts and to avoid sudden surprise changes as much as it can. True, political pressure might be brought to bear to bail out cohorts who have had unfortunate experiences under an individual accounts system, but an equitable outcome would be considerably less certain than under the traditional system. And it is not likely that cohorts with unusually high returns will be forced to help later, less fortunate cohorts.

To sum up, Social Security has certain core principles, including the following: to provide benefits to workers and their families in the form of a real annuity after the disability, retirement, or death of a family wage earner; to provide higher annual benefits relative to earnings for those with lower earnings; and to provide similar replacement rates on average to cohorts that are close in age. A system of individual accounts could well move away from all of these principles. Benefits might be provided as a lump sum that might be outlived, leaving the worker or a surviving spouse much less well off than under an annuity; any access to account balances before retirement could leave less for retirement; replacement rates, rather than being progressive, could be proportional to earnings within a cohort if its members held the same portfolios and faced the same charges; and these replacement rates could vary dramatically from one generation to the next. Finally, under the current system, the level of benefits becomes very predictable as workers approach retirement age; under an individual accounts system, benefits would be far less predictable, depending on possibly sudden changes in asset values.

Portfolio Diversification

The comparisons above assume that each individual account holds a portfolio identical in composition to that of the trust fund. One argument often made by proponents of individual accounts, however, is that such accounts would allow workers to be invested in a combination of stocks and bonds, whereas the existing trust fund is invested entirely in special-purpose Treasury bonds. A diversified portfolio comprising both stocks and bonds would be expected to yield higher returns than a portfolio consisting solely of bonds, and the higher expected return may make the individual accounts seem relatively attractive.

It is important to remember, however, that in an efficient financial market, higher expected returns are earned only by taking on greater risks. Most investors do not like risk. To induce risk-averse investors to place money in riskier assets, those assets must offer higher expected average returns. Risk is one of the principal reasons that stocks tend to have a relatively higher expected average rate of return than other financial assets.

By many common measures, stocks are relatively risky. The Standard & Poor's (S&P) 500 index has declined by more than 10 percent in twenty-one of the years since 1900.[18] (That figure is in nominal terms; in inflation-adjusted terms, the stock market declined by more than 10 percent in twenty-five of those years.) Moreover, individual stocks are considerably riskier than broad portfolios such as the S&P 500; many stocks decline even in years when the market as a whole rises.

Because individuals are averse to risk, comparing average rates of return on assets with different risk characteristics is misleading; an asset with a higher average return but substantially more risk may not be preferable to a lower-yielding, lower-risk asset. The average return on the riskier asset will be higher, but so will be the risk; some who invest in the asset will receive low returns, whereas others investing at different times will receive high returns. To analyze the relative attractiveness of different assets, virtually all economists believe it is necessary to adjust for risk.

To do this, economists calculate for risky assets a rate of return that adjusts for the risk associated with the asset. If the measured rate of return on an asset is high only because it is riskier than other assets, its risk-adjusted rate of return will not be so high: the risk adjustment will partly or fully eliminate the difference in the measured rates of return. The risk-adjusted rate of return thus allows one to evaluate the measured rates of return of different assets on a comparable basis. Only to the extent that the risk-adjusted rate of return is higher on one asset than another would that asset necessarily be preferable as an investment.

To compute risk-adjusted rates of return for various assets, economists have developed a variety of tools for measuring and correcting for risk. The task remains difficult, however. For example, the cost of bearing risk depends on a wide variety of factors, which vary from individual to individual, including especially the other risks to which they are exposed. Chapter 3 discussed some of the elements of risk that are relevant to Social Security reform. Here we focus merely on the relative returns of stocks and bonds, abstracting from the other dimensions of risk.

One critical question is whether the higher returns to stocks observed in the past can be explained solely by the greater riskiness of stocks than bonds. Some economists have concluded that they cannot—that the rate of return on stocks is higher than can be explained by their greater riskiness alone.[19] The complexities of risk adjustment make it difficult to reach a definitive conclusion. Nonetheless, in evaluating recently enacted legislation to allow the Railroad Retirement Fund to invest in equities (that is, stocks), the Bush administration's Office of Management and Budget (OMB) stated:

> Equities and private bonds earn a higher return on average than the Treasury rate, but that return is subject to greater uncertainty. . . . Economic theory suggests, however, that the difference between the expected return of a risky liquid asset and the Treasury rate is equal to the cost of the asset's additional risk as priced by the market. Following through on this insight, the best way to project the rate of return on the Fund's balances is to use a Treasury rate.[20]

In other words, in estimating the rate of return that the Railroad Retirement Fund will receive from investments in stocks, OMB concluded that the rate of return on Treasury bonds should be used rather than the higher average rate of return that stocks are expected to earn. In reaching this conclusion, OMB assumed that all of the difference between the average expected rate of return on stocks and the interest rate on Treasury bonds is due to the greater risk that stocks carry.

A similar conclusion holds for many workers covered by Social Security, namely, those who also hold significant portfolios of assets outside of Social Security to help finance their retirement. A worker accumulating assets for retirement can hold stocks and bonds in existing retirement accounts as well as outside of such accounts. Adding the opportunity to substitute stocks for bonds within Social Security, as our generic example of an individual accounts system effectively does, does not alter the overall composition of the package of assets the worker can choose unless the worker is holding few or no stocks at all outside Social Security. In other words, a worker with a diversified portfolio will generally hold both stocks and bonds, with the shares of each reflecting the worker's risk aversion. An opportunity to become more exposed to stocks through Social Security does not alter this worker's opportunities, if the worker already had the opportunity to sell some of his or her bonds and buy some more stocks. For someone already holding a diversified portfolio, the risk adjustment that is appropriate shows that stocks are worth no more than Treasury bonds.[21]

On the other hand, for workers with so little financial wealth that they are holding no stocks at all, the opportunity our generic example offers is a new one. Such workers may experience a small gain from this opportunity, but the opportunity does involve taking on additional risk.[22] Even for such workers, *some* risk adjustment is therefore appropriate, and the fact that Social Security is the primary tier of retirement income may affect the size of that adjustment. Furthermore, evidence from workers' actual 401(k) investment choices makes it clear that many workers without investing experience have trouble making sensible investment decisions in the absence of significant financial education or extremely restricted portfolio choices.[23] Ensuring that workers have adequate financial education to manage their individual accounts could be expensive, effectively adding to the administrative costs imposed under such a system.

It is worth noting that we do not object to individual accounts on grounds that the stock market is excessively risky. Indeed, if we were advising a large group of individuals saving for retirement, we would recommend a diversified portfolio, not one comprising only bonds. Our discussion of risk is intended primarily to help the reader interpret the presentations of proponents of individual accounts, some of whom regularly report the benefits that such accounts could finance without *any* adjustment for risk. Such presentations should be taken with a very large grain of salt.[24]

Finally, if the judgment were made that diversification into equities does provide benefits even after adjusting for risk, such diversification could also be undertaken directly or indirectly through the Social Security trust fund, without the need for individual accounts. Appendix E discusses this possibility.

The bottom line is that the swap of bonds for stocks inherent in our generic example of individual accounts would be of no value to many workers. For those with little financial wealth, the swap may be of some value, provided the opportunity is pursued with good investment choices and to a sufficiently limited extent, in keeping with the risk aversion appropriate for someone relying very heavily on Social Security. Any potential advantages of such a swap, however, need to be considered along with the disadvantages associated with the potential changes in how benefits are provided. It is precisely those with limited financial wealth who are likely to gain the most from the annuitized benefits provided by the current system, and from its progressivity. Thus those who stand to gain from the change in asset holdings are also those most at risk of losing from other aspects of individual accounts.

Sources of Revenue

Our generic individual accounts system assumes that a given level of revenue is available either to traditional Social Security or to the system of individual accounts. Some analysts, however, argue that an increase in revenue is more feasible politically if it is devoted to a system of individual accounts than if it is devoted to the existing system. Edward Gramlich has been perhaps the most prominent advocate of this perspective.[25] Gramlich proposes a system of individual accounts financed by contributions beyond the existing payroll tax; the mandatory additional contributions would be tantamount to a payroll tax increase that is specifically directed to the individual accounts. This implicit tax increase would then be combined with a reduction in traditional benefits sufficient for the two together to restore actuarial balance to Social Security as a whole.

It may indeed be easier to legislate an implicit tax linked to individual accounts than an explicit payroll tax increase of the same size, although it is difficult to know for sure since strong backing is not currently in evidence for either approach. Our view is that the political system can provide adequate revenue without the crutch of individual accounts and that the shortcomings of such accounts make it worthwhile to seek a reform without them. That is, we think the American public is sufficiently supportive of Social Security that it would continue to reelect legislators who voted for a modest payroll tax increase to shore up the system. To us it does not seem necessary to link payroll tax increases to individual accounts, although we acknowledge that this is a political judgment with which others may differ.

Some individual accounts proposals have not identified a specific source of contributions to the accounts but instead have simply assumed that the ultimate source will be the rest of the federal budget. For example, general revenue could be directly deposited into individual accounts, or existing payroll revenue could be diverted into the accounts and the trust fund compensated with general revenue transfers. In light of the substantial deficits projected for the federal budget, however, any proposal for transfers that does not identify a specific funding source seems strikingly irresponsible to us. Many individual accounts proposals are particularly problematic in this regard, since they rely on massive assumed general revenue transfers.

Future Legislation

It is unclear what rules Congress might impose on individual accounts if they were to be legislated. That is, without a history of legislation on individual accounts within Social Security, any attempt to predict the details of such rules is necessarily highly speculative. (Many proponents of individual accounts point to the experience of Chile for insight into how such a system would work in the United States; box 8-2, however, explains why that analogy may be a poor one.) Perhaps the best basis for assessing how the rules governing individual accounts would evolve in the United States lies in the rules adopted for IRAs and 401(k)s. To the extent that individual accounts in Social Security would be subject to similar rules, the concerns we have expressed about the undercutting of Social Security's social insurance principles are very real.

Diverting revenue into individual accounts could also affect decisions with regard to the rest of the federal budget. For example, many advocates of individual accounts argue that policymakers will treat revenue flowing into these accounts differently from revenue credited to the Social

---

Box 8-2. *Individual Accounts: The Chilean Example*

Much of the present enthusiasm for individual accounts draws on the positive experience in Chile, where such accounts were pioneered. But it is important to keep in mind some fundamental differences between circumstances in Chile in 1981, when these accounts were launched, and in the United States today. One of the most important differences is that Chile's individual accounts replaced a very badly designed social security system; the switch to individual accounts was part of ending an unsatisfactory system. By contrast, the United States enjoys a Social Security system that has been and should remain highly satisfactory once actuarial balance is restored, and restoring balance, as we have argued throughout this book, can be done without radical changes.

Furthermore, at the time, Chile was running a large government budget surplus and chose to use that surplus to finance the transition to a system that would hold more assets. The United States, in contrast, is currently running large budget deficits, raising the question of how the resources would be obtained to fund individual accounts.

Finally, Chile used the introduction of individual accounts to strengthen government reforms of its stock and bond markets. U.S. markets are already well regulated by world standards, and no one claims that the arrival of many new, inexperienced investors would improve the markets' operation. On the contrary, some observers worry that the influx of these novice investors would generate pressures for counterproductive regulatory changes.*

*See, for example, Peter Diamond and Salvador Valdés-Prieto, "Social Security Reform," in Barry Bosworth, Rudiger Dornbusch, and Raúl Labán, eds., *The Chilean Economy* (Brookings, 1994); and Peter Diamond, "Privatization of Social Security: Lessons from Chile," *Revista de Análisis Económico*, vol. 9 (June 1994), pp. 21–23, a revised version of which appears in P. Diamond, D. Lindeman, and H. Young, eds., *Social Security: What Role for the Future?* (Brookings, 1996).

Security trust fund. Whereas surpluses in Social Security tend, in this view, to be treated as available for increases in other federal spending or reductions in other taxes, revenue flowing into individual accounts would not. The fundamental issue, however, is whether the diversion of revenue into individual accounts would raise national saving. As we argued in chapter 3 and discuss further below, we remain skeptical that it would.

The design of Social Security may also influence future legislation, suggesting another difference between the generic system of individual accounts and the existing system. Under an individual accounts system, future Congresses may behave differently if the current projections of Social Security's future prove to be significantly off the mark, for example if the labor force grows more or less rapidly, or productivity increases are larger or smaller, than currently anticipated. For example, assume that revenue falls below forecasts and that part of that shortfall is to be made up by reduced traditional benefits. A proportional reduction in benefits in a system without individual accounts would have a very different distributional effect than a proportional reduction in a scaled-back traditional system combined with individual accounts. This contrast suggests that outcomes are likely to be different, with low earners more severely affected by such a scenario after the introduction of individual accounts.

A final issue involves the political sustainability of the various rules that might be established for the generic system of individual accounts. For example, the future benefit offsets represent implicit taxes on the individual accounts. Imagine the political pressure to reduce those offsets for those whose accounts have fallen sharply in value—or even for those whose accounts have not fallen at all. We are concerned that any plan involving substantial implicit taxes on individual accounts may not prove fully politically sustainable. A related political economy question involves preretirement withdrawals from the individual accounts. Although most individual accounts proposals would prohibit access to the accounts before retirement (except, under some plans, in the case of death or disability), the historical experience with IRAs suggests that there would be pressure to relax those rules. For example, individuals with substantial assets in their individual accounts but few other assets will want to dip into their accounts to pay for college, health care for a family member, or a new home. They may be sufficiently politically powerful to demand changes in the rules, changes that then might become available more widely. Indeed, the government might decide at some point to *require* individuals to tap their accounts before being granted access to government income support programs.

More generally, after almost seventy years the basic structure of Social Security is well settled: Americans have implicitly agreed to use Social Security to provide for a certain range of social insurance goals and not for other purposes. Any radical change in the program's structure would reopen largely settled questions about the broad approach through which the political process will meet this range of goals. In short, drastic changes in Social Security would alter the political environment from one of basic agreement to one of substantial flux and uncertainty. That is a risk that anyone who benefits from the current structure, or is concerned about those who rely on the current structure for their well-being, should regard as worrisome.[26] Indeed, the wide variety of rules proposed across the various individual accounts plans offered to date is itself evidence of how it is hard to predict what will come from such proposals if and when they are enacted, much less over time as political forces evolve.

Other Ways to Link to Individual Accounts

The President's Commission to Strengthen Social Security proposed a system linking individual accounts to traditional benefit reductions that is similar to our generic example. Unlike our generic example, however, both Model 2 and Model 3 as proposed by the commission would have *subsidized* the individual accounts by charging an interest rate on the liability accounts (that is, on the amounts diverted from the trust fund) that is projected to be lower than the return the trust fund earns on its reserves. Because the interest rate on the diverted funds would be lower than what the trust fund would have earned otherwise, these individual accounts proposals would worsen Social Security's financial status. Stated another way, the trust fund earns the interest rate paid on Treasury bonds on each dollar that is not diverted into an individual account; but on each dollar that is diverted into an individual account, under this proposal, the trust fund would earn only the interest rate charged on the liability account, which is lower. This amounts to a subsidy from the trust fund to the individuals who establish individual accounts. We see no good reason why such a subsidy is warranted.[27]

Other methods of linking individual accounts and traditional benefit reductions have been proposed. For example, under so-called clawback provisions, withdrawals from an individual account upon retirement would trigger proportional reductions in Social Security benefits or other transfers back to Social Security. Thus, unlike in our generic example, the returns on individual accounts subject to a clawback would affect not only the individual investor but also the financial position of Social Security. Alternatively, some plans would simply take revenue from the individual accounts without changing traditional benefits. Such a mechanism has been proposed by Representative Clay Shaw (R-FL), among others.[28]

Under the Shaw plan, a worker who retired or became disabled would receive 5 percent of his or her account balance in a lump-sum payment. The other 95 percent of the account balance would be transferred directly back to Social Security.[29] In the absence of countervailing measures, such a structure could create incentives for risky investments in the accounts, since the Social Security system would subsidize 95 percent of any losses and tax 95 percent of the gains.[30] In the Shaw plan, however, workers would be forced to invest in a specified portfolio comprising 60 percent stocks, held in broad market indexes, and 40 percent bonds, in order to avoid the potential gaming problems associated with this type of clawback.

As is apparent from this description, the individual accounts in the Shaw plan are effectively a mechanism for shifting to Social Security the risks and expected returns of investing in stocks rather than bonds. This is done in a particularly expensive way compared with trust fund investment, since individual accounts are expensive to administer, and workers are basically paid a 5 percent fee for lending their names to the accounts. The idea that giving individuals such a small stake in the accounts would dramatically change the politics of Social Security investment in stocks seems implausible. Furthermore, the Shaw plan relies on massive assumed general revenue transfers from the rest of the budget. The plan thus appears to be designed to game the actuarial evaluation of Social Security rather than to truly improve the system. As we discussed in chapter 3, merely shifting from bonds to stocks should not be presented as improving actuarial solvency.

More generally, the availability of individual accounts can be used to "justify" larger benefit cuts than would be needed without the diversion of funding from Social Security to individual accounts.

Administrative Costs and the Structure of Individual Accounts

Our generic example did not examine the administrative costs of individual accounts. Individual accounts would unquestionably entail various administrative costs not present under traditional Social Security. Thus, in order for the net returns available to finance benefits to be the same with individual accounts as with matching trust fund investments, the costs of the accounts must be implausibly low. How high those costs would be in reality would depend on a number of factors, including how centralized the system of accounts was and how limited the investment choices were; the level of service provided (for example, whether individuals enjoyed unlimited telephone calls to account representatives, frequent account balance statements, and other services); the size of the accounts; and the rules and regulations governing them (including whether participation in the accounts was voluntary or mandatory, as explained in box 8-3). The higher the administrative costs, the lower the ultimate benefit a worker would receive, all else equal, since more of the funds in the accounts would be consumed by these costs, and less would be left over to pay retirement benefits. For example, if administrative costs amounted to 1 percent of assets each year over a typical worker's career, the level of retirement benefits that could be financed would be roughly 20 percent less than what could be financed without the administrative costs. If the costs were half as large, the reduction in benefits would also be roughly half as large.[31]

Economic Effects

Replacing part of Social Security with individual accounts could affect the overall economy, through effects on national saving, work effort, and aggregate risk taking. We discussed the effects of the existing Social Security program on national saving and work effort in chapter 3. Here we briefly summarize the likely economic effects of partially replacing traditional benefits with individual accounts.

National Saving

Consider a hypothetical proposal to divert 2 percentage points of payroll tax revenue (about $90 billion a year or so) from the Social Security trust fund into private accounts. At the level of pure arithmetic, this transfer would have no net effect on national saving: government saving would decline by about $90 billion a year as payroll tax collections declined, but private saving would rise by the same amount as the $90 billion was deposited into the new accounts.

Box 8-3. *Should Accounts Be Voluntary or Mandatory?*

Our generic example of individual accounts assumes that the accounts are mandatory. Voluntary accounts linked to traditional benefit reductions raise some additional issues. First, and most obviously, the take-up rate under a voluntary accounts system may be less than 100 percent. All else equal, any effects of adopting individual accounts would then be reduced proportionately. For example, the Office of the Chief Actuary attempted to project what fraction of covered workers would take up the various alternative voluntary accounts proposed by the President's Commission to Strengthen Social Security, resulting in a scaling back of their effects to a fraction of what they would have been under a mandatory system. But reducing the size of a change does not, by itself, necessarily determine whether it is a good or a bad change. In evaluating the implications of such proposals, one also needs to consider both who would take up the accounts and who would not.

Second, voluntary accounts would have higher costs than mandatory accounts in that an additional layer of decisionmaking by the public would become necessary. This would require additional financial education and additional recordkeeping to keep track of the choices. One crucial challenge in a voluntary system is how to ensure that workers make good decisions about whether to opt into the individual accounts. In the United Kingdom, which has had a system of voluntary carve-out individual accounts since 1988, many individuals were deceived as to the benefits of individual accounts, in what has become known as the "mis-selling" scandal.* Evidence shows that the voluntary individual accounts system there has produced significantly higher administrative costs than have been incurred under mandatory systems in other countries.†

---

*High-pressure sales tactics were used to persuade workers to switch into unsuitable individual account plans. Sales agents often sought too little information from potential clients to provide proper advice. The U.K. regulatory authorities began an investigation of this mis-selling phenomenon after the problem became apparent in the early to mid-1990s. As a result of this investigation, financial firms are being forced to repay the equivalent of billions of dollars. In addition, regulators have adopted a more aggressive stance in enforcing regulations on the offering of advice to individuals. For more information on the U.K. system of individual accounts as they existed until recently, see Mamta Murthi, J. Michael Orszag, and Peter R. Orszag, "Administrative Costs under a Decentralized Approach to Individual Accounts," in R. Holtzmann and J. Stiglitz, eds., *New Ideas about Old Age Security* (Washington: World Bank, 2001). See also General Accounting Office, "Social Security Reform: Information on Using a Voluntary Approach to Individual Accounts," GAO-03-309, March 2003.

†See Peter Diamond, "Administrative Costs and Equilibrium Charges with Individual Accounts," in John Shoven, ed., *Administrative Costs and Social Security Privatization* (University of Chicago Press, 2000); and Murthi, Orszag, and Orszag, "Administrative Costs under a Decentralized Approach to Individual Accounts."

Third, with voluntary carve-out accounts, workers may be given the choice to participate on a lifetime basis or on a year-to-year basis. Would an individual be allowed to opt into the individual account system in some years and then opt back into the traditional Social Security program in others? Either approach raises potential problems. Making the choice irrevocable could strand some workers who later realize they made a mistake in opting out or in not doing so. But allowing workers to move back and forth between the two systems could increase the opportunities for gaming the system overall, as well as increase the administrative burdens and costs for the Social Security Administration, which would have to implement and track each choice.[‡] Just as some people try to time financial markets, moving funds between stocks and bonds depending on their view of market prospects, so might people move between individual accounts and traditional benefits in the hope of higher gains from timing investments in the market. By and large, such attempts at timing increase risk and do not raise returns; indeed, some argue that returns for the average investor are much lower as a consequence. Presumably, would-be timers would only be allowed to play this game with their current contributions, and not to shift funds previously invested, but even so, this could create instabilities as well as add to administrative costs.

A fourth issue is whether there would be systematic patterns in who opts into the accounts and whether any such differences in take-up would worsen or improve the social insurance provided by Social Security. The existence and degree of such an effect depend on the full implications of take-up. We have little basis for judging whether accounts would be started

[‡]The United Kingdom has chosen to allow workers to switch back and forth between the state-run system and individual accounts. This policy decision means that workers must decide on an ongoing basis whether to opt into or out of individual accounts, and it has raised the costs associated with providing advice to workers on the best option available to them. If participation in a system of individual accounts is voluntary, and if workers can switch back and forth in this way, workers will typically find it more attractive to opt into individual accounts when young and then move to the state-run system when old. To offset the incentive of younger workers to disproportionately opt into individual accounts, the United Kingdom has adopted an age-related tax rebate scheme. Workers who opt into an individual account obtain a rebate on their payroll taxes, which is used to fund the account contribution. But the rebate rate is higher for older workers and lower for younger workers. Whether or not they serve their purpose, these rebates further complicate the administration of the system and are confusing to many workers.

(Box continues on the following page.)

Box 8-3 *(continued)*

only by those for whom they make sense and not by those for whom they do not. It is possible, however, that the partial withdrawal of higher-income workers could leave behind in the traditional system a pool of disproportionately lower-income workers. Any such disproportionate withdrawal of higher-income workers from Social Security could weaken the system's ability to redistribute toward workers with lower incomes. Some designs for individual accounts would weaken the progressive benefit pattern directly; others might alter the politics of selecting earnings-varying replacement rates.[5]

[5]As David Cutler has emphasized, "We typically think that giving people choice is optimal since people can decide what is best for them. Thus, the economic bias is to believe that, if people want to opt out of social security, they should be allowed to do so. In the context of social security privatization, however, this analysis is *not* right. Allowing people to opt out of social security to avoid adverse redistribution is not efficient; it just destroys what society was trying to accomplish. . . . An analogy may be helpful. Suppose that contributions to national defense are made voluntary. Probably, few people would choose to contribute; why pay when you can get the public good for free? Realizing this, we make payments for national defense mandatory. The same is true of redistribution. Redistribution is a public good just as much as national defense; no one wants to do it, but everyone benefits from it. As a result, making contributions to redistribution voluntary will be just as bad as making contributions to national defense voluntary. We need to make redistribution mandatory, or no one will pay for it." David Cutler, "Comment on Gustman and Steinmeier, 'Privatizing Social Security: Effects of a Voluntary System,'" in Martin Feldstein, ed., *Privatizing Social Security* (University of Chicago Press, 1998), p. 358.

As emphasized in appendix A, however, in evaluating the overall effect on national saving it is important to take into account the likely responses of the government, employers, and households. The historical evidence suggests to us that changes in Social Security surpluses do not necessarily result in large changes in the non–Social Security deficits of the federal government. In that case, the offset from the rest of the budget is likely to be small. Employers might respond to the shift by changing their behavior in some way, but we are unaware of any empirical evidence on this question. Finally, households might respond to the diversion of revenue from the traditional program into individual accounts. If those accounts are more salient to households, such that they view the new accounts as raising their prospective retirement incomes, it seems reasonable to suppose that some of them will reduce their other saving.

It thus seems implausible to us to argue that individual accounts financed by diverting revenue from the existing Social Security system would cause a significant *increase* in national saving. If anything, our impression is that diverting a portion of the current Social Security surplus into individual accounts could reduce national saving.[32]

Work Effort

Substituting individual accounts for traditional defined benefits could also have an effect on work effort. Some analysts think that the greater salience of individual accounts relative to traditional Social Security benefits might generate a significant increase in work effort, if people perceived the accounts as adding to their wealth. We expressed in chapter 3 our skepticism that any significant difference would be observed. That skepticism is based in part on the general observation that younger workers are unlikely to pay a great deal of attention to retirement issues under either system, and on the offsetting theoretical effects on labor supply.[33] It is also based on the absence of significant labor supply effects in the Latin American economies that have substituted individual accounts for some or all of their defined-benefit systems.[34] Furthermore, insofar as accounts do become more salient, they will tend to reduce private saving, as argued above, at the same time that they make workers more willing to work.

Similar issues arise with regard to the decision to retire. Workers contemplating retirement seem to be generally aware that benefits under the current system will be higher if they work longer. Under an individual accounts system, delayed retirement would also increase benefits: more years of work would allow more contributions, more time for assets to accumulate, and a shorter period of retirement to be financed (thus lowering the price of an annuity upon retirement). Given the actuarial adjustments already present in Social Security, however, there is little reason to expect significant differences in an individual accounts system with similar annuitization rules.

Aggregate Risk Taking

As our discussion of the generic individual accounts system indicated, a large part of the effect of swapping trust fund bonds for stocks in individual accounts would be offset by the actions of workers who already hold both bonds and stocks in their portfolios. The net result would be little change in the economy. However, some workers would not make offsetting moves; therefore the demand for stocks would rise while that for bonds would fall. This would tend to raise the interest rate on government (and other) bonds, which in turn would raise the cost to the government of financing the outstanding public debt. In addition, both the higher interest rate on Treasury bonds and the increased demand for stocks would affect stock prices. However, these effects would be counterbalancing: the first would tend to lower stock prices, whereas the second would tend to raise them. It is not clear whether stock prices would rise or fall as a consequence; indeed, their direction would depend in part on whether national saving increased, because higher national saving tends to put downward pressure on interest rates. In any event, we expect that these effects would be small.

Conclusion

Proposals to establish a system of individual accounts within Social Security raise many issues. Diverting revenue into these accounts and away from the existing Social Security system would generate a cash-flow problem for Social Security, even if the system were eventually reimbursed for the diverted funds. Advocates of individual accounts tend to play down this cash-flow problem or simply assume it away. We, however, view the prospect of the Social Security trust fund being exhausted more than a decade sooner than otherwise as a serious political economy problem. Furthermore, the various alternatives for "solving" the problem—including transferring funds from the rest of the budget or reducing current benefits to match the reduced level of revenue—are unappealing.

Individual accounts would also make benefits much riskier and put pressure on Social Security to make changes (including earlier access to accounts, and payouts of lump sums instead of annuities) that would undercut its effective provision of social insurance. We recognize that if Congress is simply unwilling to provide sufficient revenue to preserve the program's current social insurance functions, mandatory add-on individual accounts may be a politically acceptable way to increase the payroll tax beyond what would occur without such accounts. We also recognize that some limited investment of assets in stocks as well as Treasury bonds could make Social Security more valuable. With the relatively small level of assets involved, however, and given the other shortcomings of individual accounts, any such small advantages are not worth the other costs. And we feel confident that any advantages from diversifying Social Security's portfolio—either directly through the trust fund (together with protections against political interference), or indirectly by dedicating a capital income tax to the Social Security system—could be realized without forcing individual workers to bear substantial financial risk to their basic tier of income during retirement, disability, and other times of need.

Furthermore, individual accounts would likely not generate any significant gains in overall economic efficiency. Finally, because individual accounts would fail to provide the social insurance protections that the current system offers, we do not think it makes sense to scale back that system in order to finance another system of individual accounts.

9 Questions and Answers about Our Balanced Reform Plan

Everyone has heard the saying that Social Security is the "third rail" of American politics: touch it and you die. These reports of death by political electrocution may be exaggerated, but no one would dispute that Social Security reform is highly controversial. And as we indicated in chapter 1, views on reform run the gamut. Some analysts do not favor any reform of Social Security at this point; others would destroy the program in order to save it.

Social Security reform is so controversial in part simply because so much is at stake: Social Security plays a crucial role in the lives of millions of Americans. The heatedness of the argument should not prevent us from addressing Social Security's long-term deficit in a sensible way, however, because failing to act now will make the required adjustments all the more painful in the future.

We designed our balanced approach to Social Security reform precisely with the intensity of this controversy in mind. We included both revenue increases and benefit reductions because we felt that a combination of the two would strike most people (and strikes us) as more reasonable than the extreme, polar approaches of relying on either alone. Even so, we expect that our plan will be criticized, especially because it does not take the tack, popular with some advocates, of diverting Social Security revenue into individual accounts. This chapter attempts to respond to the critics preemptively, by anticipating some of their likely criticisms. We answer these criticisms as well as a range of other questions that thoughtful readers might naturally raise. We divide these questions into several broad categories.

Actuarial Solvency

Q: Aren't the official Social Security projections unduly pessimistic? Can't we simply grow our way out of the problem?
A: The current Social Security projections will undoubtedly turn out to be incorrect, in one direction or the other, but we have no reason to suspect that they are unduly pessimistic. The actuarial deficit may turn out smaller than projected, but it may also turn out larger. One can point to certain assumptions (possibly including the productivity growth assumption) that may cause the seventy-five-year projected deficit to be overstated, but one can also point to other assumptions (possibly including the life expectancy assumption) that may understate it. On net, we think the projections are reasonable. Over the years, numerous distinguished and disinterested technical panels have examined the assumptions adopted in the Social Security projections and reached a similar conclusion. The bottom line is that the projections are a reasonable guide to the long-term deficit in Social Security, and it would be imprudent simply to disregard them and assume that the economy will be able to grow its way out of the problem.

Q: But can't we solve the problem without benefit reductions or revenue increases?
A: No. Like most real problems, the long-term Social Security deficit cannot be eliminated painlessly. Some combination of lower expenditure and higher revenue will be required. "Free lunch" solutions that rely on misleading gimmicks—assuming, for example, that trillions of dollars

will be transferred from the rest of the federal budget to Social Security despite large projected budget deficits—have to be recognized as such. Responsible analysts from across the political spectrum acknowledge that the projected deficit in Social Security will require painful choices.

Q: Isn't the problem forty years away? Why do we need to act now?
A: True, under current projections, the Social Security trust fund will not be exhausted for about another forty years. But sensible steps to reform Social Security should be taken sooner rather than later, to allow the required adjustments to be spread over a longer period. Think of Social Security as a giant supertanker. Just as it takes time to change the course of a supertanker, so, too, changing the course of Social Security must be done gradually over time, to allow the millions of people whose lives are affected by Social Security to make the proper adjustments to their retirement planning. So, even though the problem may seem far away, it makes sense to begin addressing it soon. Waiting until a crisis is imminent, as happened in 1983, may mean having to reduce benefits for those already retired, as happened in 1983. However, and at the risk of stating the obvious, acting soon represents sound policy only if the actions taken are sound.

Q: Has your plan been scored by the Office of the Chief Actuary, and has it determined that the plan will restore long-term, sustainable solvency to Social Security?
A: Yes. Everyone involved in the Social Security debate—both Democrats and Republicans—regards the Office of the Chief Actuary at the Social Security Administration as the ultimate scorekeeper on reform plans. A memorandum from the Office of the Chief Actuary attesting to our plan's achievement of long-term sustainable solvency is reprinted as appendix G.

Q: How does your plan balance benefit reductions and revenue increases?
A: Eliminating the Social Security deficit requires, by definition, either benefit reductions or revenue increases, or both. Our goal was to avoid the extremes of closing the deficit solely through one or the other, and instead to pursue a balanced approach, combining the two. Whenever appropriate, we have sought to put approximately the same weight on

benefit reductions and revenue increases. For example, our adjustment for increasing life expectancy is designed so that, in each year over a rolling seventy-five-year projection horizon, roughly half the adjustment occurs on the benefit side and half on the revenue side. Similarly, our adjustment for increased income inequality incorporates two roughly equal effects: that of subjecting a larger share of earnings to the payroll tax (a revenue change), and that of reducing benefits for the top tier of earners (a benefit change). Our universal legacy charge is likewise split roughly evenly between benefit reductions and revenue increases. Some of the reforms that we propose, however, do not lend themselves to such a split between benefit and revenue effects. Among these are our proposals that all newly hired state and local government workers and all workers with earnings above the maximum taxable earnings base share fairly in financing the legacy debt.

Q: How much of the long-term deficit does your plan close through benefit reductions and how much through revenue increases?
A: This is a more complicated question than it may seem at first. For example, part of our life expectancy adjustment and our universal legacy charge involve a reduction in benefits; the decrease in benefits for high earners in the income inequality adjustment is also a benefit reduction. Ignoring interactions, these reductions add up to 0.9 percent of payroll, or 47 percent of the 1.9 percent of payroll deficit, over the seventy-five-year horizon. The payroll tax rate component of the life expectancy adjustment and of the universal legacy charge are revenue increases, as is the legacy tax on earnings above the taxable maximum. These revenue increases add up to 1.3 percent of payroll, or 69 percent of the deficit. This accounting does not include all of our provisions and adds up to more than 100 percent of the deficit, however.

To extend the accounting further, note that two provisions of our plan would broaden the coverage of Social Security in two ways: to newly hired workers in those state and local governments whose employees are not currently covered, and to the earnings of high-earning workers that lie between the existing taxable maximum and the new taxable maximum that we propose. These components add up to 0.44 percent of payroll, or 23 percent of the seventy-five-year deficit. Both these extensions will bring in new revenue and create new benefit obligations for Social Security. But because it is awkward to classify these changes as net revenue increases, and just as awkward to classify them as *both* gross revenue increases and gross benefit increases, the overall accounting seems most naturally divided into three categories: revenue changes, benefits changes, and changes in coverage. Another set of provisions covers the benefit enhancements for long-career low earners, for survivors with low benefits, and for disabled workers and young survivors. When we allocate sufficient revenue to finance these social insurance improvements and account for the contributions of the remaining pieces of our plan, the result is that 47 percent of the 1.92-percent-of-payroll deficit is eliminated by benefit reductions, 47 percent by revenue increases, and 23 percent by coverage expansions. These add up to more than 100 percent of the deficit to be closed, because of interactions.

In summary, different methodologies suggest different answers to the question. The disparity in results illustrates the inherent difficulty in parsing the shares of the deficit reduction due to benefit and revenue components.

Q: Will a seventy-five-year deficit soon reappear under your plan, as happened following the 1983 reforms?
A: Not likely. The 1983 reforms did not address the fact that, although these reforms restored balance to Social Security over the next seventy-five years, the reformed program remained out of balance in the seventy-sixth year and thereafter. With each passing year since 1983, the seventy-five-year projection period has moved forward one year, bringing another deficit year from the far-distant future inside the projection horizon. This terminal-year phenomenon is the main culprit in the relapse of the seventy-five-year balance into deficit after the 1983 reform, explaining more than half the net increase in the deficit since 1983.

Our plan greatly reduces the terminal-year problem and thereby removes a key reason for the deficit to reappear over time. Under our plan, the trust fund balance would be growing, not falling, relative to taxable earnings at the end of the seventy-five-year period. To be sure, the future is uncertain, and one cannot rule out the need to again reform

Social Security sooner rather than later. But there is no reason to expect that a seventy-five-year deficit will reappear in the near future if our plan is passed.

A related question involves the effect of our plan over an indefinite horizon. The Office of the Chief Actuary has not evaluated our plan over such a horizon. Our plan does, however, result in a growing trust fund ratio at the end of the seventy-five-year projection period. In a loose sense, therefore, it appears to succeed in achieving balance over an indefinite horizon. As we explained in chapter 3, however, the seventy-five-year projection period is a better horizon for policymakers to focus on than an indefinite horizon.

Benefits

Retirement Benefits

Q: I am already receiving Social Security benefits. What does your plan do to my benefits?
A: Nothing. You would continue to receive, for the rest of your life, all of the benefits to which you are entitled under current law. Furthermore, since our plan would restore long-term solvency to Social Security, the potential uncertainty regarding whether the system will pay your benefits in the future (and those of your eligible surviving family members) would be resolved.

Q: I turn 55 years old in 2004. What does your plan do to my future Social Security retirement benefits?
A: Our plan does not change your future benefits. You will receive the full benefits to which you are entitled under the current benefit formula. Furthermore, since our plan would restore long-term solvency to Social Security, the potential uncertainty regarding whether the system can pay your benefits in the future would be resolved. In designing the plan, we delayed all benefit changes until 2012, the year after a 55-year-old in 2004 reaches 62, so that near-retirees would not be surprised by the changes. The benefit changes in our plan would affect only those turning 62 in 2012 and thereafter.

Q: I am 35 years old today. How does your plan affect my retirement benefits?

A: If your lifetime earnings are close to the average for all workers, your annual benefits when you retire about thirty years from now would be about 5 percent lower than under the current benefit formula. If you earn more than the average over your career, your benefit reduction would be somewhat larger; if you earn less, your reduction would be smaller.

Q: I have a newborn child. How does your plan affect my child's retirement benefits?

A: If your child turns out to be an average earner, his or her benefits at retirement in the late 2060s or early 2070s would be roughly 18 percent lower than under the current benefit formula—but roughly 50 percent higher than the inflation-adjusted benefit level for a new retiree claiming benefits today. And your child would receive those benefits, on average, over a longer retirement than new retirees today. A newborn in 2004 is projected to have a life expectancy at age 65 that is almost four years— roughly 20 percent—longer than for those turning 65 this year. If your child turns out to be a higher earner, his or her benefit reduction would be somewhat larger; if he or she turns out to be a lower earner, the reduction would be smaller.

Disability Benefits and Young Survivor Benefits

Q: How does your plan handle benefits for disabled workers?

A: Reforming the disability program under Social Security is complicated. We therefore recommend that it be the subject of a major study commissioned by Congress from the National Academy of Social Insurance or possibly some other nonpartisan group. In the absence of a more exhaustive study, we propose that, in the aggregate over the next seventy-five years, disabled workers as a group be held harmless from the benefit reductions that would otherwise apply under our plan. Our reform plan imposes *no net reduction in benefits on the disabled beneficiary population as a whole* from what they would receive under the current benefit formula over the next seventy-five years.

Q: Why don't you just maintain the current benefit formula for disabled workers?

A: We have two objectives in seeking to modify the disability benefit structure while keeping the overall cost of disability benefits unchanged over seventy-five years. The first is to allow workers who become disabled at younger ages to share partially in the benefits of aggregate productivity growth that occurs *after* they become disabled. As we discussed in chapter 6, workers who become disabled at younger ages, all else being equal, receive Social Security benefits that are lower in real terms than those received by workers who become disabled at older ages. The reason is that benefits are indexed to wage growth before the worker claims benefits, but are indexed to price inflation after benefits start. (Wages tend to grow faster than prices over time because of productivity growth.) In our view, lifetime benefits should be raised for those who become disabled at younger ages relative to those who become disabled at older ages.

The second objective is to limit the incentive for older workers to apply for disability benefits when they are already eligible for retirement benefits or will be soon. To see why this is important, consider a worker age 62. If this worker claims retirement benefits, those benefits are reduced because he or she is claiming before the full benefit age. If this worker succeeds in qualifying for disability benefits, however, his or her benefits are not reduced. Under the current system, there is thus some incentive for workers to claim disability benefits if they possibly can, rather than early retirement benefits. If retirement benefits were further reduced (as under our plan) but disability benefits were not, this incentive would be strengthened—and concerns about possible gaming of the system would be more worrisome.

Our approach accomplishes these two objectives by awarding disabled workers an annual benefit increase, after benefits begin, that exceeds inflation. Disabled workers would enjoy an enhanced annual cost-of-living adjustment, or super-COLA, that is higher than the COLA that applies to retired beneficiaries.[1] As explained in chapters 6 and 7, the result of our approach is that disabled workers as a group would be held harmless from the benefit reductions elsewhere in our plan over the seventy-five-year period—total disability benefits paid over that period would not decline compared with the current benefit formula. Some disabled workers (those who become disabled earlier in time and earlier in their lives) would enjoy higher benefits, and some would have lower benefits, but disabled workers as a group would experience no reduction in benefits.

Q: How does your plan handle benefits for the children of deceased workers?

A: Young survivor beneficiaries would be treated in the same way as disabled workers under our plan. In other words, our reform plan imposes *no net reduction in benefits on the young survivor beneficiary population as a whole* relative to what they would receive under the current benefit formula over the next seventy-five years. We would roughly hold harmless the young survivor population as a whole over the next seventy-five years by annually increasing their benefits, after they are claimed, by a super-COLA. Here, too, our approach would redistribute benefits within the young survivor population toward those who were younger when they lost a wage-earning family member and those who lost such a family member earlier in time, but it would maintain the same aggregate level of benefits for the young survivor population as a whole over the next seventy-five years.

Workers with Low Lifetime Earnings

Q: How would benefits for workers with low lifetime earnings change?

A: The goal of our low-earner benefit enhancement is to ensure that workers who have at least thirty-five years of coverage under Social Security do not live in poverty during their retirement. Specifically, workers age 54 today whose earnings are equal to what a full-time minimum wage worker earned in 2003 and have risen with average wages and will continue to do so would receive a benefit at the full benefit age that is at least equal to the poverty level in 2012. In successive generations, benefits for workers of this description would be raised *above* the official poverty line, as explained in chapters 6 and 7. For example, such a worker who first becomes eligible for retirement benefits in 2021 (and who is therefore 45 years old in 2004) would receive a benefit at the full benefit age equal to 107 percent of the poverty threshold, and such a worker who first becomes eligible for retirement benefits in 2041 (and is therefore 25 years old in 2004) would receive a benefit at the full benefit age equal to 116 percent of the poverty threshold.

Women

Q: How does your plan affect women?

A: Two facts about women in general support our approach to Social Security reform. First, women tend to have lower wages, on average, than men. As a result, the progressive nature of our benefit changes would benefit working women. For example, our proposed increase in benefits for workers with low wages on average throughout their careers would provide financial support to women who work long careers at low wages. Second, women tend to live longer than men, underscoring the importance of a source of income that is protected against inflation and against the risk of outliving one's assets. That is why our plan preserves the traditional benefits provided by Social Security, which offers these key protections, rather than scaling back those benefits to finance contributions to individual accounts, which may not (see chapter 8).

Q: What does your plan do for married women?

A: Various elements of our plan are important for married women. Perhaps the most important is the increase in relative benefits for widows. Poverty rates among widows are unacceptably high, and our proposal would raise benefit levels for widows and widowers to reduce poverty among this group.

Minorities

Q: Don't minorities get a bad deal under Social Security? Why are you preserving a system that harms them?

A: Some advocates of individual accounts have made disingenuous statements regarding the treatment of minorities under the current system. The claim that minorities get a bad deal from Social Security is misleading.

A typical claim is that minorities have shorter life expectancies than whites, and therefore collect benefits over a shorter period on average. That claim is misleading because it focuses on only one difference—average life expectancy—between minorities and white Americans. It is true that African Americans have shorter life expectancies than white Americans. (But it is not necessarily true that Hispanics have shorter life expectancies than non-Hispanics; see below.) However, several other differences between whites and minorities also affect the returns to Social Security, in ways that offset the effect of differing life expectancy.

One offsetting factor is that minorities, on average, have lower earnings than the rest of the population. They therefore gain from the progressive benefit structure of Social Security, under which benefits equal a higher percentage of previous wages for lower earners than for higher earners. Claims that minorities realize lower returns on Social Security often compare African Americans and whites *at the same earnings level.* That is misleading because African Americans, on average, have lower earnings and therefore benefit from Social Security's progressive benefit formula.[2] In other words, African Americans have *both* lower earnings and shorter life expectancies than whites. It is misleading to ignore one difference and highlight the other. Indeed, one recent study that takes both life expectancy and earnings into account suggests that the average inflation-adjusted rate of return on Social Security retirement and survivor benefits is slightly higher for blacks than for whites, and much higher for Hispanics than for non-Hispanic whites.[3]

Some minority groups, such as Hispanics, appear to have longer life expectancies than non-Hispanic whites. Since Hispanics also tend to have below-average earnings, they enjoy relatively high returns under Social Security—higher than white Americans receive, on average.

Minorities, on average, also have higher rates of disability than the rest of the population and therefore benefit disproportionately from the disability benefits that Social Security provides. For example, Social Security data show that 1.1 percent of African American workers age 50–59 became disabled in 1997, compared with 0.6 percent of all workers.[4] African-Americans account for 13 percent of working-age Americans, but 17 percent of disabled worker beneficiaries.

Social Security also provides benefits to the young children of deceased workers (as well as to other survivors). Here African American children benefit disproportionately: they constitute 15 percent of all Americans under age 18 but more than 22 percent of children receiving Social Security survivor benefits.

One factor, however, that reduces the return on Social Security to minorities is the system of spousal and widow benefits. Because African Americans are less likely to be married than white Americans, African Americans gain less from these provisions than do white Americans at the same earnings level. The bottom line is that Social Security provides crucial social insurance protections to minorities, and substantially scaling back the Social Security program would impose disproportionate harm on minorities.

Q: How does your plan affect minority workers?
A: Because minorities on average have lower earnings than other workers, the enhanced benefit under our plan for workers with long careers at low earnings would be particularly beneficial to minorities. In addition, as noted above, African Americans make up a disproportionate number of recipients of disability and young survivor benefits under Social Security. Our proposal to hold such beneficiaries harmless as a whole over the next seventy-five years would thus be substantially more advantageous to minorities than plans that would reduce these benefits in step with retirement benefits. Finally, since minorities are underrepresented among higher earners, they would bear a relatively small share of the revenue increases under our plan that are imposed on the top 6 percent of earners.

Retirement Age

Q: Does your plan raise the full benefit age (what others call the normal retirement age)?
A No. The full benefit age is the same under our plan as under current law.

Q: Does your plan raise the earliest eligibility age from 62?
A: No, although whether to include such an increase was a close call. The cost of retiring too early will increase in the future as replacement rates at age 62 decline. (This will occur in response to the already legislated increase in the full benefit age, and the proposed benefits adjustments in

our plan would reinforce that effect.) Despite this concern, we remain unconvinced that an increase in the earliest eligibility age would represent sound policy. There is great diversity among the population in life expectancy and in the profile of earnings abilities as workers age, making retirement at widely different ages sensible for different workers. Social Security needs to recognize this diversity and give workers a range of ages at which they can start benefits. Allowing access to Social Security benefits at age 62 accommodates this diversity as workers live longer and reflects the need of many workers to retire early. If Congress does change the early eligibility age, it should also explore special transitional provisions in the Disability Insurance program and Supplemental Security Income.

Payroll Revenue

Q: Does your plan include tax increases?
A: Social Security faces a long-term deficit, and our plan includes both benefit reductions and revenue increases to eliminate that deficit. The employee payroll tax rate would increase slowly from its current 6.2 percent rate to 6.35 percent in 2025 and 6.84 percent in 2045. The combined employer-employee payroll tax would rise from its current 12.4 percent rate, reaching 12.7 percent in 2025 and 13.7 percent in 2045. At that level the tax rate would still be well below those in most other industrialized countries. To be sure, some will object to any payroll tax increases, but such critics must be willing to acknowledge that without these increases, additional benefit cuts will be required to reach solvency, and they should explain why they believe those benefit cuts would be preferable to a modest payroll tax increase.

Two of our other revenue increases are not relevant to the vast majority of the population: an increase in the maximum earnings subject to payroll tax and a partial tax on earnings above this maximum. These changes would affect only the top 6 percent or so of earners in any given year.

These various revenue increases are combined with benefit reductions in our package. Eliminating the long-term deficit in Social Security in a balanced manner requires a combination of benefit reductions and revenue increases.

Q: I am an average earner making about $35,000 a year. How much more will I pay in payroll taxes under your plan?

A: Under our plan, the employee payroll tax would increase, as noted above, from its current level of 6.2 percent to 6.84 percent in 2045. In other words, you would pay an extra 0.64 percent of your $35,000 a year in earnings, or an additional $223 a year, if the tax were imposed today.

Economists typically assume that you will ultimately bear both the employer share and the employee share of the payroll tax, because market forces will adjust your wages to offset the cost of the employer share of the tax to your employer. On this assumption, the increase in the combined employer-employee payroll tax rate from 12.4 percent (the current level) to 13.7 percent (the projected level in 2045) would require you to pay an additional $447 a year in payroll taxes—or $37 a month—if it were fully in effect today. You should remember, however, that the additional revenue will help to secure the program's financing, so that you and your family can look forward to an adequate level of benefits during retirement, disability, and other times of need. In other words, the additional revenue makes your benefits more secure.

Q: I currently earn $100,000, more than the maximum subject to the Social Security payroll tax. How much more will I pay in payroll taxes under your plan because of the increase in the maximum taxable earnings base?

A: You are among the top 6 percent of wage earners, and our plan does ask you to play a somewhat larger role in financing Social Security. Part of the reason is that higher earners have enjoyed disproportionate earnings gains over the past two decades, and it therefore makes sense for higher earners to contribute somewhat more to closing the long-term deficit in Social Security. Nonetheless, the increase in the share of your earnings subject to the payroll tax would be very gradual under our plan.

In 2005, for example, the additional earnings subject to the payroll tax would amount to less than $400, so that your employee payroll tax would increase by less than $25, and your combined employer-employee payroll tax would increase by less than $50. If the increase were fully put in place immediately in 2005, the employee share of your payroll tax would increase by less than $1,000, and your combined employer-employee payroll tax would increase by less than $2,000. *But in fact that would not happen until 2063* under our plan because the change is phased in so gradually. It seems extremely unlikely that you will still be working in 2063.

Furthermore, because more of your earnings would be covered by Social Security, you would ultimately receive higher benefits than currently scheduled. For example, if the increase had been fully effective throughout your career and you retired today, you would receive about $2,000 a year more in benefits.

Q: Doesn't your plan raise the payroll tax rate by 3 percentage points? Isn't that a larger increase than the entire projected deficit as a percentage of payroll?
A: Under current projections, the combined employer-employee payroll tax necessary to finance scheduled benefits will rise to approximately 19 percent by 2075. Through gradual reductions in benefits and a gradual increase in the Social Security payroll tax rate, our plan would limit the payroll tax rate to 15.2 percent in 2075—almost 4 percentage points less than what would be required in the absence of reform. Although an increase in the payroll tax may seem unattractive, it is important to remember that restoring long-term balance to Social Security will require a combination of benefit reductions and revenue increases. Those who oppose any increase in the payroll tax rate—even a modest and gradual one—must therefore replace it with either deeper benefit cuts or other sources of revenue in order to ensure that Social Security's long-term deficit is eliminated.

Under our plan, the employee payroll tax is projected to rise gradually from 6.2 percent today to 6.35 percent in 2025, 6.6 percent in 2035, and 7.1 percent in 2055. The combined employer-employee payroll tax rate would rise gradually from 12.4 percent today to 12.7 percent in 2025, 13.2 percent in 2035, and 14.2 percent in 2055. The vast majority of workers in the labor force today will retire well before 2055 and therefore would face a combined employer-employee Social Security payroll tax of 14 percent or less throughout their careers. And because the payroll tax increase is phased in so gradually, the payroll tax rate over the next seventy-five years would average about 13.5 percent, only about 1 percentage point higher than the current 12.4 percent rate, or 0.5 percentage point higher on the employer rate and 0.5 percentage point on the employee rate. It is true that the increase is larger at the end of the seventy-five-year period. By 2075, for example, the payroll tax rate would reach 15.2 percent, but that would still be well below the approximately 19 percent rate that, in the absence of any reform, would be required to finance scheduled benefits in 2075, and well below the payroll tax rates that already apply in many other countries.

In summary, the proposed increase in the payroll tax rate is gradual and relatively modest. It would help ensure that Social Security can continue to provide an adequate level of benefits during retirement, disability, and other times of need.

Q: I am 25 years old and earn $35,000 a year, about the average wage under Social Security. I've heard I will pay almost $15,000 more in taxes over my career under your plan. Is that true?

A: No. That type of calculation is extremely misleading because it assumes that a dollar in the far distant future—such as forty years from now—is the same as a dollar today. It is standard practice in calculations involving dollar amounts that occur years apart to take both inflation and the time value of money into account; in other words, lifetime taxes and lifetime benefits should be calculated at their present discounted value.

Under our plan, if you continue to earn the average wage in the economy and retire at age 62, you would pay, over your lifetime, about $1,500 more (in present discounted value) from the employee share of the payroll tax and about $3,000 more in combined employer-employee payroll taxes. Remember, that is the total over your career, not the amount each year. The increase in the combined employer-employee payroll tax over your career amounts to 0.3 percent of your career wages, again at present value.

Q: Aren't you imposing a steep tax on millionaires?

A: A balanced Social Security reform requires some revenue increases, and individuals with very high earnings should be asked to play a key role in helping to eliminate the program's long-term deficit. Their ability to share the cost of the legacy debt is better measured by their total earnings, rather than their earnings only up to the maximum taxable earnings base. Also, they have enjoyed disproportionately rapid gains in before-tax income in recent years, and they enjoyed large tax cuts under both the 2001 and 2003 tax laws. For households with $1 million or more in earnings, the average tax increase when the changes are fully in effect would amount to about 3.5 percent of their after-tax income.

Q: Won't the legacy surcharge cause higher earners to work less?
A: We are skeptical that higher earners' work effort would change significantly in response to small changes in tax rates such as the surcharge we propose.[5] It is worth noting that the initial surcharge is about the same size as the Medicare payroll tax imposed on higher earners in 1993, which has had no noticeable effect on their work effort, and it is smaller than the marginal income tax rate cut they have enjoyed over the past three years.

General Revenue

Q: Does your plan rely on general revenue to restore long-term solvency to Social Security?
A: No. In light of today's large federal budget deficits (and those projected into the future), and given other pressing national needs, our plan relies only on dedicated revenue and, as such, would not put an increased burden on the rest of the budget. We do not assume, as do some other reform proposals, that as much as several trillions of dollars in general revenue from the rest of the budget will be transferred to restore long-term balance within Social Security. Given current budget projections, assuming such transfers without identifying how they would be financed would be fiscally reckless. It would leave Social Security dependent upon resources that may very well not materialize, prolonging the uncertainty about the program's future ability to pay benefits.

We do, however, leave open the option of using revenue specifically raised by a reformed estate or inheritance tax as an alternative to certain parts of our plan to restore long-term solvency to Social Security. This alternative differs from unspecified general revenue transfers in that it identifies the source of the revenue. We would support this alternative only if no other way could be agreed upon to retain some form of an estate or inheritance tax, which we believe valuable for the nation's long-term fiscal health and long-term balance in the distribution of wealth.

From our perspective, perhaps the key issue with regard to the use of general revenue is whether revenue from the source in question would be collected only if it were linked to Social Security. Different people will reach different judgments on that question.

Q: Why don't you propose scaling back the 2001 and 2003 tax cuts and using the proceeds for Social Security?
A: We believe that the 2001 and 2003 tax cuts were fiscally irresponsible. The revenue from fully or partially repealing them could be used in many socially beneficial ways, potentially including dedicating part to Social Security.

In light of the nation's large projected budget deficits, and the desire of the Bush administration to end the sunsets on what are ostensibly temporary tax cuts, we understand the political attraction of dedicating new revenue to Social Security rather than perpetuating tax cuts that the country cannot afford. In the perhaps naïve hope that the nation's budget will ultimately better reflect the need to avoid excessive deficits, however, we present a new source of dedicated revenue based on scaling back part of the 2001 tax cut simply as an alternative, rather than as part of our basic proposal.

Q: Haven't you supported general revenue transfers in the past? What changed?
A: We embrace the use of the estate tax to finance Social Security if the alternative is a substantial reduction in or elimination of that tax. This position is similar to President Clinton's proposal (in his 1999 State of the Union address) to use general revenue transfers when the budget was projected to be in surplus over the period when the transfers would occur, and the political debate at the time indicated that the alternative to dedicating such revenue to Social Security would be large tax cuts. The whole logic of the proposed transfers at that time was to enhance national saving by preventing large tax cuts—which were nonetheless passed in 2001 and 2003. Now, in part because of those tax cuts, the budget is projected to be in significant deficit.

At a time of surplus, it is plausible that previously legislated transfers to Social Security would actually occur. At a time of deficits, however, that is much less likely unless the transfers are specifically tied to a particular source of revenue. In other words, from a political economy perspective, dedicating projected surpluses to Social Security is an entirely different proposition from assuming that transfers will occur despite large projected deficits.

Q: Haven't you argued in the past that Social Security reform is not likely to occur without some infusion of general revenue?
A: One of us has made statements to that effect, but again, that was in the context of projected budget surpluses. The argument was fundamentally a political one: that the people affected by the painful choices required to restore long-term balance to Social Security would be less likely to accept those choices if other people were receiving substantial tax cuts at the same time. It would be like one spouse telling the other that they couldn't afford to send the kids to college, but that the new luxury car that the first spouse had just purchased was entirely affordable.

The Legacy Debt and Its Cost

Q: Does your proposal eliminate the legacy debt?
A: No. The legacy debt from Social Security's history reflects the nation's generosity to earlier generations of Social Security beneficiaries. We think it appropriate that the cost of servicing that debt be shared by all future cohorts. We also think our plan allocates that cost fairly across cohorts, neither letting the debt slide indefinitely to future generations nor concentrating the associated costs in the near term.

Q: Why is your universal legacy charge phased in over time?
A: Our ultimate goal is to stabilize the ratio of the legacy debt to taxable payroll over time. As explained in chapter 5, with the growth rate of taxable payroll projected to slow markedly in the future, the legacy charge must increase to bring us closer to this goal. When we combine the goal of reflecting the slowdown in the growth rate of taxable payroll with the

need for a smooth adjustment, the result is roughly the phase-in schedule in our plan. In addition, we delay the start of the universal legacy charge until the already legislated increase in the full benefit age is complete, since that increase, by itself, is a significant benefit reduction.

Q: Why is your legacy tax on high earners not likewise phased in over time?
A: These workers have not been paying a fair share of the legacy cost in relation to their total earnings. The sooner they start paying this tax, the fairer the allocation of that cost will be. But the subsequent increases in that tax *are* phased in over time, in step with the universal legacy charge.

Q: Why don't you reduce benefits for current and near-retirees to reduce the legacy cost?
A: Although an argument could be made that reducing the size of the legacy cost would be beneficial, it would require changes that current and near-retirees were not expecting. We avoid such changes both because current and near-retirees would not have time to offset such unexpected changes in their retirement planning, and because Social Security reform seems less politically viable if it includes such changes than if it does not.

Rate of Return

Q: Wouldn't I get a better rate of return from Social Security under individual accounts?
A: No, not on an apples-to-apples basis. Many supporters of individual accounts tout the rate of return on the stock market, which is projected to average between 6 and 7 percent a year, after inflation, in the future. Social Security, the argument goes, yields a much smaller 2 percent after inflation. This comparison, however, is fundamentally misleading. It ignores the legacy debt associated with Social Security, and it ignores the greater riskiness of stocks than of bonds.

Social Security's legacy debt imposes a cost on us all. Because previous generations received benefits that exceeded their payroll contributions plus a market rate of interest, later generations face a legacy cost in that their benefits will henceforth be smaller than their payroll contributions accumulated at a market rate of interest. The rate-of-return comparison made by some supporters of individual accounts simply ignores this point. One way of making the point clearer is to note that most payroll taxes are used to pay benefits for current beneficiaries. If that revenue is instead diverted into individual accounts, how will those benefits be paid? Either those benefits must be reduced, or some revenue must be found elsewhere to finance them. And the cost of that other revenue must be taken into account in the analysis, reducing the rate of return on total taxes, not just those that go into the individual accounts.

A second factor is that, in financial markets as efficient as those of the United States, higher expected rates of return can only be achieved by taking on more risk. Yet the rate-of-return comparison simply ignores the higher risk associated with stocks.

As many economists have realized, these two factors make the rate-of-return comparison extremely misleading. For example, in two coauthored papers, Olivia Mitchell, one of the members of President Bush's Commission to Strengthen Social Security, demonstrated these points. She and her coauthors argued that the comparison is fundamentally flawed because the rates of return are not comparable.[6] Their papers show that when analytically accurate comparisons are undertaken, the widely trumpeted gap in rates of return between individual accounts and traditional Social Security contributions essentially disappears. They write, "A popular argument suggests that if Social Security were privatized, everyone could earn higher returns. We show that this is false."[7] This same basic point holds with regard to benefit comparisons that do not adjust for risk.

Q: Couldn't the rate of return on Social Security taxes be raised by investing part of the trust fund in the stock market?
A: Yes, the expected rate of return could be increased in this way. It would still, however, be appropriate to adjust this expected rate of return for the increased risk of stocks, as explained in the two previous answers. Unlike individual accounts, investments by the trust fund would allow that risk to be spread over successive cohorts, thus reducing the risk borne by any one cohort.

Q: Why don't you include stock market investment by the trust fund in your plan?

A: Although we support investing part of the trust fund in the stock market if diversification is desired, we do not propose it in our plan simply because it seems to be too politically controversial to be viable at this point.

Much of that controversy centers on the issue of possible political interference if the trust fund were invested in the stock market. That concern, we believe, has been vastly exaggerated by some commentators. Nonetheless, if the concern proves insurmountable, policymakers could explore mechanisms for mimicking diversification of the trust fund without creating any direct corporate governance concerns. For example, Kent Smetters has shown that, in idealized settings, a tax on risky capital income, properly specified, would produce results identical to investing the trust fund in risky assets.[8] The benefits of diversifying the trust fund could thus be accomplished by dedicating revenue from capital gains or dividend taxes to the Social Security system. (Similarly, the base for the estate tax is built up from past returns on capital in the form of interest, dividends, and capital gains; hence dedicating estate or inheritance tax revenue to Social Security would also constitute a form of diversification.)

Political Economy

Q: Wouldn't your plan undermine the nation's social compact by placing too large a burden on higher earners?

A: Our plan does ask higher earners to contribute more toward putting Social Security on a sound financial footing, but it does not means-test the program, it retains a wage ceiling on the full payroll tax, and it ensures that all future workers (except some of the most vulnerable) contribute at least in some way to eliminating the projected imbalance in the program. Furthermore, by preserving the core social insurance functions of the program, our plan reflects the social compact that has sustained Social Security for seventy years.

Q: Won't politicians just dissipate the money that you are saving through your plan?

A: The changes we propose in the net cash flow to Social Security would occur slowly, as we showed in chapter 7. Under current law, the trust fund ratio reaches a peak of 4.7 times taxable earnings in 2016. Under our proposal, the peak ratio is 5.3 and is reached in 2017. Thus the effect of our plan is more to extend the life of the trust fund than to increase its balance (and thus the possibility that it would influence non–Social Security spending and taxes) at any particular time.

Q: Isn't Social Security subject to "political risk"?
A: No system of retirement income is completely immune from being undermined by future legislative action. But perhaps the greatest uncertainty comes from having, as we do now, a system that is not in long-term actuarial balance. In other words, failing to restore long-term actuarial balance within Social Security leaves current workers more uncertain about future taxes and benefits than if balance were restored. Legislating a credible, sustainable plan that restores actuarial balance would greatly reduce political risk.

Once balance is restored, "political risk" becomes a more subtle concept. In particular, given actuarial balance, the resulting greater capacity to adapt Social Security to changing circumstances in the future may make it *more* valuable to society, not less. In that case, enhanced adaptive capacity should not be viewed as a "risk" to be avoided. Furthermore, to the extent that any such "political risks" exist, they are not unique to Social Security. They also exist to some degree within the private tax-preferred retirement system and in individual accounts systems that have replaced traditional social security in other countries.

Comparisons with Proposals of the President's Commission to Strengthen Social Security

Q: How does your plan relate to the principles for Social Security reform laid out by President Bush in his mandate to the Commission to Strengthen Social Security?
A: When he established the commission in May 2001, the president put forward six principles to which the commission should adhere:
    —"Modernization must not change benefits for [current] retirees and near-retirees."

Our plan satisfies this principle.

—"The entire Social Security surplus must be dedicated to Social Security only."

This is a principle about the rest of the budget, not about Social Security. The president himself has violated this principle by proposing and signing into law tax cuts that have contributed to the large deficits outside Social Security. We view our present task as restoring actuarial balance in Social Security, not reforming the entire budget.

—"Social Security payroll taxes must not be increased."

Since this principle could be adhered to only by assuming either excessive benefit cuts or a dramatic deterioration in the long-term budget outlook outside Social Security, we chose at the outset to present a Social Security solvency plan that instead balanced increased revenue with reduced expenditure.

—"Government must not invest Social Security funds in the stock market."

Reluctantly, we abide by this principle, since we think political pragmatism calls for it.

—"Modernization must preserve Social Security's disability and survivors' components."

Unlike the commission itself, we assumed that this principle must be met in fact and not just in appearance. The commission chose to make its plans appear compassionate but also financially sound by including large cuts in benefits to disabled workers and young survivors, and then attempting to disown those cuts. Instead, we would preserve the seventy-five-year level of benefits paid to disabled workers and young survivors, so that this group of beneficiaries as a whole is held harmless from reform.

—"Modernization must include individually controlled, voluntary personal retirement accounts, which will augment the Social Security safety net."

We chose at the outset not to accept this principle, because, as explained in chapter 8 and above, we think that individual accounts would make Social Security less valuable for workers as well as make the restoration of actuarial balance more difficult.

Q: *How do retirement benefits under your plan compare with those under the reform plans proposed by the president's commission?*

A: Our plan does a better job of preserving the protections offered by Social Security than do the plans proposed by the president's commission. Under our plan, traditional Social Security benefits—benefits that protect workers against the risks of financial market collapse, of unexpected inflation, of unexpectedly low career earnings, and of disability— would be much higher than under the commission's plans that restore long-term solvency to Social Security.

For example, for a 35-year-old average earner in 2004, traditional benefits would be reduced, relative to currently scheduled benefits, by 20 percent under the commission's Model 2, and by between 10 and 20 percent under its Model 3, but by only 4.5 percent under our plan, for workers who claim benefits at or before the full benefit age (as the vast majority currently do). The age of claiming matters because Model 3 reduces benefits for early retirees by more than for later retirees. This comparison is important, because the commission's descriptions of its plans typically assume that one-third of beneficiaries would not contribute to individual accounts. That is, this comparison is a complete description of how the different plans would work for an estimated *one-third* of workers under the commission's assumed rate of participation in the individual accounts.

For the other two-thirds of workers under the commission's assumption, the comparisons are more complex, for two reasons. One is that benefits financed by individual accounts must be adjusted for financial market risk. If we make this adjustment by assuming that the entire difference in rates of return between stocks and bonds reflects their relative riskiness, then the comparison is not very different from the analysis for those not taking out accounts. For example, for a two-earner couple turning 65 in 2042, benefits would be reduced by 21 percent under the commission's Model 2, by between 7 and 24 percent under Model 3, and by 8 percent under our plan, again for workers who claimed benefits at or before the full benefit age.[9] A further complication is that the effects for one-earner couples are different from those for two-earner couples, because an individual accounts system would treat couples differently than does the current Social Security system. Appendix F provides more detail on these types of comparisons.

Q: How do disability and young survivor benefits under your plan compare with those under the commission's plans?

A: The president's commission expressed concern over the possible effects of reform on disabled workers.[10] Yet in scoring its plans, the commission assumed substantial benefit reductions for disabled workers and included the full amount of savings from these benefit cuts in making its numbers add up. In contrast, we propose that in the aggregate over the next seventy-five years, disabled workers be held harmless from the benefit reductions that would otherwise apply under our plan. For the disabled beneficiary population as a whole, our reform plan imposes no net reduction in benefits from what they would be under the current benefit formula over the next seventy-five years.

This is not to suggest that the disability program under Social Security does not need reform. But such reform is a complicated matter, and a full reform should be the subject of a major study commissioned by Congress from the National Academy of Social Insurance or some other nonpartisan group.

Q: How does the use of general revenue in your plan differ from its use by the commission?

A: We make no use of general revenue. In contrast, the commission's Model 2 assumes more than $1.5 trillion in transfers, at present value, from the rest of the federal budget, and Model 3 assumes more than $2 trillion in such transfers. (These figures follow the commission's assumption that two-thirds of all eligible workers participate in the voluntary individual accounts created under those plans. Higher participation rates would require larger transfers.) Unlike the commission's plans, moreover, our plan would succeed in restoring long-term balance to Social Security without assuming large cuts in benefits for disabled workers and young survivors, who are among the program's most vulnerable beneficiaries. Protecting such beneficiaries under the commission's plans would require even larger general revenue transfers.

Given current budget projections, assuming general revenue transfers without specifically identifying how those transfers would be financed strikes us as fiscally reckless. It would leave Social Security relying on resources that stand a good chance of not being available when needed.

Q: How does the amount of new revenue in your plan compare with the additional revenue assumed by the commission in its plans?
A: It is difficult to answer this question precisely, since it depends on the definition of "revenue" and on the participation rate in the individual accounts under the commission's plans. (For more detail on some of the ambiguities involved, see the question above regarding the share of the long-term deficit that is reduced through revenue increases under our plan.) Nonetheless, we can provide some insight into the relative magnitudes.

The revenue component of our life expectancy adjustment, the revenue component of our universal legacy charge, and the legacy tax on earnings above the maximum taxable earnings base together would increase revenue by 1.3 percent of taxable payroll in present value over the next seventy-five years. (The net effect of the increase in the maximum taxable earnings base and the expansion in coverage to include state and local workers would raise this figure to 1.8 percent of payroll, although, as discussed above, it is unclear how such expansions in coverage should be counted for this purpose.)

The present value of the revenue that the commission simply assumes would be transferred to Social Security under its Models 2 and 3 amounts to between 1.5 percent and 1.7 percent of taxable payroll, if all eligible workers participate in the individual accounts and disabled workers are protected against the substantial benefit reductions that would otherwise apply. The assumed transfer is between 1.2 percent and 1.5 percent of taxable payroll if disabled workers are not protected against those benefit reductions. (If only two-thirds of workers participate in the accounts, the transfer amounts to between 1.1 percent and 1.3 percent of taxable payroll if disabled workers are protected against benefit reductions, and between 0.8 percent and 1.2 percent of taxable payroll if they are not.)

The new dedicated revenue under our plan may thus be as much as 20 percent below the revenue assumed in the commission's plans, but it could also be substantially higher than the revenue assumed in the commission's plans, depending on the precise assumptions used to evaluate the question.

State and Local Government Workers

Q: Why do you favor universal coverage?
A: Social Security contributions in part go to pay a legacy cost, which reflects society's generosity to early beneficiaries under the program. Those early generations of beneficiaries included the parents and grandparents of state and local government workers who are not currently contributing to the system, as well as those of covered workers who are. We, as a society, must now pay that legacy cost, and we see no reason to shield some state and local government workers from bearing their fair share.

Q: Will the move to universal coverage make the system fairer?
A: Yes. In addition to sharing the legacy cost more fairly, universal coverage would make the progressive benefit structure work better. Some workers today spend part of their careers in covered work and part in noncovered work. This makes it difficult to target the progressivity in the Social Security benefit formula on those for whom it is meant: workers with low lifetime earnings. Uncovered state and local government workers who spend some time covered by Social Security in some other job may appear in Social Security's records to have low lifetime earnings, whereas they may in fact have relatively high lifetime earnings once their state and local government pay is included. Similarly, the spousal benefit under Social Security is intended to support spouses who did not work outside the home (perhaps because they were raising children) or had very low lifetime earnings. It was not meant to help spouses with careers leading to sizable pensions based on uncovered work.

Congress has already addressed these issues with the Government Pension Offset and the Windfall Elimination Provision, which reduce benefits for workers with pensions from uncovered work, but these provisions are only approximate fixes. Eventually these provisions will not be needed if all state and local government workers are covered under Social Security in the future, but that point will not be reached for a long time.

Q: *Is there a better way than the Government Pension Offset and the*
Windfall Elimination Provision to adjust benefits for time in jobs not cov-
ered by Social Security?
A: We think so, and we have made a separate proposal on this topic.[11]
Since that proposal has not yet received extended study, however, we have
not included it as part of our reform plan.

Q: *Won't all uncovered state and local government workers be hurt by*
this?
A: No. Some uncovered state and local government workers are not well
treated by the current system. Workers with short uncovered careers may
benefit from being covered by Social Security, since some state and local
government pensions do not vest for some workers with very short
careers. In contrast, Social Security is fully portable. Furthermore, most
state and local government pensions are not fully indexed for inflation. If
inflation returns as a serious problem, workers who rely on these pensions could see their real benefits fall sharply. Social Security is fully
indexed for inflation. Finally, some workers leaving uncovered work to
take a job covered by Social Security may become disabled before they
become eligible for Social Security disability benefits. With universal coverage, this would not happen.

10 Conclusions

For more than sixty years, Social Security has provided retirees with a basic, assured level of income protected against inflation, financial market fluctuations, and the risk of outliving one's assets. It protects against other risks as well, such as disability or the death of a family wage earner. And through its progressive structure, Social Security protects against the possibility of one's career not turning out as well as planned.

But Social Security also faces a long-term deficit that needs to be addressed. If we address it sooner rather than later, we will enjoy greater flexibility in the adjustments we can make and can spread those adjustments over more years and decades than if we wait. Continuing to postpone tackling the problem will just make the changes all the more painful when they can no longer be put off. Reforming the system now is much better than waiting—but only if the reform itself makes sense.

Despite general agreement among analysts and policymakers that it is better to reform Social Security today rather than tomorrow, and despite continued promises by politicians (including Presidents Clinton and Bush) and repeated claims of their commitment to reform, so far nothing has happened. One reason is that it is always difficult to focus on long-term problems such as Social Security's deficit, especially when there are other, more pressing issues to be addressed.

But another reason for the delay is that Americans have fundamental differences about the right way to go about reforming Social Security. These differences center around four issues: the role of individual accounts, the proper balance between benefit reductions and revenue increases, the use of revenue from elsewhere in the budget, and the question of how to distribute the system's legacy cost across generations. In this closing chapter we summarize our conclusions on each of these issues in turn.

Individual Accounts

Many politicians insist on the introduction of individual accounts as part of Social Security's reform. One of the Bush administration's "principles" for reform is that it include voluntary individual accounts. Individual accounts already play a very useful role in the nation's retirement system outside of Social Security, in the form of defined-contribution plans such as 401(k)s and Individual Retirement Accounts. But they cannot and should not substitute for Social Security's assured base level of income. Individual accounts do not generally provide income that is free of the risks of financial market collapse, unexpectedly high inflation during retirement, and the possibility of outliving one's assets, and they do not provide protection against having one's career or health turn out worse than expected.

It would be a mistake to replace part of Social Security with individual accounts, and it would be a further mistake to allow such carve-out accounts to be voluntary. Despite their superficial appeal, voluntary carve-out accounts would involve unnecessary levels of administrative complexity, as the United Kingdom's experience with such accounts has demonstrated. Add-on accounts, which would supplement rather than supplant the program's existing resources, might be useful in getting legislation enacted that both reforms and provides more resources for Social Security. However, voluntary add-on accounts are not essential for achieving a good reform.

Balancing Benefit Reductions and Revenue Increases

Because the benefits scheduled to be paid in the future exceed its projected revenue, Social Security faces a long-term deficit. To restore long-term balance, some combination of benefit reductions and revenue increases is necessary. But although that statement is true as a matter of simple accounting, defining the appropriate balance between the two is another matter.

The Bush administration has explicitly ruled out payroll tax increases as part of Social Security's reform. One reform plan put forth by the President's Commission to Strengthen Social Security would rely solely on benefit cuts to restore balance. Other analysts, taking the opposite tack, have suggested that reform should rely much more heavily on additional revenue.[1]

The principle of balancing revenue increases and benefit reductions served the nation well in 1983, the last time Social Security underwent significant reform. That approach helped build political consensus for reform. Our plan embraces this principle, likewise combining benefit reductions and revenue increases in roughly equal measure. It neither squeezes benefits too tightly, forcing them within the bounds of existing dedicated revenue, nor raises taxes too steeply, avoiding any and all reductions in benefits currently scheduled.

General Revenue Transfers

The Clinton administration proposed using part of the federal budget surpluses then projected to transfer resources to Social Security, thereby reducing the actuarial deficit to be closed by Social Security's own revenue or through benefit cuts. President Bush's commission, despite the reemergence of significant federal budget deficits, also proposed using general revenue to finance the deficit within traditional Social Security generated by introducing individual accounts.

Given the worsened budget outlook today, reliance on general revenue for any extended period in the future would put Social Security at risk. It is hard to know how future Congresses will react when such a call on general revenue must be honored, or to know how severe the pressures on the overall budget will be when that time comes. To avoid these uncertainties, all revenue for Social Security should continue to be dedicated revenue: specific, identified sources, such as the payroll tax or the income taxation of benefits, devoted explicitly to financing Social Security.

This then raises the question: should Social Security continue to rely solely on the revenue sources dedicated to it in the past, or should a new dedicated revenue source be added? This is fundamentally a question of whether the best alternative use of any new potential revenue source is more or less attractive than dedicating that revenue to Social Security, recognizing that Social Security must fill its actuarial gap in some fashion. In light of the nation's large projected budget deficits, and the desire of the Bush administration to end the sunsets on its ostensibly temporary tax cuts, we recognize the political attraction of dedicating new revenue to Social Security rather than perpetuating tax cuts that the country cannot afford.

If the sunsets currently in the tax code were eliminated, so that the 2001 and 2003 tax cuts were made permanent, the revenue loss over the next seventy-five years would exceed 2 percent of GDP. By contrast, the seventy-five-year actuarial deficit in Social Security is 0.7 percent of GDP, and the permanent deficit (the deficit measured over an indefinite horizon) is about 1.5 percent of GDP. If the political alternatives are either to extend the tax cuts or to use the revenue to shore up Social Security, we strongly prefer the latter. We therefore retain the option of dedicating a reformed estate or inheritance tax to Social Security as an alternative to part of the package we present: such a change would be much better policy than eliminating the estate tax, as would happen if all current tax code sunsets were repealed. We do not favor such an approach, however, if the alternative is to preserve the estate tax for general revenue, given the serious financial constraints on government to provide the other services the country needs and wants. In the perhaps naïve hope that the nation's budget will ultimately better address these needs, we endorse as an alternative, not as part of our basic proposal, the use of a reformed estate tax as a new source of dedicated revenue for Social Security.

The Legacy Debt

An issue that lies hidden beneath many discussions of Social Security reform is how the cost of servicing the program's legacy debt will be distributed across future generations. Some plans for large carve-out individual accounts would force a "transition" generation to bear all or most of that cost, exempting all later generations from any share of the burden. Other reform plans, in contrast, would push the bulk of the legacy debt onto these distant generations, excusing intervening generations from bearing their fair share of its cost. (One of the problems with using substantial general revenue transfers to Social Security rather than dedicated revenue sources is that it would make it impossible to know just how the legacy cost will ultimately be borne.)

Here, too, our plan takes a balanced approach. It avoids the extremes of either passing along the full legacy cost to far-distant generations or forcing one or a few transition generations to bear all of the cost. In addition, two groups today—those state and local government workers not now covered by Social Security and workers with earnings above the taxable maximum—are not bearing a fair share of the legacy cost. Our plan would ensure that they do.

A Final Note

The long-term deficit projected in Social Security should not serve as an excuse for destroying the program's social insurance structure. Nor should it be "fixed" with accounting or other gimmicks that promise to erase the deficit without any pain—eventually the bill for those gimmicks will come due. The American public deserves a well-informed and honest debate over Social Security's future, not obfuscation. As this book has shown, Social Security can be reformed without dismantling Social Security's important insurance protections and without resorting to accounting tricks. It can also be done without undercutting the functioning of Social Security itself or of the economy—indeed, reform can improve their functioning.

In chapter 3 we discussed five criteria to be used in evaluating proposals for Social Security reform. We conclude by underlining that our plan meets all five: It would restore actuarial balance while addressing the terminal-year problem. It would not increase the burden on the rest of the federal budget (or rely on gimmicks that take advantage of actuarial scoring rules). It would distribute the legacy cost fairly. It would preserve and improve the social insurance character of Social Security. And it would protect and improve the functioning of the economy by contributing to national saving.

Our plan comprises a moderate set of reforms that would restore long-term balance to Social Security by addressing three main sources of its long-term deficit: increases in life expectancy, increased income inequality, and the legacy debt from the system's history. The plan combines revenue increases and benefit reductions to achieve long-term solvency. Its design builds on the tradition set in 1983, when policymakers from both parties came together to embrace a balanced set of reforms.

Two decades later, the debate over Social Security reform has loomed large in presidential and other elections, but we have failed to fix the program. Extreme positions held by some and denial of the problem by others have so far impeded progress. It is time that we once again pursued a balanced approach to reforming Social Security.

Social Security and National Saving

An increase in the narrow prefunding of Social Security implies an increase in national saving unless some other sector of the economy responds by reducing its saving. Such offsetting actions could come from households, who might choose to save less if they see a stronger Social Security as reducing their need to save; or from firms, which could reduce the funding of the employee pensions they sponsor for the same reason; or from the federal government, which could choose to run larger deficits in the non–Social Security budget as a consequence of larger surpluses in the Social Security system.[1]

Household Responses

The responses of households to the provision of retirement benefits have been studied the most. There is a rough consensus that individuals will save less for their own retirement if they expect that more retirement benefits will be provided elsewhere, either by the government or by employers. However, it is believed that the offset is far less than dollar for dollar.[2]

A more relevant concern in examining reforms of different types is whether restoring actuarial balance without individual accounts would have a different effect on household saving than restoring actuarial balance with individual accounts. We are unaware of any credible empirical study of this issue; indeed, it is very difficult to think of how such a study could be conducted without an extensive national experiment. Nonetheless, our hunch is that if there is a differential effect, individual accounts would likely reduce household saving by more than would a similarly financed defined-benefit program, since individual accounts more closely resemble the other saving options already available to individuals and may therefore seem more like a replacement for such options.

Employer Responses

The size and nature of the likely response of employer-provided retirement benefits to different approaches to Social Security reform has received little study. Many private pension plans are integrated with Social Security, and reductions in Social Security benefits could therefore trigger increased employer obligations to those plans, although employers may change the plans or the Social Security reform plan could provide special provisions for such plans.[3]

Our hunch is, again, that the more similar the government program is to privately available options, the larger the potential offset. Thus individual accounts that closely mimic privately available 401(k)s or Individual Retirement Accounts may have larger offsets than the traditional Social Security system, but we are unaware of any solid empirical evidence on this issue.

Federal Budget Responses

Offsetting actions by the federal government itself are the third type of potential response to an increase in narrow prefunding for Social Security. This potential response is one that is even more difficult to study scientifically than the responses of households and employers, and one on which sharply conflicting positions have been asserted.

Some observers—typically those who support diverting existing Social Security revenue into individual accounts—argue that the accumulation of funds within the Social Security system since the 1983 reform has not contributed to national saving, and that neither would future accumulations within the trust fund. They also tend to argue, however, that the future accumulation of funds in individual accounts *would* raise national saving. In other words, according to this view, narrow prefunding undertaken through the traditional system has not accomplished and will not accomplish broad prefunding, but narrow prefunding undertaken through individual accounts would.[4]

Despite such assertions, the past two decades do not offer any clear lesson that Social Security surpluses have failed to contribute to national saving. To evaluate the effect of the Social Security surpluses on the overall federal budget and national saving, we need to know the counterfactual: what would have happened in the absence of the Social Security surpluses? Then we must compare that counterfactual with what actually did happen, given the Social Security surpluses.

It is not easy to compare what did happen with what might have happened. If the federal government always balanced its unified budget, then a Social Security surplus would not affect debt held by the public (although it still might affect the level of government investment). But this is not the case. Similarly, if the federal government always balanced its non–Social Security budget, then Social Security surpluses would reduce debt held by the public, dollar for dollar. In actuality, Congress legislates changes in expenditure programs and tax rules that affect budget balances in future years in a complex way that varies by expenditure change and by tax change. Even the presence of budgetary balance targets stated in terms of one budget or the other do not necessarily determine the impact of a Social Security surplus, since the targets themselves are chosen in light of Social Security projections, and roughly the same target can be stated in either way. Thus one needs to think explicitly about the budget process.

Those who argue that Social Security surpluses have contributed nothing to national saving believe that members of Congress and the public focus only on the unified budget, which includes both the Social Security and non–Social Security components, and that Congress seeks to hit a deficit target defined in terms of the unified budget. If that were so, larger surpluses in the Social Security component of the budget would only trigger larger deficits in the non–Social Security component, with no net effect on the overall budget. The crucial question is thus what effect the Social Security surpluses have had on the non–Social Security deficits; the President's Commission to Strengthen Social Security assumes that a $1 increase in the Social Security surplus increased the non–Social Security deficit by $1 over what it would have been otherwise. Unfortunately, this historical question is not easily answered, and different analysts have read different lessons from the history.

One approach that is not illuminating merely asserts that the unified deficits were so large that the Social Security surpluses were not likely to have been saved, because it is somehow implausible that the unified deficits could have been any larger in the absence of the Social Security surpluses.[5] This argument apparently rests on the belief that some perceived limit exists, beyond which Congress would not allow unified deficits to grow, and that that limit was binding in the 1980s. But, measured in relation to the overall economy, the largest unified deficit occurred in fiscal year 1983 (when it was 6.0 percent of GDP), a year when there was no Social Security surplus. Unless the permissible limit somehow diminished over time, for reasons that are not immediately apparent, this argument is not convincing.

Attempts to examine the question using time-series econometric analysis are also not convincing given the short time period during which there is a plausible linkage between Social Security and the rest of the budget.[6] Moreover, specific pieces of legislation imply different time patterns of revenue changes and spending changes over many subsequent years. Thus there is no simple link between deficits and lagged deficits (or between unified deficits and Social Security surpluses) that such an analysis could reliably discover. In particular, it is not credible to believe that econometric analysis could uncover the true counterfactual: the pattern of taxes and spending that would have occurred if the 1983 Social Security legislation had involved lower tax rates and therefore no buildup of the Social Security trust fund during the 1980s and beyond.

We are therefore left with nonquantitative historical analysis. Our view of the relevant history is as follows. The 1981 tax cuts, together with the defense buildup of the early 1980s, generated significant unified budget deficits. Congress did not like the size of the deficits and attempted to reduce them, but with limited success for the first decade. Throughout this period, the precise numbers reported for the unified deficits were somewhat less important than the qualitative view that the deficits were too large. Congress moved to lower deficits gradually, reflecting the political constraints on tax increases and spending reductions, the only legislative actions available to reduce the deficit. In other words, the congressional response was driven mostly by the qualitative view that the deficit was excessive, instead of being calibrated to the exact size of some measure of the deficit. In this context, it seems plausible to us that increases in the Social Security surplus did *not* generate significant increases in the non–Social Security deficit.

In the late 1990s, furthermore, unified deficits declined dramatically and then turned into surpluses. The switch to a publicly stated target in terms of the non–Social Security budget suggests that the Social Security surplus was not offset by increases in the non–Social Security deficit during that very brief period. It seems clear that, for a short time, the existence of a Social Security surplus resulted in larger unified surpluses than would otherwise have prevailed, perhaps dollar for dollar.

To round out the evaluation of the 1980s and 1990s, one more layer of analysis is necessary. Even if increases in the Social Security surpluses did result in offsetting increases in non–Social Security deficits, the Social Security surpluses may still have raised national saving. For example, to the extent that Social Security surpluses were used to reduce income taxes, the net result was basically a shift in the composition of federal revenue from income tax revenue to payroll tax revenue. Since the distribution of income tax burdens differs substantially from the distribution of payroll tax burdens (figure A-1), this shift could have increased private saving to the extent that income taxpayers have higher marginal propensities to save than payroll taxpayers; such differences in marginal propensities to save are highly plausible to us.[7] Thus the shift to higher payroll taxes reduced consumption and increased saving, whereas any concomitant and partly offsetting shift to relatively lower income taxes did not increase consumption and reduce saving by as much.

This historical perspective should caution us against simplistic statements about the likely effects of Social Security reforms on national saving.

Figure A-1. *Share of Tax Filers with Payroll Tax Exceeding Income Tax, by Income, 2003*

Percent

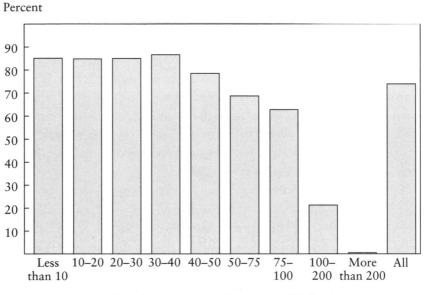

Adjusted gross income (thousands of dollars)

Source: William G. Gale and Jeffrey Rohaly, "Three Quarters of Filers Pay More in Payroll Taxes Than in Income Taxes," *Tax Notes,* January 6, 2003, p. 119.

In particular, a key question is whether including individual accounts as part of Social Security reform would raise national saving more than would devoting the same amount of revenue to the traditional system. Our interpretation of the history above leaves us uncertain as to the existence, let alone the degree, of any such difference.

Trends in Retirement Age

Historically, men have tended to retire earlier, even as they live longer. Retirement patterns for women, on the other hand, show little trend because the increased tendency of women to have careers of their own has led to an offsetting increase in labor participation.

Figure B-1 shows the historical trend in the fraction of men above age 65 who continue to work. Note that the trend toward earlier retirement has occurred over a broad span of time; on this historical scale, Social Security represents a barely discernible blip in the trend. Recently the trend appears to have ended, with the labor force participation of older men stabilizing since the mid-1980s. Whether it will pick up again or stay flat is hard to predict.

Even if the trend toward earlier retirement has ended, life expectancy *as of the age when workers retire* is very likely to continue rising. The reason is that time in the labor force is not expected to increase as rapidly as life expectancy, not just because workers' interest in and ability to work may not keep pace with increases in life expectancy,

Figure B-1. *Labor Force Participation Rates for Persons Age 65 and Above, 1850–2000*

Percent

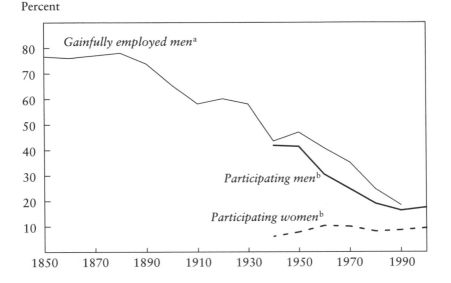

Sources: Dora L. Costa, *The Evolution of Retirement: An American Economic History, 1880–1990* (University of Chicago Press, 1998), p. 29; *Historical Statistics of the United States, Colonial Times to 1970* (Government Printing Office, 1975); *Statistical Abstract of the United States 2002*, table 561.

a. Men who worked in the years preceding the most recent census.

b. "Participating" refers to those who meet the then-current definition of labor force participation, based on their activity during the survey week.

but also because increased wealth allows more people to afford an extended period of retirement. Since wealth is likely to continue growing in the future, it seems likely that life expectancy at retirement will continue to increase steadily as well.

The picture for women is different, reflecting an interplay between growth in the number of women with substantial careers and the inducement to earlier retirement from greater wealth and the earlier retirement of one's husband. The growth in the number of divorced women also affects the trend for women: many divorcees are poorly off financially, which pushes them into the work force even if they lacked a full-time career before their divorce. Since female labor force participation at younger ages has already increased so much, the future will probably see a greater similarity in retirement patterns for men and women. This suggests that retirement ages for women are likely to remain fairly stable unless the trend to earlier retirement reappears for both men and women.

Even a moderate increase in retirement ages would not offset the cost to Social Security of increasing life expectancy. If a worker puts off retirement and continues working for another year, say, from age 62 to age 63, that decision has several effects. During the extra year of work, the worker pays additional payroll and income taxes (although the latter do not accrue to Social Security). The extra year of work may also increase the worker's AIME, and thus his or her PIA, if the earnings in that year are higher than the lowest of the thirty-five previous indexed annual earnings used to calculate the AIME. And monthly benefits will increase because they start a year later.

For the typical worker, one can compute the effect on Social Security's finances from an additional year of work at each age. For those retiring close to the earliest eligibility age (that is, at age 62 or 63), the increase in benefits from a higher AIME and a delay in benefit receipt roughly offsets the additional payroll taxes paid and the nonreceipt of benefits for one year. Thus there is little change in the financial position of Social Security, since the percentage increase in benefits is not large. With most workers retiring early in the eligibility period, the overall effect of a modest delay in retirement is not large relative to the scale of actuarial deficit.[1]

This aspect of the Social Security system—that monthly benefits are higher for people who delay receiving them—is worth emphasizing. To the degree that the increase in the monthly benefit from delayed claiming roughly offsets the decrease in the time over which benefits will be paid, extended careers, by themselves, have little effect on the financial status of Social Security. This is an attractive aspect of the system because a large financial gain for Social Security from additional work would imply a large financial cost on workers from that work, which would create a large and socially undesirable disincentive to continue working.

APPENDIX C

How the Legacy Debt Arose:
A Simplified Example

To see how the legacy debt has arisen and to understand its implications, imagine a simple pay-as-you-go retirement system in which each generation pays $1 in taxes while it is young and working and receives $1 in benefits when it is old and retired. For simplicity, we assume no population growth and no productivity growth.

Generation A is old when the system begins and receives $1 in benefits even though it never paid taxes.[1] That $1 is paid for by generation B, which is young in period 1. Then, in period 2, generation B is old and receives $1, paid for by generation C, which is young in period 2, and so on.

This simplified example illustrates the emergence of a legacy debt associated with the start-up of a pay-as-you-go system. Generation A enjoyed $1 in benefits despite not having paid into the system. All future generations must bear the cost of financing that $1 benefit, which is passed from one generation to the next in the form of lower-than-market rates of return on the system. If the market interest rate is 5 percent per generation, for example, generation

B's contribution of $1 could have instead been invested in the market and would have generated $1.05 in retirement benefits. Instead, it "generates" only $1 in retirement benefits. The reason is the legacy debt created by the initial $1 in benefits given to generation A; at a market interest rate of 5 percent, each generation effectively pays a legacy cost of 5 cents (5 percent of generation A's $1 in benefits) to finance those initial benefits.[2]

The general principle is that if some groups receive more in benefits than could have been financed by their contributions (like generation A in the example above), other groups (like generation B and subsequent generations in the example) must receive less in benefits than could have been financed by their tax contributions.

This simplified example does not involve any long-term actuarial deficit: in each year, benefit payments are exactly equal to revenue, so the deficit in each year is zero. The projected deficit over any period of time is therefore also zero. This underscores an important point: the legacy debt from the early history of a pay-as-you-go system exists even in an actuarially balanced system and is the reason why the rate of return under that system is lower than the market rate of return.

The current Social Security system is somewhat similar to the simple system presented here, except that in future years, scheduled benefits will exceed revenue—the system is *not* actuarially balanced. Different ways of restoring long-term balance to Social Security imply different distributions of the burden from the legacy debt. For example, one approach would simply freeze the current payroll tax rate and reduce benefits in future years to the level of incoming payroll revenue. This would pass the bulk of the legacy debt on to very distant generations. Another approach to restoring balance would make a single generation pay off the entire legacy debt; such an approach would saddle that transition generation with a substantial cost while exempting all subsequent generations. How the burden of the legacy debt is distributed across generations is thus a very important feature of any Social Security reform.

Characteristics of Tax-Favored Defined-Contribution Plans

Types of Individual Retirement Accounts

Traditional IRA

Year Created: 1974

Eligibility Rules: Must have earned income and not be in an employer-sponsored retirement plan, or must have adjusted gross income under $64,000 (married filing jointly) or $44,000 (single); phase-outs begin at $54,000 and $34,000, respectively. Must be under age 70½.

Contribution Limits:$3,000 for those under age 50; $3,500 for those age 50 and over.

Tax Treatment: Contributions are tax-deductible; distributions before age 59½ are subject to penalty, except in cases of death or disability, or if distributions are taken as a series of substantially equal payments or are for health insurance premiums for the unemployed, qualified higher education expenses, or qualified first-time homebuyer expenses ($10,000 maximum).

Interactions with Other Plans: Contribution limit applies to sum of contributions to all IRAs.

Nondeductible IRA

Year Created: 1974

Contribution Limits: $3,000 for those under 50; $3,500 for those 50 and over.

Interactions with Other Plans: Contribution limit applies to sum of contributions to all IRAs.

Roth IRA

Year Created: 1997

Eligibility Rules: Adjusted gross income under $160,000 (married filing jointly) or $110,000 (single); phase-outs begin at $150,000 and $95,000, respectively.

Contribution Limits: $3,000 for those under age 50; $3,500 for those age 50 and over.

Tax Treatment: Contributions are taxed; distributions are tax-free after the owner has held the account for 5 years and has reached age 59½, dies, or becomes disabled, or uses the funds for qualified first-time homebuyer expenses.

Interactions with Other Plans: Contribution limit applies to sum of contributions to all IRAs.

Types of Tax-Favored Defined-Contribution Plans

401(k)

Year Created: 1978

Eligibility Rules: Private sector employees.

Contribution Limits: Lesser of $12,000 or adjusted gross income for those under age 50; $14,000 for those age 50 and over.

Tax Treatment: Contributions are tax-deductible; distributions are taxed. Distributions are allowed upon termination of employment or plan, in case of financial hardship, or when participant reaches age 59½.

Interactions with Other Plans: Limits deductibility of a worker's IRA.

403(b)

Year Created: 1958
Eligibility Rules: Employees of certain tax-exempt and public education institutions.
Contribution Limits: Same as for 401(k).
Tax Treatment: Contributions are tax-deductible, distributions are taxed.
Interactions with Other Plans: Contribution limits apply to all plans.

457 and 457(b)

Year Created: 1978
Eligibility Rules: Non-school state and local government employees and some employees of nonprofits.
Contribution Limits: Same as for 401(k).
Tax Treatment: Contributions are tax-deductible; distributions are taxed. Distributions are allowed upon termination of employment, in case of financial hardship, or when the participant reaches 70½.
Interactions with Other Plans: Not necessary to coordinate maximum deferral with contributions to other retirement plans.

SIMPLE IRA

Year Created: 1996
Eligibility Rules: Small business employees.
Contribution Limits: $8,000 plus employer contribution; for those age 50 and over, $1,000 unmatched catch-up contribution allowed.
Tax Treatment: Contributions are tax-deductible; distribution rules are same as for traditional IRAs.
Interactions with Other Plans: Employer may not maintain any other retirement plan.

SIMPLE 401(k)

Year Created: 1996
Eligibility Rules: Small business employees.
Contribution Limits: Same as for SIMPLE IRA.
Tax Treatment: Generally same as 401(k), with additional limits on the employer deduction.
Interactions with Other Plans: Employer may not maintain any other retirement plan.

Salary Reduction Simplified Employee Pension (SARSEP)

Year Created: 1986

Eligibility Rules: Small business employees; after 1996, no employer may establish a SARSEP.

Contribution Limits: Same as for 401(k).

Tax Treatment: Contributions are tax-deductible; distributions are taxed.

Thrift Plans

Year Created: 1954

Eligibility Rules: Nonqualified plans that primarily benefit highly compensated employees who have contributed the maximum to a qualified plan; special rules apply to rank-and-file employees who participate because their employer does not offer a qualified plan that passes nondiscriminatory coverage requirements.

Contribution Limits: None.

Tax Treatment: Employer deducts contributions to a funded plan; employee pays taxes on employer contribution if substantially vested; investment income is tax-free, except for income attributable to employee contributions above employer contributions.

Sources: CCH Editorial Staff, *2003 U.S. Master Tax Guide* (Chicago: CCH Inc., 2002); and Leonard Burman, William Gale, and Peter Orszag, "The Administration's Saving Proposals: A Preliminary Analysis," *Tax Notes,* March 3, 2003.

Should the Trust Fund Invest
in the Stock Market?

Any benefits from a diversified portfolio within an individual accounts system could in principle also be achieved through investments by the Social Security trust fund itself. The argument over whether Social Security should hold private assets dates back to the system's founding in 1935.[1] Decades later, one of the three proposals in the 1997 report on Social Security reform by the 1994–96 Advisory Council on Social Security (also called the Gramlich Commission) included a provision to allow the Social Security trust fund to invest part of its reserves in equities.[2] In 1999 the Clinton administration proposed allowing stock market investments by the trust fund.[3] Other countries already allow such investments. For example, Canada recently changed the regulations governing its Canada Pension Plan to allow that system to invest a portion of its reserves in private assets. The investments are governed by a twelve-member independent investment board, with each member serving a three-year term.[4]

If diversification of the Social Security portfolio is desired, we see advantages in pursuing it through the trust fund rather than through individual accounts. First, the trust fund approach would involve lower administrative costs than diversification achieved through individual accounts. Second, investing in stocks through the trust fund, unlike investing through individual accounts, allows risk to be spread across generations. If the market should turn sharply down in some year, all generations could be made to bear some of the burden if the investments were undertaken through the trust fund. Under a system of individual accounts, some generations and individuals would bear the entire burden while others would bear none. The trust fund may therefore be a more effective means of absorbing risk than individual accounts.

One of the most commonly raised concerns about trust fund investment in stocks involves corporate governance. Ownership of a corporation's stock brings with it the right to vote for the firm's officers and on certain corporate decisions. Would trust fund ownership of stock lead to politicization of those decisions or, alternatively, to inadequate monitoring of corporate behavior? Noting such concerns, Federal Reserve Chairman Alan Greenspan argued, in testimony before the Senate Budget Committee on January 25, 2001, that allowing the government to hold private assets would risk "sub-optimal performance by our capital markets."[5]

Although this concern is a legitimate one, we are not convinced that it should preclude trust fund investments in stocks or other private sector assets. In the United States, for example, state and local government pension funds have long invested in such assets. To be sure, some research suggests that some of these investments have not been managed well, and that state and local government pension funds tend to underperform market rates of return.[6] But one major challenge in these analyses is adjusting appropriately for differences in the riskiness of the portfolios held by public and private pension funds. A recent study reexamined the evidence on state and local pension funds and concluded that "public plans appear to be performing as well as private plans."[7]

The international evidence on whether public investments in private assets are mismanaged and induce political interference in capital markets also appears mixed. In developing countries, mismanagement appears common,[8] but this experience lacks clear relevance for the United States.[9] The evidence from other industrial countries, such as Canada, New Zealand, and Sweden, suggests that investments in private sector assets by public retirement funds may not present problems any more difficult than those posed by individual accounts.[10]

Individual accounts unquestionably cost significantly more to run than trust fund investments. Thus, even if trust fund investments realized a slightly smaller risk-adjusted gross rate of return than individual accounts, the difference could well be less than the difference in administrative costs. Other research suggests that successful public investment in private assets depends on a variety of factors, including the appointment of an independent investment board and a clear, written mandate to maximize risk-adjusted returns.[11] Almost all proposals to invest the Social Security trust fund in private assets call for such an independent board and a clear legal mandate to pursue competitive returns. They would also restrict the trust fund's choice of investment vehicles to so-called market index funds, which hold a broad portfolio of assets whose composition replicates that of the market as a whole.[12] Moreover, the managers of these funds could exercise voting rights just as they do for private investors in the funds.

If corporate governance concerns nonetheless seem insurmountable, other possibilities exist, including mechanisms that would allow the trust fund to mimic the results of a diversified portfolio without actually holding private assets. For example, Kent Smetters has shown that, in idealized settings, a particular form of tax on risky capital income produces results identical to investing the trust fund in risky assets. He concludes that increasing the capital income tax rate by about 4 percentage points would be equivalent to investing the entire trust fund in equities.[13] The benefits from diversifying the trust fund could thus be accomplished by dedicating revenue from sources such as capital gains and dividend taxes to the Social Security system. In other words, one could undertake a "swap" in which Social Security gives up some revenue from taxable payroll in return for receiving some revenue from taxable capital income.

APPENDIX F

Comparisons with Models 2 and 3 of the President's Commission

This appendix undertakes various comparisons of our plan with Models 2 and 3 of the President's Commission to Strengthen Social Security. Models 2 and 3 have three basic components: changes in traditional benefits; the diversion of Social Security revenue into voluntary individual accounts; and the transfer of revenue from the rest of the budget to Social Security, to offset the adverse effects of the individual accounts on the Social Security trust fund. For more detail on the commission's plans, see the commission's final report and our separate analysis of it.[1]

Various complications arise when making comparisons between our plan and the commission's Models 2 and 3. For example:

—The plans proposed by the commission include benefit cuts for disabled workers, even though the commission emphasized that some other group needed to examine disability benefits and that its cuts in disability benefits were not to be taken as actual recommendations. Our plan holds both disabled workers and young survivors in the aggregate harmless from benefit reductions over the next seventy-five years, although benefit levels would be raised for some beneficiaries and lowered for others within these groups.

—The commission's plans assume general revenue transfers as needed to keep the trust fund ratio at 1.0 (that is, to keep the trust fund at 100 percent of annual expenditure). The transfers are needed because of the diversion of revenue into individual accounts. But because the accounts are voluntary, the amount of revenue needed depends on the rate of participation in the accounts. For some purposes, it is necessary to compute the general revenue transfers for these two plans. In doing so, however, one must make some assumption about participation in the individual accounts under the commission's Models 2 and 3; we think it makes sense to consider both a two-thirds participation rate and full participation. (Assuming a two-thirds rate, one also needs to remember that one-third of workers have no income coming from individual accounts.) The dedicated revenue under our plan, at present value, over the next seventy-five years may be more than 20 percent below the general revenue transfers under the commission's models, or may be substantially higher. The precise ratio depends on how many workers participate in the voluntary individual accounts under those plans, on whether disabled workers are protected from the substantial benefit reductions that would otherwise apply to them under Models 2 and 3, and on whether extensions of coverage are scored as "revenue."

—Our plan does not involve any investments in the stock market, and therefore the benefit levels under our plan are not subject to the risks inherent in stock investments. The income from the individual accounts under the commission's plans, on the other hand, does involve financial market risk. Since most individuals are averse to risk, almost all economists recognize that in evaluating such income, it is important to adjust for that risk. Such an adjustment attempts to evaluate different assets on an apples-to-apples basis by subtracting a penalty from the expected return on riskier assets to reflect their higher risk. As discussed in chapter 8, one overly simplified but nonetheless broadly used approach to risk adjustment is to assume that the entire difference in yields between bonds and stocks reflects risk. In comparing benefit levels, we therefore report two calculations. One adjusts for risk by treating stocks as if they had the same return as bonds. The other makes no adjustment for risk but simply reports expected returns. The "right" adjustment would lie somewhere between these two for workers with no other access to stocks, but at the lower value for those who do. We also assume that retirement income from the individual accounts is taken as a real annuity, because this facilitates direct comparison with traditional Social Security benefits.

—Model 3 requires individual deposits into individual accounts as a condition of being allowed to divert payroll tax payments into the accounts. There are two internally consistent ways to evaluate this plan: one can either not count these payments as revenue for the system and not count the benefits financed by them as part of benefits, or one can count both the revenue and the benefits. One should not include just the contributions or just the benefits in a comparison of this type.

—The commission's plans were scored by the Social Security actuaries based on the 2001 trustees' projections, whereas our plan was scored by the actuaries based on the 2003 projections. The differences in projections could have modest effects on the results. Furthermore, the commission's plans were released in 2001 but have not been implemented. It is therefore unclear whether the best basis for comparison is to assume that the commission's plans would have been implemented as scheduled in its 2001 report, or would instead be implemented on a delayed basis to reflect the passage of time since that report. We generally assume the former, to facilitate use of the official analysis of those plans, but we also make some indication of the effects of delayed implementation.

Despite these and other important obstacles to making comparisons across different reform plans, readers may still find the comparisons illuminating. In comparing benefits we focus on average earners. Both the commission's plans and ours contain benefit enhancements for low earners and for survivors with low benefits. We do not compare those. We also do not compare benefits for higher earners; our plan and the commission's Model 3 include benefit reductions for high earners, but the commission's Model 2 does not.

Traditional Retirement Benefits for Average Earners

We begin with traditional benefit comparisons for average earners. We use the term "traditional benefits" to refer to the benefits provided by the traditional Social Security system, and "combined benefits" to refer to the

Table F-1. *Changes in Traditional Benefits for Average Earners under Alternative Reform Proposals*[a]

Percent change from scheduled benefits

Age at end of 2004	Authors' plan	Model 2[c]	Model 3[b]	
			At full benefit age	*At age 62*
55	0.0	−3.0	−1.5	−11.3
45	−0.6	−3.9	−2.0	−11.8
35	−4.5	−20.6	−10.9	−19.8
25	−8.6	−28.2	−15.2	−23.7
15	−12.4	−35.1	−19.4	−27.5
5	−16.0	−41.3	−23.3	−31.0
0	−17.7	−44.2	−25.2	−32.7

Source: Authors' calculations.

a. Models 2 and 3 are those of the President's Commission to Strengthen Social Security.

b. Assumes Model 3 is implemented as scheduled in the commission's 2001 report and therefore computes the benefit reduction at full benefit age as $1 - 0.995^{y-2008}$, where y is the entitlement year. The benefit reduction at age 62 is calculated as $1 - 0.9*(0.995^{y-2008})$. If implementation is delayed by three years, traditional benefit reductions are reduced at each age by about 1 to 2 percentage points. For example, the benefit reduction for a newborn in 2004 claiming benefits at the full benefit age would then be 24.1 percent rather than 25.2 percent.

c. Assumes 1.0 percent real wage growth per year and that the model is implemented as scheduled in the commission's 2001 report, and therefore computes the benefit reduction as $1 - 0.99^{y-2008}$, where y is the entitlement year. If implementation is delayed by three years, traditional benefit reductions are reduced at each age by about 2 to 3 percentage points. For example, the benefit reduction for a newborn would then be 42.5 percent rather than 44.2 percent.

combination of traditional benefits and income from individual accounts.[2]

Table F-1 shows the reduction in traditional benefits under our plan and under the commission's Models 2 and 3 for average earners. For Model 3, we show the benefit reduction both at the full benefit age and at age 62, since Model 3 includes additional benefit reductions at age 62. (It also includes benefit enhancements for those who claim benefits after the full benefit age. But few workers currently claim benefits after that age.) As the table shows, the traditional benefit reductions under our plan are substantially smaller than those under either Model 2 or Model 3. For example, for a 35-year-old average earner in 2004, traditional benefits would be reduced by 4.5 percent under our plan, by slightly more than 20 percent under Model 2, and by between 10 and 20 percent under Model 3, for workers who claim benefits at or before the full benefit age (as the vast majority currently do). If two-thirds of workers start individual accounts, this table fully compares the results for those average earners who do not open accounts—assumed to be one-third of such workers in the commission's presentations.

Combined Retirement Benefits for Average Earners

The comparison above excludes the income from individual accounts that would be available to participating workers under Models 2 and 3. Here we compare benefit levels under our plan with the combination of traditional Social Security benefits and expected income from the individual accounts under Models 2 and 3. In evaluating these comparisons, several points are important to remember:

—*Participation rates*. If two-thirds of workers participate in individual accounts under Models 2 and 3, then, for the remaining one-third, the calculations in this section are irrelevant, since these workers would receive no income from such accounts. The results of the traditional benefit comparison above are the relevant results for these workers.

—*Annuitization*. To facilitate the comparisons with traditional Social Security benefits, we assume that workers convert their full account balances upon retirement to a fixed real annuity, that is, one that pays a constant amount of inflation-adjusted dollars in each period that the annuitant is alive. For married couples, we assume a joint-and-two-thirds annuity, that is, one in which the surviving spouse receives a benefit equal to two-thirds what the couple received when both were alive. For further details on these assumptions, see our previous papers on the commission's plans.

—*Risk*. As emphasized above and in chapter 8, Social Security benefits are not subject to the same financial market risks as benefits that depend on stock market returns. Virtually all economists would agree that it is misleading to present benefit levels based on assets of widely differing risk without making any adjustment for that risk. We therefore present the figures in two ways: with no risk adjustment and with a simplified

Table F-2. *Changes in Benefits for Average-Earning Two-Earner Couples: Authors' Proposal and President's Commission Model 2*[a]

Percent change from scheduled benefits

Year turning age 65	Authors' plan	Traditional benefits	Model 2 Expected combined benefits Not adjusted for risk	Adjusted for risk[b]
2012	−0.0	−0.9	0.0	−0.5
2022	−0.6	−9.9	−6.1	−8.5
2032	−3.7	−18.2	−8.3	−15.2
2042	−7.8	−25.7	−5.9	−20.5
2052	−11.7	−32.5	−6.3	−26.1
2075	−19.7	−45.9	−20.5	−39.6

Source: Memorandum from the Office of the Chief Actuary and authors' calculations.

a. Model 2 is that of the President's Commission to Strengthen Social Security.

b. As measured by the "low yield" calculations undertaken by the Social Security actuaries.

risk adjustment that assumes that stocks earn no more than bonds on a risk-adjusted basis. The right adjustment for many workers is somewhere between these two numbers, but we think it is closer to the fully adjusted numbers.

—*Additional contributions under Model 3.* In order to participate in an individual account under the commission's Model 3, workers are required to deposit 1 percent of their taxable earnings in their accounts, in addition to the payroll revenue that is automatically diverted to the accounts. That additional contribution boosts the expected income from the account in retirement. We show the results both with and without that additional contribution.

We begin with comparisons between our plan and Model 2 for medium earners in two-earner couples. As table F-2 shows, the reduction in expected *combined* benefits under Model 2 is more substantial than the reduction in benefits under our plan for two-earner couples turning 65 in 2022 and 2032, even without adjusting for risk.[3] Thereafter the combined benefit reduction under Model 2 for two-earner couples continues to be larger than under our plan when the benefits under Model 2 are adjusted for financial market risk.

Table F-3. *Changes in Benefits for Average-Earning One-Earner Couples: Authors' Proposal and President's Commission Model 2*[a]

Percent change from scheduled benefits

		Model 2		
			Expected combined benefits	
Year turning age 65	*Authors' plan*	*Traditional benefits*	*Not adjusted for risk*	*Adjusted for risk*[b]
2012	–0.0	–0.9	–0.3	–0.6
2022	–0.6	–9.9	–7.3	–9.0
2032	–3.7	–18.2	–11.5	–16.2
2042	–7.8	–25.7	–12.3	–22.2
2052	–11.7	–32.5	–14.8	–28.1
2075	–19.7	–45.9	–28.7	–41.7

Source: Memorandum from the Office of the Chief Actuary and authors' calculations.
a. Model 2 is that of the President's Commission to Strengthen Social Security.
b. As measured by the "low yield" calculations undertaken by the Social Security actuaries.

Table F-3 presents the corresponding results for couples in which one spouse works in covered employment and the other does not (perhaps because of the need to care for children or elderly relatives). As the table shows, the combined benefit reductions under Model 2 for such a one-earner couple with medium earnings are more severe than under our plan, regardless of whether the income from the individual accounts under Model 2 is adjusted for risk or not.

Tables F-4 through F-6 present the results for medium-earning two-earner and one-earner couples under the commission's Model 3 and under our plan. Model 3 differs from Model 2 in two important ways. First, it includes additional benefit reductions for those who claim benefits before age 65; since the vast majority of beneficiaries currently do claim benefits before age 65, we present results both for those who claim benefits at age 65 and for those who claim benefits at age 62. Second, Model 3 requires an additional 1-percent-of-payroll contribution from those workers who choose to have payroll revenue diverted into their individual accounts. Without the additional 1 percent contributions, Model 3 assumes between 1.16 percent and 1.68 percent of payroll in general revenue transfers over the next seventy-five years, compared

Table F-4. *Changes in Benefits for Average-Earning Two-Earner Couples Claiming Benefits at Age 65: Authors' Proposal and President's Commission Model 3*[a]

Percent change from scheduled benefits

Year turning age 65	Authors' plan	Traditional benefits at age 65	Not adjusted for risk	Adjusted for risk[b]	Adjusted for risk without additional 1 percent contribution[c]
			Model 3		
			Expected combined benefits		
2012	–0.0	–0.9	0.9	0.4	–0.8
2022	–0.6	–8.0	–0.9	–4.1	–7.7
2032	–3.7	–13.5	2.8	–6.2	–12.7
2042	–7.8	–17.7	10.3	–7.2	–16.3
2052	–11.7	–21.7	11.9	–10.0	–20.1
2075	–19.7	–29.9	2.7	–18.5	–28.3

Source: Memorandum from the Office of the Chief Actuary and authors' calculations.

a. Model 3 is that of the President's Commission to Strengthen Social Security.

b. As measured by the "low yield" calculations undertaken by the Social Security actuaries.

c. Assumes "low yield" calculations undertaken by the actuaries and reduces annuity size by 1/3.5 to reflect the 1 percent additional contribution as a share of the 3.5 percent total contribution rate (2.5 percent payroll tax diversion plus 1 percent additional contribution rate).

with approximately 1.3 to 1.8 percent of payroll in additional, dedicated revenue under our plan. In other words, without the additional 1 percent contributions, the assumed revenue under Model 3 and under our plan is roughly comparable. With the additional 1 percent contributions, however, Model 3 effectively assumes substantially more revenue than our plan. The additional assumed revenue naturally raises the expected benefit level under that plan, implying that the comparisons need to reflect the additional revenue.

Tables F-4 and F-5 present the results for two-earner couples. For medium-earning two-earner couples, the combined benefit reductions under Model 3 are smaller than under our plan if no risk adjustment is made, benefits are claimed at age 65, and the retirement income from the additional 1 percent contribution to the individual accounts is included;

Table F-5. *Changes in Benefits for Average-Earning Two-Earner Couples Claiming Benefits at Age 62: Authors' Proposal and President's Commission Model 3*[a]

Percent change from scheduled benefits

Year turning age 65	Authors' plan	Model 3			
		Traditional benefits at age 62	*Expected combined benefits*		
			Not adjusted for risk	Adjusted for risk[b]	Adjusted for risk without additional 1 percent contribution[c]
2012	–0.0	–10.9	–9.7	–9.7	–10.6
2022	–0.6	–17.9	–12.0	–13.5	–17.1
2032	–3.7	–23.5	–8.8	–14.6	–21.6
2042	–7.8	–27.7	–1.8	–12.4	–24.3
2052	–11.7	–31.7	–0.4	–16.4	–27.8
2075	–19.7	–39.9	–9.5	–25.0	–36.1

Source: Memorandum from the Office of the Chief Actuary and authors' calculations.

a. Model 3 is that of the President's Commission to Strengthen Social Security.

b. As measured by the "low yield" calculations undertaken by the Social Security actuaries.

c. Assumes "low yield" calculations undertaken by the actuaries and reduces annuity size by 1/3.5 to reflect the 1 percent additional contribution as a share of the 3.5 percent total contribution rate (2.5 percent payroll tax diversion plus 1 percent additional contribution rate).

none of these assumptions, however, strikes us as the most reasonable basis for comparison. As table F-4 shows, if benefits are claimed at age 65, but the return to stocks is risk-adjusted and the retirement income from the additional 1 percent contributions is excluded, combined benefits are lower under Model 3 than under our plan. For example, under these assumptions, combined benefits for those turning 65 in 2042 are 16 percent less than under the current benefit formula under Model 3, and 8 percent less than benefits under our plan.

Table F-5 shows the corresponding results for those claiming benefits at age 62, which is currently the most common age for claiming benefits. The combined benefit reduction under Model 3 for these beneficiaries exceeds that under our plan on a risk-adjusted basis. When, in addition, the returns to stocks are risk-adjusted and the retirement income from the

Table F-6. *Changes in Benefits for Average-Earning One-Earner Couples Claiming Benefits at Age 65: Authors' Proposal and President's Commission Model 3*[a]

Percent change from scheduled benefits

		Model 3			
			Expected combined benefits		
Year turning age 65	Authors' plan	Traditional benefits at age 65	Not adjusted for risk	Adjusted for risk[b]	Adjusted for risk without additional 1 percent contribution[c]
2012	–0.0	–0.9	0.3	0.0	–0.8
2022	–0.6	–8.0	–3.2	–5.4	–7.8
2032	–3.7	–13.5	–2.5	–8.5	–12.9
2042	–7.8	–17.7	1.2	–10.6	–16.7
2052	–11.7	–21.7	1.0	–13.8	–20.6
2075	–19.7	–39.9	–7.9	–22.2	–28.8

Source: Memorandum from the Office of the Chief Actuary and authors' calculations.

a. Model 3 is that of the President's Commission to Strengthen Social Security.

b. As measured by the "low yield" calculations undertaken by the Social Security actuaries.

c. Assumes "low yield" calculations undertaken by the actuaries and reduces annuity size by 1/3.5 to reflect the 1 percent additional contribution as a share of the 3.5 percent total contribution rate (2.5 percent payroll tax diversion plus 1 percent additional contribution rate).

additional 1 percent contributions is excluded, the combined benefit reduction for those turning 65 in 2042 is 24 percent under Model 3, but only 8 percent under our plan.

Finally, table F-6 presents the results for one-earner couples claiming benefits at age 65. When the analysis is undertaken on a risk-adjusted basis, the benefit reductions are again larger under Model 3 than under our plan. The difference would be even larger for one-earner couples claiming benefits at age 62.

It may not be clear why, on a risk-adjusted basis, the benefit reductions for average earners are smaller under our plan than under, say, the commission's Model 2, even though the total revenue assumed in the two reform plans is arguably similar (if one compares the general revenue

Figure F-1. *Trust Fund Ratios under Proposed Reform and under President's Commission Model 2, 2004–80*

Percent

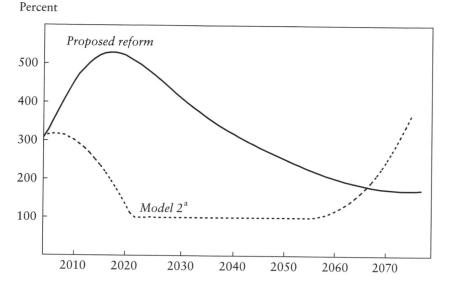

Source: Office of the Chief Actuary, Social Security Administration.
a. Assumes all eligible workers participate in individual accounts.

transfers under Model 2, assuming universal participation in the accounts and protection of disabled workers, with the additional, dedicated revenue under our plan). Two factors explain this result. First, like Model 3 but unlike Model 2, our plan imposes relatively larger benefit reductions on higher earners than on average earners. Because of this, the required benefit reduction for average earners is more modest than that required for average earners under Model 2. Second, Model 2 imposes large benefit reductions over the next seventy-five years in order to accumulate substantial assets in individual accounts and a large and growing trust fund in 2077. Figure F-1 shows the different time paths of the trust fund under our plan and under Model 2 (assuming that all eligible workers participate in the individual accounts established under that plan and that revenue is transferred from the rest of the budget to maintain the trust fund at 100 percent of benefits).

Memorandum from the
Office of the Chief Actuary

The Office of the Chief Actuary at the Social Security Administration serves as the ultimate arbiter of whether a reform plan restores long-term balance to Social Security. It agreed to provide actuarial estimates for the reform plan proposed in this volume. Many aspects of our plan had not been included in previous plans and therefore required extensive new analysis by the Office of the Chief Actuary. In the spirit of promoting transparency in the Social Security debate, this appendix reprints in full the resulting memorandum.

As the memorandum indicates, the Office of the Chief Actuary concluded that our "proposal would, through a combination of increases in taxes and coverage, reductions in the general growth in benefit levels, and certain enhancements to benefit protections, restore solvency to the OASDI program over the 75-year projection period under the intermediate assumptions of the 2003 Trustees Report. Moreover, as the projected trend in the ratio of Trust Fund assets to the annual cost of the program would be stabilized and even rising slowly at the end of the period, the OASDI program would be made sustainably solvent under these assumptions for the foreseeable future."

Social Security

Memorandum   Refer to: TCA

Date: October 8, 2003

To: Peter Diamond, Professor, Massachusetts Institute of Technology
           Peter Orszag, Senior Fellow, Brookings Institution

From: Stephen C. Goss, Chief Actuary

Subject: Estimates of Financial Effects for a Proposal to Restore Solvency to the
           Social Security Program--INFORMATION

This memorandum provides a description of and financial estimates of the effect of a proposal that you have developed. The description that follows represents our understanding of your intent for the provisions of this proposal. Development of the specifics of these provisions and the estimates presented here were only possible through the creativity and extraordinary efforts of Jason Schultz, Alice Wade, Chris Chaplain, Seung An, Michael Clingman, Lesley Reece, Bill Piet, and many others in the Office of the Chief Actuary.

This proposal would, through a combination of increases in taxes and coverage, reductions in the general growth in benefit levels, and certain enhancements to benefit protections, restore solvency to the OASDI program over the 75-year projection period under the intermediate assumptions of the 2003 Trustees Report. Moreover, as the projected trend in the ratio of Trust Fund assets to the annual cost of the program would be stabilized and even rising slowly at the end of the period, the OASDI program would be made sustainably solvent under these assumptions for the foreseeable future.

The balance of this memorandum provides a detailed description of our understanding of the provisions of the proposal, followed by a description of the financial effects of enactment of the proposal, as indicated in the attached tables.

2

I. Provisions of the Proposal

Provision 1: Mortality adjustment

Under this provision, the Social Security Administration would compute successive adjustments to the PIA formula factors (90, 32, 15) and the OASDI payroll tax rates beginning with 2012. The first ratio adjustment factors would be computed in 2009, with ratios of values from the 2009 Trustees Report to values from the 2008 Trustees Report. The annual calculation would be done in October of each year 2009 and later as described below.

Compute the ratio of two expected present values of lifetime retirement benefits starting at the NRA of an individual who will attain age 59 in the current year (2009). Use the interest rates for the current Trustees Report for both present values. The numerator of the ratio would be the present value reflecting mortality from the period life table of the prior year's (2008) Trustees Report for the year TRyear -3 (2005). The denominator of the ratio would be based on mortality from the life table of the current (2009) Trustees Report for TRYear -3 (2006). Based on the intermediate projections of the 2003 Trustees Report, this ratio is expected to average about 0.9976 over the next 75 years. The PIA multiplicative factor applicable for those becoming eligible in the third following year (2012) would be one half of the change reflected in the ratio of expected present value amounts, or an average reduction of about 0.12 percent per year.

Compute the tax-rate multiplicative factor using the "85 percent" rule:
tax rate multiplier=(1+.85*(1-PIA multiplicative factor)) and apply that multiplier to the tax rates for the second following year, to determine the tax rates applicable for the third following year.

For years where the NRA will be changing for those who attain 59 in that year, (a) retain the tax rate multiplier from step 1; (b) for the PIA multiplier, evaluate the effect on benefits at the NRA from the change in the NRA and set PIA multipler=1 for those years if the effect on benefits from the NRA increase is larger than the effect on benefits at the NRA from step 1; if the effect from step 1 is larger, then reduce the PIA multiplier from step 1 to net out the effect of the NRA increase. For years of new benefit eligibility (at age 62) 2017 through 2022, the normal retirement age increase in current law is expected to exceed the reduction indicated by the ratios described above, and so the PIA multiplier is expected to be 1 for these years.

Implementation of this provision for all OASDI benefits would increase the OASDI long-range actuarial balance by an amount estimated to be 0.55 percent of taxable payroll.

Provision 2: Taxable maximum earnings base

Increase the maximum taxable earnings base by an additional 0.5% (by a factor of 1.005) for years 2005 through 2063 so that the percentage of OASDI covered earnings that falls below the maximum taxable amount would be projected to be 87 percent for years 2063 and later under the intermediate assumptions of the 2003 Trustees Report. Implementation of this provision would increase the OASDI long-range actuarial balance by an amount estimated to be 0.25 percent of taxable payroll.

3

Provision 3: Upper bracket PIA factor

Reduce the 15 percent PIA factor by 0.25 percentage point each year 2012 through 2031. The PIA factor would thus decline to 10 percent for beneficiaries newly eligible in years 2031 and later. This modification would be applied to the PIA factor before other adjustments described in this proposal. Implementation of this provision would increase the OASDI long-range actuarial balance by an amount estimated to be 0.18 percent of taxable payroll.

Provision 4: State and local workers

Cover all new State and local government employees hired in 2008 or later under the OASDI program. Implementation of this provision would increase the OASDI long-range actuarial balance by an amount estimated to be 0.19 percent of taxable payroll.

Provision 5: "Legacy charge"

Apply a 3-percent tax rate (1:5 for employers and employees each, and 3 percent for the self employed) to all OASDI covered earnings above the OASDI taxable maximum amount, as modified above. Benefit levels would not reflect the additional earnings subject to taxation. Implementation of this provision would increase the OASDI long-range actuarial balance by an incremental amount (after the effects of provisions 2 and 4 above) estimated to be 0.55 percent of taxable payroll.

Provision 6: Low-Earner PIA Enhancement

This provision would increase the PIA for workers becoming newly eligible for benefits in 2012 and later who have more than 20 years of work (or work for more than half the years since reaching age 22) at a relatively low earnings level. The provision would raise the PIA by 11.9 percent for a retiree becoming eligible in 2012 with 35 years of full-time work at the minimum wage level.[1] This would raise the PIA for this retiree to the projected aged poverty level for 2012.

The provision would provide the same 11.9-percent increase for 35-year workers with average earnings below that of the 35-year minimum wage worker. This 11.9 percent increase would be reduced for 35-year workers with higher career-average earnings levels (AIME), reaching 0 for those with AIMEs at the level of the SSA average wage index for the second year prior to their eligibility. For workers with more than 35 years of work, the percentage increase is maintained

---

[1] The "minimum wage worker" is assumed to work 2000 hours each year at a minimum hourly wage rate of $5.15 in 2003 and indexed thereafter by growth in the Social Security average wage index. The minimum wage worker is assumed not to work after the calendar year in which age 60 is attained.

4

at the same level as specified for workers with the same AIME level and only 35 years of work. However, the percentage increase is reduced for workers with fewer than 35 years of work, reaching 0 for those with 20 or fewer years of work. Thus, no enhancement is provided by this provision for retirees with 20 or fewer years of employment. The year-of-work requirements would be "scaled" to the length of the elapsed period from age 22 to benefit eligibility for workers who become disabled or die before reaching age 62.[2] The incremental effect of this provision after provisions 1 and 3 would be to reduce the size of the long-range OASDI actuarial balance by an estimated 0.14 percent of taxable payroll.

The table below illustrates the effect of the benefit enhancement for workers with low earnings.

Effect of Provision 6: Percentage Increase in PIA for Retirees with No Period of Disability, New Eligibility in 2012 or Later

		Average Earnings Level in Years Worked (2004 wage levels)						
			Minimum Wage		Minimum Wage X 2			
Number of Years of Work	Quarters of Coverage (QCs)	$5,000	$11,139	Low $16,291	$22,277	Medium $36,203	High $57,924	Maximum $88,500
		Percentage Increase in PIA Due to Provision 6						
10	40	0	0	0	0	0	0	0
15	60	0	0	0	0	0	0	0
20	80	0	0	0	0	0	0	0
25	100	4.0	4.0	3.9	3.2	1.6	0	0
30	120	7.9	7.9	7.0	5.4	1.6	0	0
35	140	11.9	11.9	9.5	6.6	0	0	0
40	160	11.9	11.9	9.5	6.6	0	0	0

Based on intermediate assumptions of the 2003 Trustees Report.

The benefit enhancement under this provision would be computed according to the following formula:

For all workers whose AIME is less than twice the AIME for a medium scaled worker, the PIA is multiplied by

$$1 + \text{applicable percentage} \times \text{AIME factor} \times \text{coverage factor.}$$

---

[2] For example, the PIA of a 21-year minimum wage worker, who becomes disabled at age 46 in 2012 or later, would be increased 11.9 percent because this worker had OASDI covered earnings in seven eighths of the 24 elapsed years.

5

In the above formula,

- "Applicable percentage" is equal to 11.9 percent for beneficiaries initially eligible in 2012 and later,

- "AIME factor" is equal to
$$\begin{cases} 1 & \text{if } AIME \leq M \\ (A - AIME)/(A - M) & \text{if } M < AIME < A \\ 0 & \text{if } AIME \geq A. \end{cases}$$
Here,
A = AIME of a scaled medium worker and
M = AIME for a 35-year minimum wage worker.

- "Coverage factor" is equal to
$$\begin{cases} 0 & \text{if } QCs \leq 2 \times \text{elapsed years} \\ 1 + (QCs - 3.5 \times \text{elapsed years})/\text{elapsed years} & \text{if } 2 \times \text{elapsed years} < QCs < 3.5 \times \text{elapsed years} \\ 1 & \text{if } QCs \geq 3.5 \times \text{elapsed years}. \end{cases}$$
In the above formula for the coverage factor, "QCs" represents the number of quarters of coverage earned by the worker prior to benefit eligibility. "Elapsed years" represents the number of years starting with the year the worker attains age 22 through the year prior to benefit eligibility, excluding periods of disabled worker entitlement.

Provision 7: 75-Percent of Couple Benefit for Aged Widow/Widowers

This provision applies to a surviving spouse who is eligible for both a worker benefit and an aged surviving spouse benefit. This provision would provide, beginning in 2012, the option to receive 75 percent of the benefit that the married couple would be receiving if both were still alive. Calculation of the couple benefit would reflect all age-related reductions for such benefits. If the deceased spouse is not already entitled for OASDI benefits at death, then it will be assumed that the deceased spouse would have become entitled for benefits on the date of death, or the earliest eligibility date, if later. The potential benefit for survivors under this provision would be limited to what the survivor would receive as a retired worker beneficiary with the average Primary Insurance Amount for all worker beneficiaries with benefits in current payment in the year of eligibility for this provision. Implementation of this provision would increase the OASDI actuarial deficit by an estimated 0.08 percent of taxable payroll.

Provision 8: Residual legacy benefit and tax adjustments

This provision has three parts. It is designed to provide sufficient additional revenue and benefit reduction so that, in conjunction with all other provisions of this proposal, the OASDI program

6

would be restored to solvency for the 75-year long-range period, and that this solvency would meet the criteria for sustainable solvency.

1. For years 2023 and later, reduce the three PIA formula factors annually by an additional 0.30 percent (multiply by the factor 0.997).
2. For years 2023 and later, increase the combined OASDI payroll tax rate annually by 0.255 percent (multiply by the factor 1.00255). This annual increase is 85 percent as large as the annual decrease applied to PIA factors.
3. For years 2023 and later, increase the 3-percent legacy payroll tax rate (applicable for covered earnings in excess of the taxable maximum, see provision 5) annually by 0.51 percent (multiply by the factor 1.0051). This increase is specified to be twice the increase applied to the basic payroll tax rate applicable to OASDI covered earnings below the taxable maximum.

The estimated incremental effect of provision 8 on the long-range OASDI actuarial balance after application of provisions 1-7 is 0.97 percent of taxable payroll.

Provision 9: Disability benefits

Compute a 75-year cost saving (present value for 2003-77) from applying all benefit changes in Provisions 1-8 to disabled workers and their auxiliary beneficiaries in 2012 and thereafter (the quarters of coverage necessary to receive the low-earner enhanced benefit would be scaled for disabled workers).

This provision is intended to provide an increment to benefits payable to beneficiaries under the DI program that will accumulate throughout their period of entitlement to such benefits, and will convey to any continuation of benefits payable under the OASI program after the death or conversion (at NRA) of the disabled worker. The increment is designed so that the net present value of the cost of such increments over the 75-year period 2003-77 would equal the net present value of the benefit reductions from Provisions 1-8 applied to all disabled worker beneficiaries and their auxiliaries (see above).

The provision would apply a "super-COLA" to disabled worker beneficiaries and their auxiliaries by increasing PIA for all DI beneficiaries by a factor of 1.009 (or 0.9 percent), applied cumulatively for each year of benefit receipt under the DI program, in 2012 and thereafter. Super COLAs received while a disabled worker beneficiary would be retained after conversion of retired worker status at NRA (or after the death of the worker), but no further super COLAs would be earned after such conversion or death. The excess of the super-COLA over the COLA will be treated as an increase in PIA for purposes of all auxiliary benefits and subsequent survivor benefits based on the worker's record.

The super COLA as computed above would also apply for years of benefit receipt as a child survivor or as a surviving spouse with an entitled child in care.

7

The estimated incremental effect of provision 9 on the long-range OASDI actuarial balance after application of provisions 1-8 is a reduction in the size of the long-range OASDI actuarial balance of 0.21 percent of taxable payroll.

II. Estimated Financial Effects of the Proposal

The attached tables provide estimates of the effects of enactment of this proposal on the actuarial status of the OASDI program, on the Federal Government Unified Budget, and on the cash flow between the combined OASDI Trust Funds and the General Fund of the U.S. Treasury over the next 75 years. All estimates are based on the intermediate assumptions of the 2003 OASDI Trustees Report.

Table 1 indicates that the long-range OASDI actuarial balance would be increased by an estimated 2.00 percent of taxable payroll, from a deficit of 1.92 percent of payroll under current law to a positive balance of 0.09 percent of payroll with enactment of the proposal. Expressed on a present-value basis as of the beginning of 2003, the 75-year unfunded obligation of $3.5 trillion for the OASDI program under current law would be replaced by an estimated combined Trust Fund balance at the end of the period of $0.5 trillion in present value discounted to January 1, 2003. Moreover, the solvency for the 75-year long range period would be deemed sustainable for the foreseeable future as indicated by the stable ratio of Trust Fund Assets to annual program cost (TFR) at the end of the period. The pattern of annual OASDI balances at the end of the period indicates that a rising TFR might be expected beyond the 75-year period if the provisions of the proposal are extended.

Table 1a provides a comparison of estimated combined OASDI Trust Fund assets at the end of each year under current law and under the proposal in constant 2003 dollars. Under the proposal, Trust Fund assets are projected to be rising in constant dollars at the end of the period. This table also provides a comparison of the estimates of OASDI effective taxable payroll under current law and under the proposal in constant 2003 dollars. By 2077, the effective taxable payroll is projected to be increased by over 12 percent.

Table 1b provides the estimated effect of enactment of the proposal on the Federal Government Unified Budget balance. The change in the annual unified budget cash flow would be positive for all years starting 2005. As a result, the proposal would have a substantial impact on the amount of Federal debt held by the public by the end of the period. This value, like the change in the annual Unified Budget balance as a result of the proposal, reflects the cumulative effects of reduced service on the debt under the proposal.

Table 1c provides a comparison of the annual cash flow from the combined OASDI Trust Funds to the General Fund of the Treasury under the proposal, and under a "Theoretical Social Security with PAYGO Transfers". Under this Theoretical Social Security, it is assumed that the law is changed so that the General Fund would make transfers to the Trust Funds as needed just sufficient to permit continued full payment of scheduled benefits after the exhaustion of the Trust Fund assets in 2042. Values are shown as a percentage of payroll (equal to the annual balances

8

in table 1), in current (nominal) dollars, in present value discounted to January 1, 2003, and in constant 2003 dollars. The total cash flow for the period 2003 through 2077 is indicated in present value. Under the *Theoretical Social Security with PAYGO Transfers*, the total cash flow needed from the General Fund would be $4.9 trillion, that is, $3.5 trillion in transfers in addition to the $1.4 trillion for redemption of assets held by the Trust Funds at the beginning of the period. Under the proposal, net cash flow from the General Fund is estimated at $0.9 trillion for the period, or $4 trillion less than under the Theoretical Social Security with PAYGO Transfers.

Stephen C. Goss

Attachments

Table 1. *Projected OASDI Financial Status under Diamond-Orszag Proposal with Ult Real TF Int Rate of 3.0*

Year	Cost Rate	Income Rate	Annual Balance	TFR 1-1-yr	OASDI Contrib Rate
2003	10.89	12.70	1.81	288	12.4
2004	10.82	12.69	1.88	309	12.40
2005	10.27	12.69	2.43	330	12.40
2006	10.18	12.69	2.51	357	12.40
2007	10.18	12.71	2.53	383	12.40
2008	10.21	12.72	2.51	408	12.40
2009	10.28	12.73	2.45	432	12.40
2010	10.39	12.75	2.36	454	12.40
2011	10.53	12.81	2.28	474	12.40
2012	10.78	12.82	2.04	489	12.41
2013	11.00	12.85	1.85	502	12.42
2014	11.25	12.88	1.63	513	12.44
2015	11.51	12.91	1.40	522	12.45
2016	11.81	12.94	1.13	527	12.46
2017	12.12	12.97	0.85	529	12.48
2018	12.45	13.01	0.56	529	12.49
2019	12.78	13.04	0.26	527	12.51
2020	13.12	13.07	−0.05	522	12.52
2021	13.48	13.11	−0.37	515	12.54
2022	13.82	13.14	−0.68	507	12.55
2023	14.12	13.21	−0.91	498	12.60
2024	14.42	13.28	−1.14	488	12.65
2025	14.70	13.34	−1.36	478	12.69
2026	14.96	13.41	−1.55	468	12.74
2027	15.21	13.47	−1.73	457	12.79
2028	15.44	13.54	−1.90	445	12.84
2029	15.64	13.60	−2.03	434	12.89
2030	15.81	13.66	−2.14	423	12.94
2031	15.95	13.72	−2.22	412	12.99
2032	16.06	13.78	−2.28	401	13.04
2033	16.16	13.84	−2.32	390	13.08
2034	16.23	13.90	−2.33	380	13.13
2035	16.27	13.95	−2.32	370	13.18
2036	16.30	14.01	−2.30	360	13.23
2037	16.31	14.06	−2.25	351	13.28
2038	16.32	14.11	−2.21	343	13.33
2039	16.32	14.16	−2.15	334	13.38
2040	16.31	14.22	−2.09	326	13.43
2041	16.30	14.27	−2.03	319	13.48
2042	16.28	14.32	−1.96	312	13.53
2043	16.28	14.37	−1.91	304	13.58

Year	Cost Rate	Income Rate	Annual Balance	TFR 1-1-yr	OASDI Contrib Rate
2044	16.28	14.42	−1.86	298	13.63
2045	16.28	14.47	−1.81	291	13.68
2046	16.29	14.53	−1.76	284	13.73
2047	16.29	14.58	−1.72	278	13.78
2048	16.31	14.63	−1.68	272	13.83
2049	16.33	14.68	−1.64	266	13.88
2050	16.34	14.74	−1.61	260	13.93
2051	16.37	14.79	−1.58	254	13.98
2052	16.39	14.84	−1.55	248	14.03
2053	16.42	14.90	−1.52	243	14.08
2054	16.44	14.95	−1.49	237	14.13
2055	16.46	15.01	−1.46	232	14.18
2056	16.49	15.06	−1.43	226	14.23
2057	16.51	15.11	−1.40	221	14.28
2058	16.52	15.17	−1.36	216	14.33
2059	16.53	15.22	−1.31	212	14.38
2060	16.54	15.27	−1.26	207	14.43
2061	16.54	15.32	−1.21	203	14.48
2062	16.54	15.38	−1.16	199	14.53
2063	16.54	15.43	−1.11	195	14.58
2064	16.54	15.48	−1.06	192	14.63
2065	16.54	15.53	−1.01	189	14.69
2066	16.55	15.59	−0.96	186	14.74
2067	16.55	15.64	−0.91	183	14.79
2068	16.55	15.69	−0.86	181	14.84
2069	16.55	15.75	−0.81	178	14.89
2070	16.56	15.80	−0.76	177	14.94
2071	16.56	15.85	−0.71	175	14.99
2072	16.56	15.90	−0.66	174	15.05
2073	16.56	15.96	−0.60	173	15.10
2074	16.55	16.01	−0.55	172	15.15
2075	16.55	16.06	−0.49	172	15.20
2076	16.54	16.11	−0.43	172	15.25
2077	16.54	16.17	−0.37	172	15.31
2078	16.53	16.22	−0.31	173	15.36

Summarized

	CostRt OASDI	IncRt OASDI	ActBal OASDI	Change in ActBal
2003 −2077	14.44	14.52	0.09	2.00

Based on Intermediate Assumptions of the 2003 Trustees Report with Ult Real Int Rate of 3.

Office of the Actuary
Social Security Administration
October 6, 2003

Table 1a. *Comparison of Trust Fund Assets and Effective Taxable Payroll for the Diamond-Orszag Proposal*

| Year | OASDI Trust Fund Assets (EOY) | | OASDI Effective Taxable Payroll | |
	Present Law	Proposal	Present Law	Proposal
	(In billions of Constant 2003 Dollars)			
2003	1,543	1,543	4,387	4,387
2004	1,683	1,683	4,504	4,504
2005	1,833	1,859	4,628	4,838
2006	1,990	2,045	4,749	4,968
2007	2,154	2,240	4,860	5,090
2008	2,323	2,444	4,967	5,218
2009	2,493	2,654	5,069	5,344
2010	2,664	2,868	5,167	5,465
2011	2,835	3,087	5,261	5,582
2012	3,001	3,301	5,348	5,691
2013	3,161	3,511	5,439	5,800
2014	3,312	3,717	5,526	5,905
2015	3,452	3,915	5,611	6,008
2016	3,579	4,104	5,694	6,109
2017	3,691	4,281	5,779	6,209
2018	3,786	4,444	5,862	6,312
2019	3,863	4,594	5,948	6,414
2020	3,921	4,728	6,033	6,516
2021	3,957	4,844	6,120	6,619
2022	3,971	4,941	6,206	6,721
2023	3,964	5,023	6,292	6,825
2024	3,936	5,091	6,379	6,930
2025	3,885	5,143	6,467	7,036
2026	3,813	5,181	6,557	7,144
2027	3,718	5,205	6,648	7,253
2028	3,601	5,214	6,741	7,365
2029	3,461	5,211	6,836	7,480
2030	3,300	5,196	6,933	7,597
2031	3,119	5,172	7,033	7,716
2032	2,917	5,139	7,134	7,837
2033	2,696	5,099	7,236	7,960
2034	2,457	5,053	7,340	8,086
2035	2,200	5,004	7,445	8,213
2036	1,925	4,951	7,552	8,342
2037	1,634	4,898	7,660	8,473
2038	1,326	4,843	7,769	8,601
2039	1,001	4,788	7,880	8,732
2040	661	4,734	7,990	8,862
2041	303	4,681	8,101	8,993

Year	OASDI Trust Fund Assets (EOY)		OASDI Effective Taxable Payroll	
	Present Law	Proposal	Present Law	Proposal
	(In billions of Constant 2003 Dollars)			
2042	—	4,629	8,214	9,126
2043	—	4,578	8,327	9,256
2044	—	4,528	8,440	9,388
2045	—	4,478	8,555	9,521
2046	—	4,428	8,669	9,653
2047	—	4,378	8,784	9,787
2048	—	4,328	8,900	9,922
2049	—	4,277	9,018	10,058
2050	—	4,225	9,136	10,196
2051	—	4,173	9,256	10,335
2052	—	4,119	9,377	10,475
2053	—	4,064	9,499	10,617
2054	—	4,007	9,623	10,762
2055	—	3,950	9,749	10,908
2056	—	3,891	9,877	11,053
2057	—	3,832	10,008	11,199
2058	—	3,773	10,140	11,348
2059	—	3,715	10,274	11,499
2060	—	3,658	10,409	11,651
2061	—	3,603	10,546	11,805
2062	—	3,550	10,685	11,962
2063	—	3,499	10,826	12,120
2064	—	3,450	10,967	12,280
2065	—	3,405	11,111	12,441
2066	—	3,362	11,256	12,604
2067	—	3,322	11,402	12,769
2068	—	3,285	11,550	12,936
2069	—	3,251	11,699	13,105
2070	—	3,222	11,850	13,274
2071	—	3,196	12,002	13,446
2072	—	3,175	12,156	13,619
2073	—	3,159	12,311	13,794
2074	—	3,150	12,468	13,972
2075	—	3,146	12,627	14,151
2076	—	3,149	12,788	14,332
2077	—	3,159	12,950	14,515
2078	—	3,178	13,115	14,701

Based on Intermediate Assumptions of the 2003 Trustees Report with Ult Real Int Rate of 3.

Office of the Actuary
Social Security Administration
October 6, 2003

Table 1b. *Projected Unified Budget Effect on Diamond-Orszag Proposal*

Year	Change in OASDI CashFlow	Change in Annual UnifBudg CashFlow	Change in Debt Held by Public 1/ (EOY)	Change in Annual UnifBudg Balance
		(In billions of Constant 2003 Dollars)		
2004	0.0	0.0	0.0	0.0
2005	25.2	25.2	−26.0	26.0
2006	27.3	27.3	−54.9	29.7
2007	28.7	28.7	−86.2	32.9
2008	31.3	31.3	−121.1	37.4
2009	34.1	34.1	−160.1	42.5
2010	36.9	36.9	−203.1	47.7
2011	41.0	41.0	−251.7	54.5
2012	38.3	38.3	−298.9	54.5
2013	40.6	40.6	−349.8	59.7
2014	42.6	42.6	−404.3	64.7
2015	44.4	44.4	−462.3	69.8
2016	46.3	46.3	−523.9	75.1
2017	47.9	47.9	−589.0	80.3
2018	49.8	49.8	−658.0	86.2
2019	51.5	51.5	−730.8	91.9
2020	53.0	53.0	−807.3	97.8
2021	54.2	54.2	−887.4	103.6
2022	55.6	55.6	−971.2	109.7
2023	59.2	59.2	−1,061.3	118.4
2024	63.1	63.1	−1,158.2	127.8
2025	67.4	67.4	−1,262.3	137.9
2026	71.9	71.9	−1,374.3	148.7
2027	76.7	76.7	−1,494.5	160.3
2028	81.8	81.8	−1,623.6	172.6
2029	87.5	87.5	−1,762.4	186.1
2030	93.5	93.5	−1,911.6	200.5
2031	100.0	100.0	−2,072.0	216.0
2032	107.0	107.0	−2,244.4	232.8
2033	114.1	114.1	−2,429.3	250.3
2034	121.7	121.7	−2,627.6	269.0
2035	129.8	129.8	−2,840.1	289.1
2036	138.3	138.3	−3,067.8	310.4
2037	147.4	147.4	−3,311.6	333.2
2038	155.7	155.7	−3,571.3	356.2
2039	164.5	164.5	−3,847.9	380.5
2040	173.6	173.6	−4,142.1	406.4
2041	183.3	183.3	−4,455.2	433.7
2042	193.5	193.5	−4,788.2	462.7

Year	Change in OASDI CashFlow	Change in Annual UnifBudg CashFlow	Change in Debt Held by Public 1/ (EOY)	Change in Annual UnifBudg Balance
	(In billions of Constant 2003 Dollars)			
2043	203.1	203.1	−5,141.0	492.3
2044	213.1	213.1	−5,514.8	523.5
2045	223.7	223.7	−5,910.7	556.5
2046	234.8	234.8	−6,329.8	591.3
2047	246.4	246.4	−6,773.5	628.0
2048	257.8	257.8	−7,242.2	666.0
2049	269.6	269.6	−7,737.2	705.9
2050	282.1	282.1	−8,259.8	748.0
2051	295.0	295.0	−8,811.5	792.2
2052	308.6	308.6	−9,393.7	838.8
2053	322.3	322.3	−10,007.4	887.4
2054	336.4	336.4	−10,654.2	938.2
2055	351.1	351.1	−11,335.5	991.6
2056	365.7	365.7	−12,052.2	1,046.9
2057	380.6	380.6	−12,805.8	1,104.6
2058	396.0	396.0	−13,597.8	1,165.0
2059	411.7	411.7	−14,429.8	1,228.1
2060	427.9	427.9	−15,303.4	1,293.9
2061	444.4	444.4	−16,220.3	1,362.6
2062	461.5	461.5	−17,182.3	1,434.4
2063	479.3	479.3	−18,191.5	1,509.6
2064	497.6	497.6	−19,249.7	1,588.1
2065	516.3	516.3	−20,359.0	1,669.9
2066	535.5	535.5	−21,521.3	1,755.3
2067	555.3	555.3	−22,738.9	1,844.4
2068	575.8	575.8	−24,014.2	1,937.6
2069	597.0	597.0	−25,349.5	2,034.7
2070	618.5	618.5	−26,747.1	2,135.9
2071	640.7	640.7	−28,209.4	2,241.4
2072	663.3	663.3	−29,738.9	2,351.1
2073	686.9	686.9	−31,338.5	2,465.8
2074	711.0	711.0	−33,011.0	2,585.3
2075	735.7	735.7	−34,759.1	2,709.6
2076	760.9	760.9	−36,585.6	2,838.9
2077	786.7	786.7	−38,493.5	2,973.5
2078	813.5	813.5	−40,486.2	3,113.9

Based on Intermediate Assumptions of the 2003 Trustees Report with Ult Real Int Rate of 3.

Office of the Actuary
Social Security Administration
October 6, 2003

Table 1c. OASDI Cash Flow to General Fund of the Treasury— Diamond-Orszag Proposal vs. Theoretical OASDI

	Diamond-Orszag Proposal				Theoretical Social Security with PAYGO Transfers			
	Net Amount of Cash-Flow from the OASDI Trust Funds to the General Fund of the Treasury During the Year 1/				Net Amount of Cash-Flow from the OASDI Trust Funds to the General Fund of the Treasury During the Year 1/			
	Billions of Dollars —				Billions of Dollars —			
	Annual Balance	Current $	PV Jan 1, 03	Constant 2003$	Annual balance	Current $	PV Jan 1, 03	Constant 2003$
2003	1.81	77	75	77	1.8	77	75	77
2004	1.88	83	76	81	1.9	83	76	81
2005	2.43	121	105	115	2.0	95	82	90
2006	2.51	133	108	123	2.1	103	84	95
2007	2.53	142	109	127	2.1	110	84	99
2008	2.51	148	107	129	2.0	112	81	98
2009	2.45	152	104	129	1.9	112	76	95
2010	2.36	154	99	127	1.8	110	70	90
2011	2.28	158	95	126	1.6	106	64	85
2012	2.04	148	84	115	1.4	99	56	76
2013	1.85	141	76	106	1.2	87	47	65
2014	1.63	130	66	95	1.0	72	37	52
2015	1.40	117	56	83	0.7	54	26	38
2016	1.13	99	45	68	0.4	31	14	21
2017	0.85	77	33	51	0.1	5	3	3
2018	0.56	52	21	34	−0.3	−25	−9	−16
2019	0.26	24	10	15	−0.6	−57	−21	−36
2020	−0.05	−7	−2	−5	−0.9	−94	−33	−58
2021	−0.37	−44	−14	−26	−1.3	−135	−44	−80
2022	−0.68	−82	−25	−47	−1.6	−178	−55	−103
2023	−0.91	−114	−33	−64	−1.9	−220	−64	−123
2024	−1.14	−149	−41	−81	−2.2	−265	−73	−144
2025	−1.36	−184	−48	−97	−2.5	−312	−81	−164
2026	−1.55	−220	−54	−113	−2.8	−361	−88	−184
2027	−1.73	−257	−59	−127	−3.1	−411	−95	−204
2028	−1.90	−294	−64	−142	−3.3	−463	−101	−223
2029	−2.03	−329	−67	−154	−3.5	−516	−106	−241
2030	−2.14	−362	−70	−165	−3.7	−568	−110	−258
2031	−2.22	−393	−72	−174	−3.9	−620	−113	−274
2032	−2.28	−421	−72	−181	−4.0	−671	−116	−288
2033	−2.32	−448	−72	−186	−4.1	−722	−117	−300
2034	−2.33	−471	−72	−190	−4.2	−773	−118	−312
2035	−2.32	−491	−71	−193	−4.3	−823	−119	−323
2036	−2.30	−509	−69	−194	−4.4	−872	−119	−332
2037	−2.25	−522	−67	−193	−4.4	−921	−118	−340
2038	−2.21	−535	−64	−192	−4.5	−969	−117	−348
2039	−2.15	−546	−62	−190	−4.5	−1,018	−116	−355
2040	−2.09	−555	−59	−188	−4.5	−1,069	−115	−361
2041	−2.03	−562	−57	−185	−4.5	−1,121	−113	−368
2042	−1.96	−569	−54	−181	−4.5	−1,176	−112	−375

	Diamond-Orszag Proposal				Theoretical Social Security with PAYGO Transfers			
	Net Amount of Cash-Flow from the OASDI Trust Funds to the General Fund of the Treasury During the Year 1/				Net Amount of Cash-Flow from the OASDI Trust Funds to the General Fund of the Treasury During the Year 1/			
	Billions of Dollars —				Billions of Dollars —			
	Annual Balance	Current $	PV Jan 1, 03	Constant 2003$	Annual balance	Current $	PV Jan 1, 03	Constant 2003$
2043	−1.91	−578	−52	−179	−4.6	−1,234	−111	−382
2044	−1.86	−588	−50	−177	−4.6	−1,297	−110	−390
2045	−1.81	−598	−47	−174	−4.6	−1,365	−109	−398
2046	−1.76	−609	−46	−172	−4.7	−1,438	−108	−407
2047	−1.72	−620	−44	−170	−4.7	−1,515	−108	−417
2048	−1.68	−633	−42	−169	−4.8	−1,598	−107	−427
2049	−1.64	−647	−40	−168	−4.8	−1,687	−106	−437
2050	−1.61	−661	−39	−166	−4.9	−1,782	−106	−448
2051	−1.58	−677	−38	−165	−5.0	−1,884	−106	−460
2052	−1.55	−694	−36	−165	−5.0	−1,995	−105	−473
2053	−1.52	−712	−35	−164	−5.1	−2,111	−105	−486
2054	−1.49	−730	−34	−163	−5.2	−2,234	−105	−500
2055	−1.46	−746	−33	−162	−5.2	−2,363	−105	−513
2056	−1.43	−763	−31	−161	−5.3	−2,498	−104	−526
2057	−1.40	−778	−30	−159	−5.4	−2,638	−104	−540
2058	−1.36	−790	−29	−157	−5.4	−2,783	−103	−553
2059	−1.31	−798	−28	−154	−5.5	−2,932	−103	−566
2060	−1.26	−803	−26	−150	−5.5	−3,088	−102	−578
2061	−1.21	−805	−25	−146	−5.6	−3,249	−101	−591
2062	−1.16	−806	−23	−142	−5.6	−3,420	−100	−604
2063	−1.11	−805	−22	−138	−5.7	−3,602	−99	−617
2064	−1.06	−802	−21	−133	−5.7	−3,793	−99	−631
2065	−1.01	−798	−19	−129	−5.8	−3,994	−98	−645
2066	−0.96	−793	−18	−124	−5.8	−4,207	−97	−660
2067	−0.91	−787	−17	−120	−5.9	−4,433	−97	−675
2068	−0.86	−777	−16	−115	−6.0	−4,672	−96	−691
2069	−0.81	−764	−14	−110	−6.0	−4,923	−95	−707
2070	−0.76	−749	−13	−104	−6.1	−5,188	−95	−723
2071	−0.71	−731	−12	−99	−6.1	−5,466	−94	−740
2072	−0.66	−709	−11	−93	−6.2	−5,759	−93	−756
2073	−0.60	−680	−10	−87	−6.3	−6,066	−93	−774
2074	−0.55	−646	−9	−80	−6.3	−6,389	−92	−791
2075	−0.49	−607	−8	−73	−6.4	−6,727	−91	−809
2076	−0.43	−562	−7	−66	−6.4	−7,082	−91	−826
2077	−0.37	−509	−6	−58	−6.5	−7,453	−90	−844
Total 2003–77		−929				−4,927		

1/ Equals net investment in special Treasury Bonds by the Trust Funds minus transfers from the General Fund of the Treasury. Results for PAYGO GR borrowing would be equivalent. Based on Intermediate Assumptions of the 2003 Trustees Report

Office of the Actuary
Social Security Administration
October 6, 2003

Notes

Chapter One

1. President George W. Bush, announcing the formation of the President's Commission to Strengthen Social Security, in the Rose Garden at the White House, May 2, 2001 (www.csss.gov/press/press050201.html).

2. See, for example, Dean Baker and Mark Weisbrot, *Social Security: The Phony Crisis* (University of Chicago Press, 1999).

3. See, for example, the interim and final reports of the President's Commission to Strengthen Social Security (www.csss.gov/reports/Report-Interim.pdf and www.csss.gov/reports/Final_report.pdf). For detailed critical analyses of the commission's proposals, see Peter A. Diamond and Peter R. Orszag, "Assessing the Plans Proposed by the President's Commission to Strengthen Social Security," *Tax Notes,* July 2002, and "An Assessment of the Proposals of the President's Commission to Strengthen Social Security," *Contributions to Economic Analysis and Policy,* vol. 1, issue 1, article 10 (2002).

4. For other recent discussions of Social Security reform, see C. Eugene Steuerle and Jon M. Bakija, *Retooling Social Security for the 21st Century: Right and Wrong Approaches to Reform* (Washington: Urban Institute, 1994); Edward Gramlich, *Is It Time to Reform Social Security?* (University of Michigan Press,

1998); Sylvester J. Schieber and John B. Shoven, *The Real Deal: The History and Future of Social Security* (Yale University Press, 1999); Robert Ball, *Insuring the Essentials* (New York: Century Foundation, 2000); and Henry J. Aaron and Robert D. Reischauer, *Countdown to Reform: The Great Social Security Debate* (New York: Century Foundation, 2001).

5. Table 5-3 in chapter 5 and table 6-6 in chapter 6 list the elements in other recent reform plans that are similar or identical to components of our plan.

6. The legacy charge would begin only in 2023, because the scheduled increases in the full benefit age end for those turning 62 in 2022.

7. The objective of maintaining a relatively constant ratio of legacy debt to taxable payroll across time resembles an objective of stabilizing the government debt-GDP ratio across time. The universal legacy charge would be adjusted as necessary to achieve this objective beyond the seventy-five-year period covered by Social Security's official actuarial projections.

8. The 1983 reforms gradually increased the full benefit age (formally but misleadingly called the normal retirement age), as explained in chapter 2. Our plan changes Social Security taxes and benefits without altering the full benefit age. We also do not alter the age of first eligibility for retirement benefits.

9. Workers born in 1958 were 25 years old in 1983. The 1983 reforms reduced benefits for such workers by 11.1 percent if benefits were first claimed at age 65, and by 10.4 percent if at age 62.

Chapter Two

1. Before 1940, limited payments were made to individuals on a lump-sum basis. The first applicant for a lump-sum benefit was Ernest Ackerman of Cleveland, Ohio, who was covered by Social Security for one day and received a lump-sum payment in 1937 of 17 cents. See www.ssa.gov/history/briefhistory3.html.

2. Jeffrey R. Brown, Olivia S. Mitchell, and James M. Poterba, "Role of Real Annuities and Indexed Bonds in an Individual Accounts Retirement Program," in M. Feldstein and J. Liebman, eds., *Risk Aspects of Investment-Based Social Security Reform* (University of Chicago Press, 2001).

3. These figures are for recipients who initially claimed benefits at the age of 65 and reflect the worker's benefit only. They do not reflect any additional benefits for the worker's spouse or family.

4. Some researchers have noted that the progressivity of Social Security's annual benefit formula is reduced when other factors are taken into account. For example, workers with higher earnings tend to live longer than lower earners of the same sex, so that, on average, higher earners collect retirement benefits for longer. Social Security is therefore somewhat less progressive on a lifetime basis than it is on annual basis. On the other hand, workers with lower earnings are more likely to become disabled and receive disability benefits before retirement

age. On balance, Social Security remains somewhat progressive and a valuable source of social insurance even after these factors and others are taken into account.

5. Earnings in years after age 60 are not indexed; instead the actual nominal earnings in those years go into the calculation of the AIME.

6. For workers who initially become eligible for retirement or disability benefits in 2003, the PIA is determined as 90 percent of the first $606 of the AIME, plus 32 percent of the AIME between $606 and $3,653, plus 15 percent of the AIME over $3,653. The same formula is used to determine the PIA for disabled workers and the spouses and children of workers who die in 2003 before claiming benefits.

7. In addition, workers younger than the full benefit age have their benefits further reduced if their earnings exceed a specified level, which was $11,520 in 2003. This is referred to as an earnings test. A worker whose benefits are further reduced because of the earnings test receives a larger benefit when he or she stops working or reaches the full benefit age.

8. In addition, a family maximum limits the total benefit that may be paid to members of a family based on any one worker's earnings history. For the family of a worker who reaches age 62 in 2003, or who dies in 2003 before attaining age 62, the maximum family benefit payable is equal to 150 percent of the first $774 of the worker's PIA, plus 272 percent of the worker's PIA over $774 through $1,118, plus 134 percent of the worker's PIA over $1,118 through $1,458, plus 175 percent of the worker's PIA over $1,458.

9. We say "approximately" because the employer portion of the payroll tax is excluded from compensation in computing the employer tax payment and in computing federal income taxes for the worker. For a given 12.4 percent payroll tax rate, a wage of $106.20 would generate more than $12.40 in payroll tax liability ($0.124 \times \$106.2 = \$13.17$). Also, the exclusion of the employer share of the payroll tax from taxable compensation under the income tax means that the worker would be worse off if he or she were responsible for $12.40 in Social Security payroll tax and received a before-tax wage of $106.20. To avoid such a result, taxable compensation could be computed in a manner similar to that currently applied to self-employed workers (for whom this issue is relevant under current law). The methodology for computing self-employment taxes is technically flawed, however. Under current law, the income base on which self-employed people calculate their tax equals total compensation less 7.65 percent (one-half of the combined Social Security and Medicare Hospital Insurance payroll tax rate), rather than total compensation divided by 1.0765. The result is that the self-employed pay lower payroll taxes than employed workers with the same level of total compensation. The Congressional Budget Office has estimated that correcting the manner in which compensation for the self-employed is computed would raise more than $5 billion over the next ten years, $2.2 billion of

which would accrue as payroll revenue. See Congressional Budget Office, *Budget Options*, March 2003, REV-14.

10. An exception to this statement occurs when a worker has more than one employer and total wages from all employers exceed $87,000. The employee share of the excess payroll taxes paid by such a worker is rebated when the worker files an income tax return, but the employer share is not.

11. Social Security Administration, *Fast Facts and Figures about Social Security, 2002.*

12. What we refer to collectively throughout this volume as the Social Security "trust fund" is actually two trust funds: the Old-Age and Survivors Insurance Trust Fund and the Disability Insurance Trust Fund.

Chapter Three

1. In fact, three projections are made: one assuming that the system will incur relatively low costs, one that assumes relatively high costs, and an intermediate projection, on which we will focus. The Office of the Chief Actuary undertakes these projections in conjunction with the Social Security trustees. By law the trustees include the secretaries of the Treasury, labor, and health and human services and two public trustees, traditionally one Democrat and one Republican.

2. An alternative projection, in which benefits are reduced to equal contemporaneous revenue once the trust fund reaches zero, is referred to as "payable benefits."

3. This is in contrast with much of the past history of Social Security: future payroll tax rate increases were on the books from the creation of the program until 1990. The modest rise in the income rate shown in figure 3-1 reflects the income taxation of benefits. The thresholds for taxation of benefits are not indexed, contributing to the modest rise in the income rate.

4. We do not think it necessary, as some have proposed, for this traditional measure to be amended by ignoring the assets currently in the trust fund or by requiring that the projected annual net cash flow in each year be zero (that is, that revenue exactly match expenditure in each future year). Either of these approaches would effectively rule out using the trust fund to smooth timing differences between revenue and expenditure.

5. The Office of the Chief Actuary has established a set of criteria that must be met in order for the system to be deemed in actuarial balance. If the system's short-run finances (current revenue plus the trust fund balance) are insufficient to pay scheduled benefits, the system is clearly not in balance. Over longer periods, however, the reliability of the projections declines. Actuarial balance based on long-run considerations therefore allows some small degree of shortfall; if the shortfall is modest enough, corrective action is not necessarily warranted and the system is deemed to be in balance.

6. As the baby-boom generation is conventionally defined, the youngest baby-boomers were born in 1964; the vast majority are expected to have died by 2064. But the cost rate for scheduled benefits in 2064 is expected to be 19.1 percent (that is, benefits and administrative costs are expected to amount to 19.1 percent of taxable payroll), compared with 10.8 percent today, and to continue increasing after 2064.

7. We recognize that fully eliminating the terminal-year problem implicitly represents a form of permanent balance. See Ronald Lee and Hisashi Yamagata, "Sustainable Social Security: What Would It Cost?" *National Tax Journal*, vol. 56 (March 2003), pp. 27–43.

8. The Office of the Chief Actuary also uses a concept called "sustainable solvency." For a reform plan to meet this test, it must restore actuarial balance over the seventy-five-year horizon and result in a trust fund balance that is not falling relative to expenditure at the end of the horizon. It is important to avoid a severe terminal-year problem, in which Social Security promptly returns to imbalance after a reform as the rolling projection period moves forward. But the sustainable solvency criterion seems to us overly stringent, since we do not think that Social Security needs to be fixed "forever." For example, we would find it acceptable if the trust fund balance were sufficiently large at the end of a given seventy-five-year period that, even with moderate declines, it would remain above a reasonable precautionary level for a decade or two. In sum, we recognize the importance of looking beyond seventy-five years, but we think there is more than one way of satisfying the reasonable requirement that projected deficits not reemerge too quickly following a reform.

9. The degree to which such pressure exists under the scheduled benefit baseline is somewhat ambiguous, since it is unclear whether the gap between scheduled benefits and revenue is assumed in that baseline to be met through general revenue transfers or payroll tax increases.

10. For estimates of the long-term budget imbalance, see Alan J. Auerbach, William G. Gale, Peter R. Orszag, and Samara Potter, "Budget Blues: The Fiscal Outlook and Options for Reform," in Henry Aaron, James Lindsay, and Pietro Nivola, eds., *Agenda for the Nation* (Brookings, 2003).

11. Since its appearance in the early 1980s, the term "magic asterisk" has come to refer to any proposed solution to a budget gap that invokes insufficiently specified revenue increases or spending cuts.

12. Under the 2003 Social Security trustees' assumptions, such revenue infusions would not be needed until 2042. Such legislation could be further cloaked in the label of a debt to be paid back by Social Security beyond the seventy-five-year horizon.

13. Such a shift was proposed by one faction of the 1994–1996 Advisory Council on Social Security, was contemplated by President George W. Bush's Commission to Strengthen Social Security, and was proposed by Robert Pozen, a

member of that commission. As this book was being drafted, Congress was considering eliminating this component of the income taxation of benefits. If the alternative were indeed elimination of the provision (as opposed to its continuing to provide revenue for Medicare), then retaining the provision and dedicating the revenue to Social Security would not represent a gimmick.

14. Various reform plans have proposed a national value added tax to be dedicated to Social Security. See, for example, Laurence J. Kotlikoff and Jeffrey Sachs, "It's High Time to Privatize," *Brookings Review,* vol. 15, no. 3 (summer 1997), pp. 16–23; and Kotlikoff and Sachs, "The Personal Security System: A Framework for Reforming Social Security," Federal Reserve Bank of St. Louis *Review,* March/April 1998, pp. 11–13.

15. The degree to which reforms grandfather the benefits for workers currently nearing retirement does affect the size of the legacy debt, but there seems to be general agreement that these workers (mainly those in their mid-fifties) should be largely or entirely protected from future benefit cuts, because they will not have had time to adapt their saving behavior in response to those cuts.

16. Whether a reform raises national saving is closely related to how the legacy cost is distributed across generations under that reform. For example, a reform that generates higher national saving in the near term imposes larger legacy costs on today's workers than on workers in the distant future. Thus the previous perspective on reform is closely related to this one.

17. A more complex structure could better balance incentives and insurance by using a more complicated weighting scheme than simply counting or not counting individual years of earnings, as under the current system. We do not discuss such a basic overhaul because of its complexity and because the research needed to derive a good weighting scheme is lacking; instead we focus on changes that are more readily understood, in the hope that this less ambitious approach will allow reform to be achieved sooner rather than later.

18. Not punishing earlier retirement excessively and not rewarding later retirement excessively are mirror images of each other. That is, for someone considering working longer, the larger the increase in benefits from a delayed start, the greater the incentive to delay. But from the perspective of someone eager to retire early, a large increase in benefits from a delayed start is naturally seen as a large punishment for choosing early retirement.

19. Gary Burtless, testimony before the Subcommittee on Social Security of the House Committee on Ways and Means, hearing on "Social Security and Pension Reform: Lessons From Other Countries," July 31, 2001. In addition to the individual risk inherent in individual stock investment, widely varying replacement rates over a short period would create political pressures to offset such an outcome.

20. For discussions of political risk, see Hugh Heclo, "A Political Science Perspective on Social Security Reform," in R. Douglas Arnold, Michael J. Graetz, and Alicia H. Munnell, eds., *Framing the Social Security Debate: Values, Politics,*

and Economics (Washington: National Academy of Social Insurance, 1998); and Peter Diamond, ed., *Issues in Privatizing Social Security, Report of an Expert Panel of the National Academy of Social Insurance* (MIT Press, 1999). For additional political economy analysis, see Henning Bohn, "Will Social Security and Medicare Remain Viable as the U.S. Population Ages?" University of California at Santa Barbara, April 2003.

21. For a history of earlier legislation in Chile, see Peter A. Diamond and Salvador Valdés-Prieto, "Social Security Reform," in Barry P. Bosworth, Rudiger Dornbusch, and Raúl Labán, eds., *The Chilean Economy: Policy Lessons and Challenges* (Brookings, 1994). Since the creation of the Chilean individual accounts system in the early 1980s, laws reforming the initial decree have occurred almost once per year, on average.

22. Medicare part B covers physicians' services, outpatient hospital care, and some other non-hospital-provided medical services. For further discussion see Alicia Munnell, "The Declining Role of Social Security," Just the Facts #6, Center for Research, Boston College, February 2003, and Lawrence H. Thompson, "Sharing the Pain of Social Security and Medicare Reform," Retirement Project Brief no. 11, Urban Institute, August 2000.

23. Given declining replacement rates, a similar question is how to apportion whatever benefit reductions are planned among different cohorts.

24. See Karen Holden and Cathleen Zick, "Insuring against the Consequences of Widowhood in a Reformed Social Security System," in Arnold, Graetz, and Munnell, eds., *Framing the Social Security Debate,* pp. 157–81; and Melissa M. Favreault, Frank J. Sammartino, and C. Eugene Steuerle, "Social Security Benefits for Spouses and Survivors," in Favreault, Sammartino, and Steuerle, eds., *Social Security and the Family* (Washington: Urban Institute Press, 2002), table 6.1, p. 183.

25. For data on the circumstances of the disabled, see Virginia Reno, Jerry Mashaw, and Bill Gradison, eds., *Disability: Challenges for Social Insurance, Health Care Financing, and Labor Market Policy* (Washington: National Academy of Social Insurance, 1997).

26. See, for example, Chad Newcomb, "Distribution of Zero-Earnings Years by Gender, Birth Cohort, and Level of Lifetime Earnings," Research and Statistics Note no. 2000–02, Social Security Administration, Office of Policy, Office of Research, Evaluation, and Statistics, November 2000. It should be noted that the official poverty standard is very low and is indexed to inflation, not average earnings in the economy. Thus it is not an adequate representation of great need, and this has led many analysts to also consider those whose incomes are modestly above the poverty line. For a discussion of the measurement of poverty, see National Research Council, Commission on Behavioral and Social Sciences and Education, "Measuring Poverty: A New Approach" (Washington: National Academy Press, 1995).

27. Another approach to aiding those in serious need could come through changes in the program targeting benefits to the needy elderly and disabled: the Supplemental Security Income (SSI) program. We discuss in chapter 6 some relatively minor changes to the SSI program that could accompany our reform plan, but broader changes may also be warranted. It is worth noting that one could try to finance benefit changes targeted to the needy by altering existing benefit rules that help some of the needy but are not well targeted. In particular, researchers have identified Social Security's spousal benefit as disproportionately benefiting the families of higher earners. See, for example, C. Eugene Steuerle and Jon M. Bakija, *Retooling Social Security for the 21st Century* (Washington: Urban Institute Press, 1994), pp. 208–10. Such changes would be more controversial than financing targeted changes through broad reductions in benefits or out of additional dedicated revenue.

28. For further discussion of this point, see Peter Diamond, "The Economics of Social Security Reform," in R. Douglas Arnold, Michael J. Graetz, and Alicia H. Munnell, eds., *Framing the Social Security Debate: Values, Politics, and Economics* (Brookings, 1998); and Peter Orszag and Joseph Stiglitz, "Rethinking Pension Reform: Ten Myths about Social Security Systems," in R. Holzmann and J. Stiglitz, eds., *New Ideas about Old Age Security* (Washington: World Bank, 2001).

29. Peter Diamond and Jonathan Gruber, "Social Security and Retirement in the United States," in Jonathan Gruber, and David A. Wise, eds., *Social Security and Retirement around the World* (University of Chicago Press, 1999). A significant literature examines the effect of Social Security on labor supply. See, for example, Alan L. Gustman and Thomas L. Steinmeier, "The Social Security Early Entitlement Age in Structural Model of Retirement and Wealth," Working Paper 9183 (Cambridge, Mass.: National Bureau of Economic Research, September 2002); John Rust and Christopher Phelan, "How Social Security and Medicare Affect Retirement Behavior in a World of Incomplete Markets," paper no. 9406005 in the Public Economics series of the Economics Working Paper Archive at Washington University in St. Louis; Courtney Coile and Jonathan Gruber, "Social Security and Retirement," Working Paper 7830 (Cambridge, Mass.: National Bureau of Economic Research, August 2000); and Alan B. Krueger and Bruce D. Meyer, "Labor Supply Effects of Social Insurance," Working Paper 9014 (Cambridge, Mass.: National Bureau of Economic Research, June 2002).

30. For a summary of the literature on the effects of Social Security on labor supply, see Krueger and Meyer, "Labor Supply Effects of Social Insurance." Those authors conclude that studies that use a plausible identification strategy find a "very modest impact" on labor supply. See also the other papers referenced in the previous footnote.

31. As discussed above, individual labor supply decisions affect taxes paid and future benefits received under Social Security. Thus the program has a direct effect

on labor market incentives and these decisions. Poorly designed rules could greatly distort labor supply decisions in the sense of reducing economic efficiency. In contrast, neither Social Security taxes nor Social Security benefits vary directly with individual saving, although a recipient's taxable asset income can change the rate at which Social Security benefits are taxed under the income tax. Thus Social Security affects national saving primarily because of redistribution across cohorts (the legacy cost), not through distortions in individual decisions. Hence there is little efficiency cost associated with the effect of Social Security on national saving.

32. See, for example, Orszag and Stiglitz, "Rethinking Pension Reform: Ten Myths about Social Security Systems." See also Diamond, ed., *Issues in Privatizing Social Security.*

Chapter Four

1. For precise definitions of the mortality rate and of how the Social Security Administration constructs its assumptions, see "Life Tables for the United States Social Security Area, 1900–2100," Social Security Administration, Office of the Chief Actuary, Actuarial Study no. 116, August 2002.

2. At the same time that retirees are enjoying an inflation-adjusted benefit, people still in the work force are typically experiencing increases in wages that exceed inflation. (Although nominal wages have at times risen less rapidly than the consumer price index for short periods, wages over the long haul have risen faster than prices and are expected to do so in most years in the future.) Thus, over many years, the Social Security income of retirees tends to decline relative to the average earnings of contemporaneous workers. Those living a long time into retirement tend to fall further and further behind those still in the work force. Some other countries recognize this concern and, in their social security systems, raise benefits for retirees in line with wage rather than price increases, or in line with an average of the two.

3. See, for example, Henry J. Aaron and William B. Schwartz, eds., *Coping with Methuselah: The Impact of Molecular Biology on Medicine and Society* (Brookings, 2003).

4. Social Security does not currently adjust the level of annual benefits according to how long the beneficiary is expected to live. This is in sharp contrast with how an individual accounts system would work. In such a system, each worker reaching retirement age has an accumulated sum in his or her name that is available to finance that worker's retirement. That sum could, at the worker's option, be used to purchase a lifetime annuity that is indexed for inflation, thus closely mimicking today's Social Security benefit structure. However, given the way annuities are currently marketed, the price of such an annuity will depend in large part on the worker's life expectancy. In this sense an individual accounts system, unlike Social Security, is completely indexed for life expectancy, and the cost

of a longer life expectancy is borne by the individual worker. Under the current Social Security system, by contrast, if people live longer after retirement, it is Social Security that bears the increase in cost.

5. See, for example, Karen Smith, Eric Toder, and Howard Iams, "Lifetime Distributional Effects of Social Security Retirement Benefits," presented at the Third Annual Conference of the Retirement Research Consortium, Washington, May 17–18, 2001; and Lee Cohen, C. Eugene Steuerle, and Adam Carasso, "Social Security Redistribution by Education, Race, and Income: How Much and Why," presented at the same conference.

6. See, for example, Sherwin Rosen, "The Economics of Superstars," *American Economic Review,* vol. 71, no. 5 (December 1981), pp. 845–58; and Kevin Murphy and Finis Welch, "Wage Differentials in the 1990s: Is the Glass Half Full or Half Empty?" in Finis Welsh, ed., *The Causes and Consequences of Increasing Inequality* (University of Chicago Press, 2001). On a possible role for social norms, see Thomas Piketty and Emmanuel Saez, "Income Inequality in the United States, 1913–1998," Working Paper 8467 (Cambridge, Mass.: National Bureau of Economic Research, September 2001).

7. It is possible that all of the increased earnings for higher earners represented net additions to total earnings rather than a redistribution of earnings that would otherwise have accrued to workers lower in the earnings distribution. In that extreme case, the level of earnings subject to the payroll tax would be unaffected by the rapid growth in inequality. But even then, Social Security would have benefited if it were somehow possible to have that more rapid economic growth without all of the gains accruing to the highest earners. It is impossible to determine the precise extent to which the higher earnings at the top of the earnings distribution reflected net increases in total earnings, as opposed to shifts within a given total. But we believe that at least part of the increase at the top of the earnings distribution is associated with a reduction in earnings elsewhere, relative to what would have occurred in the absence of the increase in inequality. Finally, even if all of the increased inequality were due to increased aggregate earnings, it would still represent a positive change in the ability of the economy as a whole to support incomes in retirement.

8. A recent Social Security Administration paper studies changes in the earnings distribution between 1982 and 1995. It concludes that the Gini coefficient (a commonly used measure of inequality, which equals 1 if one worker receives all the earnings in the economy and 0 if all workers have equal earnings) increased by only about 1 percent between 1982 and 1995 if the top 1 percent of earners are excluded, and by about 4 percent if the highest earners are included. Kelvin R. Utendorf, "The Upper Part of the Earnings Distribution in the United States: How Has It Changed?" *Social Security Bulletin,* vol. 64, no. 3 (2001/02), pp. 1–11.

9. Workers who become seriously ill experience a reduction in their earnings and a shortening of their life expectancy. Furthermore, workers can choose

whether to stop working, which then affects their earnings. These factors complicate the analysis of the relationship of mortality rates to earnings. Relating mortality rates to education levels, however, has the advantage that education is highly correlated with potential lifetime earnings and yet is largely if not entirely unaffected by the confounding effects of ill health (on both earnings and mortality) and work choices (on earnings). Demographers have therefore tended to focus on the connection between education and mortality rather than earnings and mortality.

10. The trend toward an increase in this differential holds regardless of whether an absolute measure (those who have achieved a certain grade level) or a relative measure (those at a certain percentile of the population ranked by education) is used for educational attainment. We prefer the relative measure, since the absolute measures are affected by changes in the average education level in the population. For example, the persons who do not complete high school today tend to have different characteristics from those who did not complete high school forty years ago.

11. The relative index of inequality (RII) depicted in the figure is equivalent to the slope of the log of mortality rates when plotted on a cumulative educational distribution function. Since the change in the log of a variable is approximately equal to the percentage change in the variable (for small changes), we refer to the RII in terms of percent differentials. Note that mortality differences by education are more extreme for younger people and have also widened over time, but by less than the differences for older people. See Gregory Pappas, Susan Queen, Wilbur Hadden, and Gail Fisher, "The Increasing Disparity in Mortality between Socioeconomic Groups in the United States, 1960 and 1986," *New England Journal of Medicine*, vol. 329, no. 2 (July 8, 1993), pp. 103–09, and the correction that appeared in the October 7, 1993, issue.

12. See also Diane S. Lauderdale, "Education and Survival: Birth Cohort, Period, and Age Effects," *Demography*, vol. 38, no. 4 (November 2001), pp. 551–61; J. J. Feldman, Diane Makuc, Joel Kleinman, and Joan Cornoni-Huntley, "National Trends in Educational Differences in Mortality," *American Journal of Epidemiology*, vol. 129 (1989), pp. 919–33; S. H. Preston and I. T. Elo, "Are Educational Differences in Adult Mortality Increasing in the United States?" *Journal of Aging and Health*, vol. 7 (1995), pp. 476–96; and K. Stenland, Jane Henley, and Michael Thun, "All-Cause and Cause-Specific Death Rates by Educational Status for Two Million People in Two American Cancer Society Cohorts, 1959–1996," *American Journal of Epidemiology*, vol. 156, no. 1 (2002), pp. 11–21. See also the article and correction by Pappas and others cited in the previous note. For data on similar experiences in the United Kingdom, see L. Hattersley, "Trends in Life Experience by Social Class—An Update," *Health Statistics Quarterly*, vol. 2 (Summer 1999), pp. 16–24; and A. Donkin, P. Goldblatt, and K. Lynch, "Inequalities in Life Expectancy by Social Class 1972–1999," *Health Statistics Quarterly*, vol. 15 (Autumn 2002), pp. 5–15.

13. That support includes the cost of providing space in one's home for one's elderly parents to live. Elderly persons who have more income tend to use that income to live independently, rather than with their children. See, for example, Dora L. Costa, *The Evolution of Retirement: An American Economic History 1880–1990* (University of Chicago Press, 1998), pp. 106–32.

14. This ignores some additional debt that would arise if changes to the program were phased in slowly rather than immediately. It also ignores any additional taxes that might be paid by workers currently age 55 and over if tax rates are changed before they retire.

15. This calculation reflects only the impact on the Social Security budget; it does not include the value to the worker of the insurance provided against serious lifetime risks. Because private insurance companies have administrative expenses, people buying insurance expect to get back from insurance companies less than they pay in premiums. This does not mean that insurance is not a valuable asset to purchase; so, too, with Social Security.

16. Trustees' Report, 2003, table IV.B8. In other words, without the tax increase assumed in figure 4-8, the net transfer to future cohorts would be zero. Although the aggregate net cost for those under 15 is zero, the results vary by income and by cohort. For example, the aggregate zero cost for those under 15 reflects the sum of positive net revenue from the older cohorts in this group (those presently close to age 15), followed by negative ones thereafter (those born in the distant future). Since we discount future dollars at a 3 percent interest rate (which exceeds the 1.5 percent growth in taxable payroll), the negative transfers in the distant future are of limited present discounted value.

17. If D is the legacy debt this year, T is taxable payroll this year, r is the interest rate, and n is the growth rate in taxable payroll, then the legacy debt will increase to $D(1 + r)$ next year, and taxable payroll will increase to $T(1 + n)$. To keep the ratio D/T constant, it is necessary to finance an amount equal to $D(1 + r)/(1 + n)$, which is approximately equal to $D(r - n)$ for small values of r and n.

18. The total fertility rate for a given year is defined as the average number of children who would be born to a woman in her lifetime if she were to experience the birth rate by age for that year, and assuming that she survives the entire childbearing period.

19. Both of these trends contribute to the terminal-year effect discussed in more detail in chapter 3, because later years in the seventy-five-year projection period are more fully affected by the fertility transition than earlier years, and because beneficiaries in those later years will have lower average mortality.

Chapter Five

1. See, for example, Lawrence H. Thompson, "Sharing the Pain of Social Security and Medicare Reform," The Retirement Project Brief no. 11 (Washington: Urban Institute, August 2000).

2. See *Strengthening Social Security and Creating Personal Wealth for All Americans: The Final Report of the President's Commission to Strengthen Social Security,* available at www.csss.gov/reports/Final_report.pdf.

3. For example, one could instead undertake all of the adjustment to longer life expectancy by extending one's career. However, such a plan would not make economic sense unless one's opportunities and willingness to work increased in proportion to life expectancy. It is not clear how one would measure these, but we think that a proportional change does not seem likely, especially when combined with the incentive for earlier retirement that comes with higher earnings. Indeed, the fact that those cohorts expected to live longer are also expected to have higher earnings is an important dimension in evaluating any adjustment of Social Security.

4. One way to think about this issue is in terms of a net replacement rate, defined as the ratio of annual benefits to annual earnings net of the payroll tax. (This ignores any role of income taxation of both earnings and benefits and side-steps the issue of how to average earnings over different ages in determining the denominator.) That is, instead of the usual replacement rate, b/w, consider the net replacement rate, $b/(1 - t)w$. For someone relying solely on Social Security (that is, who has done no other saving), this is the same as the consumption replacement rate. This concept is well defined only after one has selected a retirement age at which to evaluate benefits. Consideration of successive cohorts then requires selecting how the age at retirement for evaluation purposes should be chosen. Although one could derive a balance between tax and benefit responses to increased life expectancy in this way, it simply moves the critical issue to a particular place in the analysis, one that does not seem more informative than our approach.

5. For example, under the current system, benefits are increased by 8 percent if benefits are claimed one year after the full benefit age and decreased by 6 2/3 percent if benefits are claimed one year before the full benefit age. If the benefit at the full benefit age is $10,000, and the full benefit age is 65, then workers claiming benefits at age 66 receive a benefit equal to $10,800. But if the full benefit age is 67, then workers claiming benefits at age 66 receive a benefit equal to $9,333. The increase in the full benefit age similarly reduces benefits at any other age of first claiming, although the degree of reduction varies across ages, and the relationship between benefits and the age at which they are first claimed is altered.

6. See, for example, C. Eugene Steuerle and Jon Bakija, *Retooling Social Security for the 21st Century: Right and Wrong Approaches to Reform* (Washington: Urban Institute Press, 1994); American Academy of Actuaries, "Raising the Retirement Age for Social Security," Issue Brief, October 2002; and Social Security Administration, "Social Security Fact Sheet: Increase in Retirement Age," available at www.ssa.gov/pressoffice/IncRetAge.html.

7. Specifically, using the period mortality table for the most recent available period and the one available for the previous year, and using the interest rates projected the current year, the Office of the Chief Actuary would determine the

percentage reduction in the PIA for that cohort that would keep unchanged the lifetime cost, at present value, of a dollar of benefits commencing at the full benefit age. With this approach, changes in benefit levels do not depend on assumed changes in life expectancy, but rather on actual changes in mortality by age. See the memorandum from the Social Security actuaries in appendix G for further detail.

8. Since adjustments would be made on an ongoing basis, any unexpected changes in benefits that a cohort would encounter as it nears retirement age are likely to be small. Furthermore, workers would know how their earnings history would relate to their future benefit levels with certainty once they reached age 60.

9. This does not result in precisely a 50-50 balance between changes in taxes and changes in benefits over the initial seventy-five-year period. Rather, our thought was to produce a rolling seventy-five-year balance from each annual change, recognizing that the initiation of this policy involves anticipation of many future changes. In addition, to avoid the administrative complexities associated with de minimis changes, the tax rate would change only when the accumulated computed change from this provision and later ones since the last adjustment exceeded 0.05 percent of payroll.

10. If the already-legislated benefit is larger than the automatic adjustment, the legislated change would take effect with no alteration from the new provision. The adjustment in the tax rate would happen nevertheless. Our approach implies a different pattern of redistribution across cohorts that have different life expectancies than does current law. This pattern may not optimally reflect the distribution of burdens across cohorts, but we have chosen to adopt a simple criterion (and want to preserve a uniform payroll tax rate for everyone) rather than a complex principle. It would indeed be complex to determine how differing earnings levels and differing life expectancies should be reflected in net benefits (benefits less revenue) for different cohorts.

11. Interestingly, Model 3 of President Bush's Commission to Strengthen Social Security also implicitly proposed a similar change in the maximum taxable earnings base to increase revenue. Although the commission was prohibited from recommending any tax increases, Model 3 included revenue that matched what would be generated if the taxable maximum were increased. Specifically, the scoring of the general revenue transfers under Model 3 assumed that the fraction of covered earnings subject to tax increased to 86 percent between 2005 and 2009 and was then maintained at that level thereafter. In what may be the only dissenting words in the report, the commission noted that "Some members . . . believed that a substantial portion of this [revenue transfer to Social Security under Model 3] should come from an increase in the payroll tax base. . . . However, this suggestion was deemed inconsistent with the principles in the executive order establishing the Commission" (*Strengthening Social Security and Creating Personal Wealth for All Americans,* p. 131, note 41).

12. In terms of the seventy-five-year projection horizon, raising the maximum taxable earnings base has a further positive effect because some of the benefit increases as a consequence of more taxable earnings within the horizon would be paid beyond the horizon.

13. We ignore the revenue side. The payroll tax rate is the same for everyone. If the effect of longer life expectancy on retirement ages does not vary much, on average, with earnings levels, a change in relative life expectancies does not have much effect on relative taxes paid.

14. Specifically, for each year we take the benefit level in the law, multiply it by the probability that a typical member of the group we are analyzing is alive, and then discount the product of that calculation by the government interest rate back to age 65. The result is a number that represents how much, on average, it costs Social Security to provide the benefits for workers at a particular earnings level.

15. See the 2003 Trustees' Report, table VI.F11, available at www.ssa.gov/OCACT/TR/TR03/lr6F11-1.html.

16. A rigorous calculation for a unisex mortality table would make an adjustment for the slightly higher number of males born each year than females. Adjusting the figures in table 5-1 to reflect this difference does not appreciably change the results.

17. John Geanakoplos, Olivia S. Mitchell, and Stephen P. Zeldes, "Would a Privatized Social Security Really Pay a Higher Rate of Return?" in R. Douglas Arnold, Michael J. Graetz, and Alicia H. Munnell, eds., *Framing the Social Security Debate* (Washington: National Academy of Social Insurance, 1998), p. 148. See also the discussion in chapter 3.

18. Much of the material in this section is drawn from Alicia H. Munnell, "The Impact of Mandatory Social Security Coverage of State and Local Workers: A Multi-State Review," Revised Final Report, AARP, 2000.

19. With universal coverage, the Government Pension Offset and Windfall Elimination Provision under current Social Security law will eventually no longer be needed. These provisions were legislated so that those covered by Social Security for only part of their careers, or whose spouses were not fully covered by Social Security, did not receive unwarranted benefits from the program's progressive benefit formula. Some have argued instead for eliminating these provisions, but we think that in the absence of universal coverage they serve an important role in targeting higher benefits on those intended to receive them. These provisions could be improved. See Peter A. Diamond and Peter R. Orszag, "Reforming the GPO and WEP in Social Security," *Tax Notes*, November 3, 2003.

20. This number is only an approximation to the precise cost of the legacy debt. The charge would be initially imposed through a 1.5 percent employer payroll tax and a 1.5 percent employee payroll tax on earnings above the taxable maximum, with the tax rate increasing over time as described in the text. The

time profile of this legacy charge from 2023 on matches the time profile of the universal legacy charge described below.

21. Pozen would impose a 3.9 percent payroll tax on earnings above the taxable maximum but would allow those taxed earnings to be partly counted for benefit purposes. See Robert C. Pozen, "Arm Yourself for the Coming Battle over Social Security," *Harvard Business Review* (November 2002), pp. 52–62. This is roughly equivalent in its net impact on Social Security finances to a tax of 2.9 percent with no change in benefit determination.

22. Especially given the reduction in dividend and capital gains tax rates enacted in the 2003 tax legislation, an increase in the tax imposed on high earnings might cause some diversion of wage income into dividend and capital gains income. We are, however, unaware of any estimates of the elasticity of this diversion in the vicinity of the current dividend and capital gains tax rates.

23. One could instead allow full or partial inclusion of such earnings in benefit calculations. We chose not to pursue this approach because those with such high earnings are not likely to be crucially reliant on Social Security for benefits. Thus a higher tax rate with partial benefit credits would not serve an important social insurance purpose beyond ensuring that high earners bear a fair share of the legacy cost.

24. The existing tax has loopholes that should be closed. A more radical reform would convert the estate tax into an inheritance tax.

25. See William G. Gale and Joel Slemrod, "Life and Death Questions about the Estate and Gift Tax," *National Tax Journal*, vol. 53, no. 4 (December 2000), pp. 889–912; and Gale and Slemrod, "Rethinking the Estate and Gift Tax: Overview," in William G. Gale, James Hines, and Joel Slemrod, eds., *Rethinking Estate and Gift Taxation* (Brookings, 2001).

26. Paine also wanted to use part of the revenue to give a grant to those turning 21 to help launch their careers. See Thomas Paine, "Agrarian Justice" (1797), in William Van der Weyde, ed., *The Life and Works of Thomas Paine*, Patriot's Edition (New Rochelle, N.Y.: Thomas Paine National Historical Association, 1925).

27. Delaying the tax provides a form of annuity, which even those planning on leaving bequests should value unless their intended heirs are completely risk-neutral. Wojciech Kopczuk, "The Trick Is to Live: Is the Estate Tax Social Security for the Rich?" Working Paper 9188 (Cambridge, Mass.: National Bureau of Economic Research, September 2002).

28. Capital gains held until death currently escape the income tax. Taxing them before taxing estates thus has considerable logic, although it runs into complications of recordkeeping that the current structure avoids. The proposed treatment of partial gains under the 2001 tax act, with a carryover of basis, creates an unmanageable recordkeeping nightmare, as was recognized in the rapid repeal of the previous attempt to carry over bases in the late 1970s. The Tax Reform Act

of 1976 stipulated that the basis for inherited assets carry over to the heir; before the provision took effect, however, it was repealed.

29. For example, those with high marginal tax rates and substantial capital gains could gift their assets to trusted friends or family members with lower marginal tax rates. The capital gains could then be realized at a lower tax rate, and the assets transferred back to the original owner. Gift and inheritance taxes may thus protect much more revenue than they collect directly. See Jonathan G. Blattmachr and Mitchell M. Gans, "Wealth Transfer Tax Repeal: Some Thoughts on Policy and Planning," *Tax Notes*, January 15, 2001; John Buckley, "Transfer Tax Repeal Proposals: Implications for the Income Tax," *Tax Notes*, January 22, 2001; David Cay Johnston, "Questions Raised on New Bush Plan to End Estate Tax," *New York Times,* January 29, 2001; and Iris Lav, "If Estate Tax Is Repealed, Repeal of Gift Tax Would Not Be Far Behind," Center on Budget and Policy Priorities, May 3, 2001.

Chapter Six

1. The poverty threshold has been the subject of controversy. See, for example, National Research Council, Commission on Behavioral and Social Sciences and Education, "Measuring Poverty: A New Approach" (Washington: National Academy Press, 1996).

2. The Supplemental Security Income program provides monthly income to people with disabilities and those over 65 who have income and assets below specific thresholds. However, this program does not provide sufficient benefits to keep the targeted group out of poverty. At the same time, Social Security's targeting in protecting against poverty is necessarily imperfect, because the program bases benefits solely on covered earnings, not uncovered earnings or nonearned income.

3. Kelly Olsen and Don Hoffmeyer, "Social Security's Special Minimum Benefit," *Social Security Bulletin*, vol. 64, no. 2 (2001/2002), pp. 1–15.

4. Under the Kolbe-Stenholm approach, workers with a twenty-year history of covered earnings under Social Security would receive a benefit at the full benefit age of at least 60 percent of the poverty level. The minimum benefit would increase for workers with longer careers; for workers with at least forty years of covered earnings, the minimum benefit at the full benefit age would equal 100 percent of the poverty level. The minimum benefit target would be indexed to prices over time under the Kolbe-Stenholm plan, as is the poverty level.

5. The commission's Model 2 proposed a new minimum benefit for low-wage workers with at least twenty years of covered earnings. This benefit would increase with years of additional covered earnings. For workers with at least thirty years of covered earnings, the benefit at the full benefit age was expected to reach 120 percent of the poverty threshold by 2018 and then stabilize at approximately that level. Model 3 also proposed a minimum benefit for workers with at

least twenty years of covered earnings. This benefit, too, would increase with additional years of coverage; for workers with at least thirty years of covered earnings, the minimum benefit at the full benefit age would equal 100 percent of the poverty threshold in 2018 and exceed the threshold thereafter.

6. The Primus proposal would replace the 90, 32, and 15 percent PIA factors (see chapter 2) with a single 75 percent factor. This factor would be applied to a special AIME; earnings for the purpose of this special AIME would be limited to 45 percent of the average wage. For a further description of the Primus proposal, see Kilolo Kijakazi, "Low-Wage Earners: Options for Improving Their Retirement Income," in Peter Edelman, Dallas Salisbury, and Pamela Larson, *The Future of Social Insurance* (Washington: National Academy of Social Insurance, 2001).

7. Steven H. Sandell, Howard M. Iams, and Daniel Fanaras, "The Distributional Effects of Changing the Averaging Period and Minimum Benefit Provisions," *Social Security Bulletin*, vol. 62, no. 2 (1999), pp. 4–13. This minimum benefit was simulated assuming that Social Security had been modified to take forty years into account in computing regular benefits, rather than thirty-five years as under current law. Since that assumption reduces regular benefits, the marginal effect of the minimum benefit is somewhat exaggerated relative to adding a minimum benefit to the scheduled benefit level. Our plan, however, would also involve some reduction in regular benefits relative to the scheduled benefit level; the results presented here may therefore still provide at least some insight into the marginal effect of a minimum benefit of this type under our plan.

8. For workers who become disabled or die before age 62, the years of coverage required to receive (or for their survivors to receive) the minimum benefit would be scaled to the length of the elapsed period from age 22 to the year of benefit eligibility.

9. As specified, this provision would create a "notch" between those becoming eligible in 2011 and before and those becoming eligible in 2012 and thereafter. The notch could be eliminated by phasing the provision in over time rather than having it take full effect in 2012, or by raising benefits for already eligible workers in the relevant income ranges.

10. Karen Holden and Cathleen Zick, "Insuring against the Consequences of Widowhood in a Reformed Social Security System," in R. Douglas Arnold, Michael J. Graetz, and Alicia H. Munnell, *Framing the Social Security Debate: Values, Politics, and Economics* (Washington: National Academy of Social Insurance, 1998), pp. 157–81.

11. Melissa M. Favreault, Frank J. Sammartino, and C. Eugene Steuerle, "Social Security Benefits for Spouses and Survivors," in Favreault, Sammartino, and Steuerle, eds., *Social Security and the Family* (Washington: Urban Institute Press, 2002), table 6.1, p. 183.

12. U.S. Department of Health, Education, and Welfare, *Social Security and the Changing Roles of Men and Women* (Washington, 1979); U.S. Department of

Health and Human Services, *Report on Earnings Sharing Implementation Study* (Washington, January 1985); Congressional Budget Office, *Earnings Sharing Options for the Social Security* System (Washington, January 1986); U.S. House of Representatives Select Committee on Aging, *How Well Do Women Fare under the Nation's Retirement Policies?* Comm. Pub. 102-879 (Washington: GPO, September 1992).

13. It is thus common to cite the range of one-half to two-thirds for the survivor's replacement rate, ignoring actuarial adjustments. But replacement rates in some cases lie above this range once adjustments for the age of claiming benefits are included. For example, consider a worker claiming benefits at age 70 whose spouse claims spousal benefits at age 62. Once the normal retirement age reaches 67, claiming worker benefits at age 70 will generate a monthly benefit equal to 124 percent of the worker's PIA, and claiming spousal benefits at age 62 will generate a monthly benefit equal to 32.5 percent of the worker's PIA (half of 65 percent). The couple's total benefit is thus 156.5 percent of the PIA. After the death of the worker, provided the surviving spouse has reached the full benefit age, he or she would receive 124 percent of the PIA (since the delayed retirement credits from the worker transfer to the widow or widower). Thus the survivor would receive 124/156.5 = 79.2 percent of what the couple had received before the death of the worker.

14. Richard Burkhauser and Timothy Smeeding, "Social Security Reform: A Budget Neutral Approach to Reducing Older Women's Disproportionate Risk of Poverty," Policy Brief 2/94, Syracuse University Center for Policy Research, 1994.

15. Specifically, each year the Office of the Chief Actuary would produce tables that would indicate, for any couple, the change in benefits on a break-even basis that would achieve the proposed survivor replacement rate. That is, when the second member of a couple claims benefits, the Office of the Chief Actuary would first determine what the benefits would be under current law (adjusted for any legislated changes in benefit levels). Then it would adjust the time profile of benefits to ensure a target survivor replacement rate of 75 percent. To do so, it would proportionately reduce the benefits of both members of a couple while alive in order to finance the higher survivor benefit level after one spouse dies. There would also be a need for rules to cover the possible return of one of the retirees to work. We envision the use of a period mortality table for this calculation to avoid disputes about the mortality rate projection and to allocate slightly more benefits to later in life.

16. For further details, see Kilolo Kijakazi, "Women's Retirement Income: The Case for Improving Supplemental Security Income," Center on Budget and Policy Priorities, June 8, 2001.

17. When Social Security added disability benefits in 1956, the basic benefit formula was modified to allow for an incomplete earnings history. For disabled workers the AIME is determined by the number of years of potential work less a number of dropout years, paralleling the use of thirty-five years for determining

benefits for retirees who had the opportunity to work between ages 21 and 62. A disabled worker's benefit is equal to the PIA regardless of the age at which benefits are claimed; this treatment provides a benefit that is the same as if the disabled worker were at the full benefit age.

18. For data on the circumstances of people with disabilities, see Virginia Reno, Jerry Mashaw, and Bill Gradison, eds., *Disability: Challenges for Social Insurance, Health Care Financing, and Labor Market Policy* (Washington: National Academy of Social Insurance, 1997).

19. Peter A. Diamond, Stephen C. Goss, and Virginia P. Reno, "Shifting from Defined Benefit (DB) to Defined Contribution (DC) Benefits: Implications for Workers' Disability and Survivor Benefits," National Academy of Social Insurance, October 1998, p. 13.

20. A somewhat more sophisticated version of this idea would allow, after the initial claim of disability benefits, a larger weight to be attached to wages as opposed to prices for younger workers; the weight on wages would then decline as the disabled worker aged. Thus the younger the disabled beneficiary, the closer the indexation of benefits would be to wage growth. The average weight attached to wage growth relative to price growth would be chosen so that the resultant actuarial cost of the benefit increases for disabled workers matched the actuarial value of the benefit reductions that would apply to disabled workers from the other provisions in our plan.

21. Since our reform relies less on benefit cuts than do other proposals (in part by placing more reliance on revenue increases, and in part by not providing for individual accounts, which are more valuable for retirees than for disabled workers), our plan to restore actuarial balance has much less effect on disability benefits than other proposals we have analyzed.

22. The indexing in the 1972 legislation was not done properly, leading to an increase in benefits during the 1970s well in excess of what Congress had intended. The 1977 legislation changed the nature of the indexing of Social Security to correct the problems from the 1972 approach.

23. Technically, the inflation rate is defined as the increase in the CPI-W (a version of the consumer price index that measures prices for urban wage earners and clerical workers) from the third quarter of the preceding year to the third quarter of the year in which the cost-of-living adjustment became effective (for benefits payable the following January).

24. Another gap in indexing occurs in the calculation of the AIME. Earnings after the year of turning 60 are *not* indexed back to age 60 when calculating the AIME. This enhances the increase in benefits from additional work. However, it does so in an erratic way depending on the inflation rate. These later earnings could be indexed back to age 60 using the CPI instead of the wage index. If this were thought to lower the incentive to continued work by too much (since older

workers are more likely to have thirty-five years with positive earnings, and thus a reduced payoff from additional work compared with someone with less than thirty-five years), the erratic nature of the current system could be adjusted by indexing by the inflation rate less the expected long-run inflation rate, currently 3 percent. Indeed, detailed study might turn up an economic efficiency argument for using some other baseline than expected inflation for this calculation.

Chapter Seven

1. We could also compare benefits under our plan with what benefits would be if they were reduced, year by year, so as to cost no more than the current tax structure could finance with no help from general revenue. However, this baseline of payable benefits has so little chance of actually happening and encounters such a sharp discontinuity when the trust fund reaches zero that it does not seem a useful basis for comparison. More broadly, two plans that would each restore long-term balance to Social Security will generally differ from each other in terms of both revenue and benefits, making it important to keep both in mind when doing comparisons. In chapter 9 we undertake some comparisons of our plan with the plans proposed by President Bush's Commission to Strengthen Social Security. Here we focus simply on how our plan compares with current law.

2. The aggregate adjustment (taxes plus benefits) for life expectancy under our plan is also smaller than under some plans. One reason is that the size of the adjustment depends in part on whether the full benefit age is adjusted (or an equivalent adjustment in the PIA is made) or whether the PIA is adjusted for an unchanging full benefit age once it has reached age 67 (as provided for under current law). Our plan produces a smaller aggregate change than some other plans because it does not adjust the age for full benefits (or make an equivalent change in the PIA).

3. We present the effects on the payroll tax rate only through 2055 because the vast majority of today's workers will have departed the work force by then. In chapter 9 we also present results for years after 2055.

4. For more details on the Urban-Brookings tax model, see www.taxpolicycenter.org.

5. Specifically, we provide a deduction to the individual for the employer's share of the payroll tax. We also apply the similar deduction under the income tax for half of payroll taxes paid by the self-employed. For a discussion of why these factors are slightly imprecise, see the notes to chapter 2.

6. We show benefit levels for those who are 15 years old and above in 2004, because that age range covers current workers and those about to enter the work force. In chapter 9 we also discuss the benefit changes for even younger people, including newborns.

Chapter Eight

1. This is not to say that benefits as described by current law will never be changed; indeed, we are proposing to make changes to the benefit structure. But Social Security can be designed so that the need for legislation is infrequent. With advance planning, legislated changes can protect those nearing retirement and involve only moderate and gradual changes for others active in the labor market. In contrast, financial market changes can be large and sudden and affect those on the verge of retirement, and even those already retired if they continue to rely on a diversified portfolio of assets. For one recent study of how older workers have reacted to substantial financial market fluctuations, see Jonathan Gardner and Mike Orszag, "How Have Older Workers Responded to Scary Markets?" Watson Wyatt Technical Paper 2003-LS05, June 2003.

2. Social Security benefits also do not depend on whether one's (wage-indexed) high-earning years come early or late in one's career. The assets accumulated in an individual account, by contrast, do depend on whether one's high-earning years came early or late: they will tend to be higher if the high-earning years come earlier.

3. Moreover, the progressivity of the Social Security benefit formula tends to balance the tendency of higher earners to live longer than lower earners of the same sex, so that Social Security is much more progressive on a lifetime basis than a generic individual accounts plan that requires annuitization (to ensure that workers do not outlive their savings). Under both Social Security and the individual accounts plan, the longer life expectancy of higher earners would increase their expected *lifetime* benefits relative to lower earners, since they would receive their annual benefit for more years, on average. But under Social Security, the monthly benefit itself is progressive, offsetting the effects of differences in life expectancy on expected lifetime benefits.

4. Many workers with short periods of coverage cash out their pension accumulations well before reaching retirement age. See Leonard E. Burman, Norma B. Coe, and William G. Gale, "Lump Sum Distributions from Pension Plans: Recent Evidence and Issues for Policy and Research," *National Tax Journal*, vol. 52, no. 3 (September 1999), pp. 553–62; and William G. Gale, Leonard E. Burman, and Norma B. Coe, "What Happens When You Show Them the Money? Lump Sum Distributions, Retirement Income Security, and Public Policy," Brookings, January 3, 2001.

5. See William G. Gale and Peter R. Orszag, "Private Pensions," in Henry Aaron, James Lindsay, and Pietro Nivola, eds., *Agenda for the Nation* (Brookings, 2003), table 3.

6. Robert Carroll, "IRAs and the Tax Reform Act of 1997," Office of Tax Analysis, Department of the Treasury, January 2000.

7. General Accounting Office, "Private Pensions: Issues of Coverage and Increasing Contribution Limits for Defined Contribution Plans," GAO-01-846, September 2001. The agency also found that 85 percent of those who would benefit from an increase in the 401(k) contribution limit earn more than $75,000.

8. See, for example, Craig Copeland, "IRA Assets and Characteristics of IRA Owners," *EBRI Notes*, December 2002; and David Richardson and David Joulfaian, "Who Takes Advantage of Tax-Deferred Saving Programs? Evidence from Federal Income Tax Data," Office of Tax Analysis, Department of the Treasury, 2001.

9. This design was applied in somewhat different form in the plans proposed by the President's Commission to Strengthen Social Security. A form of this approach was originally proposed by the General Accounting Office in response to requests from Representative John Porter (R-IL). See General Accounting Office, "Social Security: Analysis of a Proposal to Privatize Trust Fund Reserves," GAO/HRD-91-22, December 12, 1990. We ignore the complications arising from workers who die before starting retirement benefits.

10. The mechanism would involve having the Social Security Administration keep records of the amount of payroll tax revenue that each worker diverted to an individual account. These amounts would be entered as balances in a "liability account" for the worker. Each year, Social Security would update the results on the amount diverted and would charge interest on the balance in the liability account. Upon the worker's retirement, the balance would be paid off by reducing his or her traditional Social Security benefits. Specifically, Social Security would convert the accumulated balance in the liability account into an equivalent amount per month. The debt to Social Security would then be repaid by subtracting that computed monthly payment from the worker's Social Security benefit.

11. More specifically, we assume that payroll is diverted into individual accounts for workers aged 54 and younger at the beginning of 2002. We also base the projections on the 2001 intermediate cost assumptions of the Social Security trustees' report. These assumptions allow us to use a variety of calculations already undertaken by the Office of the Chief Actuary for Model 1 of the President's Commission to Strengthen Social Security. To ensure that the Social Security trust fund is held harmless over a worker's lifetime, the benefit offset must reflect the diverted revenue accumulated at a 3 percent real interest rate, which is the real interest rate assumed to be earned by the trust fund. To compute the benefit offsets, we combine the figures calculated by the Office of the Chief Actuary for Model 1, which assumed a 3.5 percent real interest rate for the benefit offsets, and for Model 3, which assumed a 2.5 percent rate. The figures for Model 3 are scaled by 2.0/2.965, because the offset amounts under Model 3 are based on a total 2.965 percent-of-payroll contribution rate (including 1 percent of payroll in add-on contributions).

12. For example, many people choose nominal annuities, rather than annuities that adjust for inflation or the returns on assets. Such a choice exposes the annuitant to the risk of inflation. Many people choose to have a bequest built into the annuity if they die earlier rather than later in their life expectancy. Such a bequest is necessarily highly variable in value, depending on the age at death. A less risky bequest could be financed by paying less for an annuity of the same size that does not include a bequest feature; the money saved could then be accumulated and bequeathed.

13. The current system does not preclude bequests. Even if workers did not save outside Social Security, accumulating wealth that could be bequeathed, they could purchase life insurance policies to finance such bequests, with the premiums for these policies financed out of their monthly Social Security benefits.

14. More complicated annuities could provide a payment to heirs, but that would require that the retiree receive a lower monthly annuity payment and thus have less to live on in old age. The iron laws of finance demand such an outcome, since the same dollars can be used for only one purpose. Thus, each dollar that a pensioner can bequeath to heirs means a dollar less to support retirement income, because the pool of funds available to finance retirement benefits is reduced. This iron law holds for all types of pensions—Social Security, private pensions, and individual accounts.

15. Some taxpayers might receive even more than their contributions if Congress provides bailouts to cohorts who suffer from poor financial market performance close to retirement. The cost of such bailouts would be paid by younger cohorts in the future.

16. Social Security provides spouse and survivor benefits without reducing the worker benefit for a worker with a spouse. In contrast, individual account annuitization pricing would reduce worker annuities to finance spouse and survivor benefits. The current structure is controversial, with some analysts believing that the current structure is too generous to married workers relative to single workers and makes benefits too dependent on the division of earnings between husband and wife.

17. See, for example, Gary Burtless, Testimony before the Subcommittee on Social Security of the House Committee on Ways and Means, Hearing on Social Security and Pension Reform: Lessons from Other Countries, July 31, 2001.

18. This measure reflects the change in the index from January of one year to January of the next. If the measure instead reflects the change in the *average* stock price from one year to the next, the number of years with nominal declines is seventeen. Also, although bonds held to maturity have little or no risk in nominal terms, they do have risk in real (inflation-adjusted) terms: if inflation turns out to be higher than expected, the real value of the bond's principal is reduced. That means that unexpected inflation poses a risk to bondholders. In the 1990s the Treasury Department began issuing inflation-indexed bonds that protect investors against such risk.

19. Rajnish Mehra and Edward Prescott, "The Equity Premium: A Puzzle," *Journal of Monetary Economics*, vol. 15, no. 2 (March 1985), pp. 145–61. But see also Ellen R. McGrattan and Edward C. Prescott, "Is the Stock Market Overvalued?" *Federal Reserve Bank of Minneapolis Quarterly Review*, vol. 24, no. 4 (Fall 2000), pp. 20–40; Ravi Jagannathan, Ellen R. McGrattan, and Anna Scherbina, "The Declining U.S. Equity Premium," *Federal Reserve Bank of Minneapolis Quarterly Review*, vol. 24, no. 4 (Fall 2000), pp. 3–19; and Ellen R. McGrattan and Edward C. Prescott, "Taxes, Regulations, and Asset Prices," Working Paper 8623 (Cambridge, Mass.: National Bureau of Economic Research, December 2001), which find otherwise.

20. Office of Management and Budget, *Budget Systems and Concepts*, Fiscal Year 2003, pp. 15–16. The actuary of the railroad retirement system did not assume this adjustment.

21. One also needs to consider tax differences across different ways of holding assets. This may generate some differences between holding stocks in an account outside Social Security and holding stocks in an account linked to Social Security, but we do not think that providing opportunities to take advantage of any such differential taxation is a primary purpose of Social Security reform.

22. See, for example, John Geanakoplos, Olivia S. Mitchell, and Stephen P. Zeldes, "Would a Privatized Social Security Really Pay a Higher Rate of Return?" in R. Douglas Arnold, Michael J. Graetz, and Alicia H. Munnell, eds., *Framing the Social Security Debate* (Washington: National Academy of Social Insurance, 1998), and Peter Diamond and John Geanakoplos, "Social Security Investment in Equities I: The Linear Case," *American Economic Review*, vol. 93, no. 4 (September 2003), pp. 1047–74.

23. For example, many workers seem to have difficulty understanding the value of diversification, recognizing the meaning of different points on a risk-return frontier, and avoiding risk-increasing attempts to time markets. Many of these problems could be avoided by allowing little or no discretion in portfolio choice, but that might not be politically sustainable.

24. Furthermore, we would not recommend that individuals with small retirement savings borrow in order to invest in stocks. That seems too risky. But carve-out accounts as proposed by President Bush's Commission to Strengthen Social Security would effectively allow for such borrowing. One of the major objectives of Social Security reform should be to put Social Security on a firm footing, to ensure that future retirees can more readily rely on a basic, assured stream of income. Carve-out accounts are inconsistent with this objective.

25. See the Individual Accounts plan proposed by Gramlich and Mark Twinney in the report of the 1994–1996 Advisory Council on Social Security. A description is available at www.ssa.gov/history/reports/adcouncil/report/gramlich.htm. See also Edward Gramlich, *Is It Time to Reform Social Security?* (University of Michigan Press, 1998).

26. See Hugh Heclo, "A Political Science Perspective on Social Security Reform," in Arnold, Graetz, and Munnell, eds., *Framing the Social Security Debate*.

27. For a further description of the commission's proposals, see Peter A. Diamond and Peter R. Orszag, "An Assessment of the Proposals of the President's Commission to Strengthen Social Security," *Contributions to Economic Analysis and Policy*, vol. 1, issue 1, article 10 (2002).

28. Martin Feldstein earlier proposed a similar mechanism. See the memorandum from Stephen C. Goss, Deputy Chief Actuary, Social Security Administration, "Long-Range OASDI Financial Effects of Clawback Proposal for Privatized Individual Accounts—INFORMATION," December 3, 1998.

29. For a more complete analysis of the Shaw plan, see Kilolo Kijakazi, Richard Kogan, and Robert Greenstein, "The Shaw Social Security Proposal: The Role of Massive General Revenue Transfers," Center on Budget and Policy Priorities, September 2002.

30. Even stronger incentives could arise if the clawback were limited to the level of traditional benefits and the account were large enough so that the clawback would simply eliminate the traditional benefit. In evaluating the actuarial effects of the Shaw plan, the Office of the Chief Actuary took this possibility into account. For further detail, see Stephen C. Goss, Alice H. Wade, and Chris Chaplain, "OASDI Financial Effects of the Social Security Guarantee Plus Act of 2003," Office of the Chief Actuary, Social Security Administration, January 7, 2003.

31. These examples were chosen because equity mutual funds currently charge more than 1 percent a year on average, but individual accounts can avail themselves of mechanisms to lower the charges. For details on the relationship between charges and benefits, see Peter Diamond, "Administrative Costs and Equilibrium Charges with Individual Accounts," in John Shoven, ed., *Administrative Costs and Social Security Privatization* (University of Chicago Press, 2000); and Mamta Murthi, J. Michael Orszag, and Peter R. Orszag, "Administrative Costs under a Decentralized Approach to Individual Accounts: Lessons from the United Kingdom," in R. Holzmann and J. Stiglitz, eds., *New Ideas about Old Age Security* (Washington: World Bank, 2001).

32. This discussion focuses on the effects associated with the diversion of revenue from the trust fund to individual accounts. Looking well ahead into the future, one may be impressed that the individual accounts proposed by the President's Commission to Strengthen Social Security are projected to hold more assets than the trust fund's traditional long-run target of just meeting the level of expenditure projected for the following year. But this projection is more accurately a measure of the financial crisis looming for Social Security than of an increase in national saving. That is, projecting a larger level of assets raises the question of where the funds will come from to purchase those assets.

33. In a simulation, Gustman and Steinmeier find that if the defined-benefit structure of Social Security were completely replaced by individual accounts,

labor force participation would barely change for those under age 60, and that "labor force participation by those in their sixties might increase slightly as a result of privatization, with a maximum increase in participation at age sixty-five amounting to 2 percentage points." See Alan L. Gustman and Thomas L. Steinmeier, "Privatizing Social Security: Effects of a Voluntary System," in Martin Feldstein, ed., *Privatizing Social Security* (University of Chicago Press, 1998), pp. 332–33. See also Congressional Budget Office, "Analysis of a Proposal by Professor Martin Feldstein to Set Up Personal Retirement Accounts Financed by Tax Credits," August 1998.

34. Writing about Argentina, Rafael Rofman finds that "The stagnation in the number of contributors to the SIJP is worrisome, since it was expected that the introduction of the individual account scheme and the reductions in employers' contributions established in recent years would act as incentives to increase participation." Klaus Schmidt-Hebbel does find less growth in informal work in Chile than in other Latin American countries, and he attributes this to pension reform. Even if this attribution is correct, it should be noted that the Chilean reform lowered the payroll tax rate as well as changing the social security system from a defined-benefit to a defined-contribution system. Thus one cannot separate the effect of lower taxes per se from the effect of a change in the form of benefits. See Rafael Rofman, "The Pension System in Argentina Six Years after the Reform," World Bank, 2000, p. 19; Klaus Schmidt-Hebbel, "Latin America's Pension Revolution: A Review of Approaches and Experience," Central Bank of Chile, 1999.

Chapter Nine

1. Even in the absence of our reform plan, we see a strong case for adjusting benefits for disabled workers more rapidly than merely keeping pace with inflation, accompanying the larger increase in benefits with a lower level of initial benefits. Similarly, there may be a case for having benefits for retirees rise more rapidly than inflation, likewise financed by lower initial benefits, although the appropriate rate of increase would be lower than for disabled workers.

2. President Bush's commission, citing the same study, argues that an African American receives $21,000 less from Social Security on a lifetime basis than a white person with the same level of earnings and marital status.

3. See Jeffrey Liebman, "Redistribution in the Current U.S. Social Security System," in Martin Feldstein and Jeffrey Liebman, eds., *The Distributional Aspects of Social Security and Social Security Reform* (University of Chicago Press, 2002), table 2, part 2. The difference in rates of return for retirement and survivor benefits between African Americans and whites is of marginal statistical significance. African Americans benefit disproportionately from Social Security

disability insurance benefits, however, which are not included in the study. If disability benefits were included, the difference in rates of return would increase.

4. Office of Policy, Office of Research, Evaluation, and Statistics, Social Security Administration, "Earnings of Black and Nonblack Workers: Who Died or Became Disabled in 1996 and 1997?" Note No. 2000-01, November 2000.

5. See, for example, Robert A. Moffitt and Mark O. Wilhelm, "Taxation and the Labor Supply Decisions of the Affluent," in Joel B. Slemrod, ed., *Does Atlas Shrug? The Economic Consequences of Taxing the Rich* (Harvard University Press, 2002). Moffitt and Wilhelm conclude, "High-income taxpayers are often thought to have more opportunities to respond to tax law changes and to have a greater incentive to do so because of their high marginal tax rates. Our analysis of changes in the hours of work of such men between 1983 and 1989, in response to the marginal tax rate reductions legislated in the 1986 Tax Reform Act, finds essentially no evidence of any such response" (p. 221). See also Austan Goolsbee, "It's Not about the Money: Why Natural Experiments Don't Work on the Rich," in Slemrod, *Does Atlas Shrug?* for a critique of the methodology typically used to examine the responsiveness of high earners to tax changes.

6. John Geanakoplos, Olivia S. Mitchell, and Stephen P. Zeldes, "Would a Privatized Social Security System Really Pay a Higher Rate of Return?" in R. Douglas Arnold, Michael J. Graetz, and Alicia H. Munnell, eds., *Framing the Social Security Debate: Values, Politics, and Economics* (Brookings, 1998), also available as Working Paper 6713 (Cambridge, Mass.: National Bureau of Economic Research, August 1998); and Geanakoplos, Mitchell, and Zeldes, "Social Security Money's Worth," Working Paper 6722 (Cambridge, Mass.: National Bureau of Economic Research, September 1998), also available in Mitchell, Robert J. Myers, and Howard Young, eds., *Prospects for Social Security Reform* (University of Pennsylvania Press, 1999).

7. Geanakoplos, Mitchell, and Zeldes, "Social Security Money's Worth," in Mitchell, Meyers, and Young, *Prospects for Social Security Reform*, p. 80.

8. Kent Smetters, "The Equivalence of the Social Security Trust Fund's Portfolio Allocation and Capital Income Tax Policy," Working Paper 8259 (Cambridge, Mass.: National Bureau of Economic Research, April 2001).

9. The range reflects both the variation caused by the range of ages at which workers may claim benefits under Model 3 and whether one includes the income from the additional contributions to the individual accounts required under Model 3 in order to participate in the accounts. We also assume that the commission's models are implemented on the same schedule as envisioned in its report; a delay in implementation to reflect the passage of time since the report was released would make the traditional benefit reduction smaller (since the benefit reductions would begin later), while also making the income from the individual accounts smaller (since the accumulation of funds in the accounts would begin later). See appendix F for further details.

10. The commission's report states: "DI [disability insurance] beneficiaries may not have their full adult lives in which to accumulate a retirement account, so this is a rationale for maintaining their traditional benefits. However, if benefits were changed for OASI [old-age and survivors' insurance] but not DI, this might lead to an increase in DI applicants. The Commission urges the Congress to consider the full range of options available for addressing these concerns. In the absence of fully developed proposals, the calculations carried out for the Commission and included in this report assume that defined benefits will be changed in similar ways for the two programs. *This should not be taken as a Commission recommendation for policy implementation.*" *Strengthening Social Security and Creating Personal Wealth for All Americans*, p. 149 (italics in original).

11. See Peter A. Diamond and Peter R. Orszag, "Reforming the GPO and WEP in Social Security," *Tax Notes,* November 3, 2003.

Chapter Ten

1. See, for example, Lawrence H. Thompson, "Sharing the Pain of Social Security and Medicare Reform," The Retirement Project Brief 11, Urban Institute, August 2000.

Appendix A

1. We ignore possible general-equilibrium effects. One treatment of such effects is in Peter Diamond, "National Debt in a Neoclassical Growth Model," *American Economic Review*, vol. 55, no. 5, part 1 (December 1965), pp. 1126–50.

2. Even Martin Feldstein, a prominent critic of the present Social Security system, finds that the offset is less than one for one. See Martin Feldstein, "Social Security, Induced Retirement, and Aggregate Capital Accumulation," *Journal of Political Economy,* vol. 82, no. 5 (September/October 1974), pp. 905–26. Dean Leimer and Selig Lesnoy, correcting a computational error in the Feldstein paper, found that the effect of Social Security wealth was half as large as Feldstein's original estimate and that the estimate was not statistically different from zero. See Dean R. Leimer and Selig D. Lesnoy, "Social Security and Private Saving: New Time-Series Evidence," *Journal of Political Economy,* vol. 90, no. 3 (June 1982), pp. 606–29. Feldstein argues that this insignificant estimate results from extending the period examined to 1974 and not adjusting for a change in the benefit formula in 1972. He also updates some of the estimates for new data. See Martin Feldstein, "Social Security and Saving: New Time Series Evidence," *National Tax Journal,* vol. 49, no. 2 (June 1996), pp. 151–64. In any case, we remain extremely skeptical that such time-series analyses give answers with any reliability to this question.

3. For further information on integrated plans, see Pamela Perun, "Social Security and the Private Pension System: The Significance of Integrated Plans,"

prepared for the Fifth Annual Conference of the Retirement Research Consortium, Washington, May 2003; and General Accounting Office, "Social Security Reform: Implications for Private Pensions," GAO/HEHS-00-187, September 2000.

4. For example, the President's Commission to Strengthen Social Security argued, "The Commission agrees that advance funding cannot be reliably accomplished through a Social Security Trust Fund invested wholly by the federal government. While it is theoretically possible to build up a fund in this manner, the past two decades have taught our nation a clear lesson about how unlikely this is in practice. The availability of Social Security surpluses provided the government with an opportunity to use these surpluses to finance other government spending, rather than saving and investing them for the future. A failure to increase national saving means that future taxpayers will bear a higher tax burden without the benefit of the increase in productivity that such saving might have stimulated." *Strengthening Social Security and Creating Personal Wealth for All Americans: Final Report of the President's Commission to Strengthen Social Security* (December 2001), p. 38. It should be noted, however, that the report identifies no study with which the commission "agrees" on this point.

5. For example, Schieber and Shoven write, "The answer to our question whether the Social Security trust fund balance represents wealth that can benefit future generations depends on unobservable or counterfactual behavior. What would federal government spending have been and, for that matter, what would tax collections have been, if the government hadn't had access to Social Security's cash-flow surplus over the last fifteen years or so? The question cannot be answered with certainty, but Figure 13.5 provides some clues. There we see the excess of [Social Security] revenues, not including interest on the previously accumulated bonds, over costs and the on-budget surplus of the federal government. The figure shows that for the years 1985–1997 the Social Security cash-flow surplus was dwarfed by the deficits in the rest of the federal government budget. To be sure, this doesn't directly answer our question, but it does add to the likelihood that the $757 billion pile of government bonds has not made the future population wealthier." Sylvester Schieber and John Shoven, *The Real Deal: The History and Future of Social Security* (Yale University Press, 1999), pp. 204–05.

6. For an attempt at such an econometric examination, see Kent Smetters, "Is the Social Security Trust Fund Worth Anything?" presented at the conference on "The Social Security Trust Fund: Lock Box or Leaky Bucket," American Enterprise Institute, December 9, 2002, and Smetters, "Is the Social Security Trust Fund Worth Anything?" Working Paper 9845 (Cambridge, Mass.: National Bureau of Economic Research, July 2003). Smetters's results are extremely sensitive to the time period studied and the econometric specification adopted.

7. Peter Diamond, "Social Security, the Government Budget and National Savings," Working Paper (Massachusetts Institute of Technology, December 2003).

Appendix B

1. See Peter Diamond and Jonathan Gruber, "Social Security and Retirement in the United States," in Jonathan Gruber and David Wise, eds., *Social Security and Retirement around the World* (University of Chicago Press, 1999), p. 437–74.

Appendix C

1. From the beginning, Social Security benefits have gone only to workers who paid some payroll tax, and to their families. But the taxes paid by the first generation of recipients were so small relative to the benefits they received that this stylized model captures the essence of what happened. The model should be interpreted in terms of the excess of what they received over what they paid.

2. If the interest rate were never higher than the growth rate of taxable payroll, there would be no increase in the ratio of the legacy debt to taxable payroll, and no need to pay a legacy cost. Thus the debt could be left to continue indefinitely. But this is not projected to be the case: instead, real interest rates are projected to be roughly twice the long-run rate of growth of real taxable payroll.

Appendix E

1. Sylvester Schieber and John Shoven, *The Real Deal: The History and Future of Social Security* (Yale University Press, 1999), p. 70.

2. See the description of a "public-private investment strategy" in the Maintain Benefits plan in *Report of the 1994–1996 Advisory Council on Social Security* (Washington, 1997), pp. 83–87.

3. For a description of the Clinton administration's deliberations on this issue, see Douglas W. Elmendorf, Jeffrey B. Liebman, and David W. Wilcox, "Fiscal Policy and Social Security Policy during the 1990s," in Jeffrey Frankel and Peter Orszag, eds., *American Economic Policy in the 1990s* (MIT Press, 2002).

4. See the website of the Canada Pension Plan at www.cppib.ca.

5. Alan Greenspan, "Outlook for the Federal Budget and Implications for Fiscal Policy," testimony before the Committee on the Budget, U.S. Senate, January 25, 2001.

6. Olivia Mitchell and Roderick Carr, "State and Local Pension Plans," in J. Rosenbloom, ed., *Handbook of Employee Benefits* (Chicago: Irwin, 1996); Olivia Mitchell and Ping-Lung Hsin, "Public Pension Governance and Performance," in Salvador Valdés-Prieto, ed., *The Economics of Pensions: Principles, Policies, and International Experience* (Cambridge University Press, 1997); Alan Greenspan, "Social Security," testimony before the Committee on Budget, U.S. Senate, January 28, 1999; and Celinda Franco, Edward Rappaport, and James Storey, "State and Local Pension Plans: Economically Targeted Investments and

Social Responsibility Screening," CRS Report for Congress RL 30218, Congressional Research Service, May 25, 1999.

7. Alicia Munnell and Annika Sundén, "Investment Practices of State and Local Pension Funds: Implications for Social Security Reform," in Olivia S. Mitchell and Edwin C. Hustead, eds., *Pensions in the Public Sector* (University of Pennsylvania Press, 2000), p. 154. For other views, see also John Nofsinger, "Why Targeted Investment Does Not Make Sense!" *Financial Management,* vol. 27, no. 3 (Autumn 1998), pp. 87–96; Roberta Romano, "Pension Fund Activism in Corporate Governance Reconsidered," *Columbia Law Review,* vol. 93, no. 4 (1993), pp. 795–853; Mark A. Sarney, "State and Local Pension Plans' Equity Holdings and Returns," *Social Security Bulletin,* vol. 63, no. 2 (2000), pp. 12–16; Government Accounting Office, "Public Pension Plans: Evaluation of Economically Targeted Investments," 1995; and Franco, Rappaport, and Storey, *State and Local Pension Plans.*

8. Estelle James, "Pension Reform: An Efficiency-Equity Tradeoff?" in Nancy Birdsall, Carol Graham, and R. Sabot, eds., *Beyond Tradeoffs* (Brookings, 1998).

9. More recent research suggests that even after undertaking some risk adjustment, public trust funds in developing countries tend to underperform private funds in developing countries. See Augusto Iglesias and Robert J. Palacios, "Managing Public Pension Reserves: Evidence from the International Experience," in Robert Holzmann and Joseph E. Stiglitz, eds., *New Ideas about Old Age Security* (Washington: World Bank, 2001).

10. R. Kent Weaver, "Whose Money Is It Anyhow? Governance and Social Investment in Collective Investment Funds," Working Paper 2003-07 (Center for Retirement Research, Boston College, May 2003).

11. Robert Palacios, "Securing Public Pension Promises through Funding," Pension Research Council Working Paper 2002-19 (University of Pennsylvania, 2002).

12. Henry Aaron and Robert Reischauer, *Countdown to Reform: The Great Social Security Debate* (New York: Century Foundation, 2001); and Theodore Angelis, "Investing Public Money in Private Markets: What Are the Right Questions?" in R. Douglas Arnold, Michael J. Graetz, and Alicia H. Munnell, eds., *Framing the Social Security Debate: Values, Politics, and Economics* (Washington: National Academy of Social Insurance, 1998). On index funds, see Ajay Shah and Kshama Fernandes, "The Relevance of Index Funds for Pension Investment in Equities," in R. Holzmann and J. Stiglitz, eds., *New Ideas about Old Age Security* (Washington: World Bank, 2001).

13. Kent Smetters, "The Equivalence of the Social Security Trust Fund's Portfolio Allocation and Capital Income Tax Policy," Working Paper 8259 (Cambridge, Mass.: National Bureau of Economic Research, April 2001).

Appendix F

1. We do not discuss Model 1 because that proposal would not restore long-term solvency. The commission's report is available at www.csss.gov. For our analysis of the commission's plans, see Diamond and Orszag, "Assessing the Plans Proposed by the President's Commission to Strengthen Social Security," *Tax Notes,* July 2002, and "An Assessment of the Proposals of the President's Commission to Strengthen Social Security," *Contributions to Economic Analysis and Policy,* vol. 1, no. 1, article 10, 2002.

2. Note that traditional benefits and combined benefits are identical for workers who choose not to contribute to individual accounts. The basic changes in traditional benefits that would result from the commission's plans represent the overall effect the plans would have on workers who elect not to participate in the accounts.

3. As emphasized above, we assume that the commission's models are implemented as scheduled in its final report. If implementation were delayed to reflect the passage of time since that report was issued, the traditional benefit reduction would be larger, but the annuity provided by the individual account would be smaller, under the commission's models than as presented here.

Index

Actuarial balance: over 75 years, 8, 30–34, 97, 114; over the very long term, 32–33; recent reform proposals, 98; restoring without stock market returns, 42

Actuarial deficit, change since *1983*, 56–57

Actuarial effects, 117–19, 165–69; and stock market returns, 42

Administrative costs of individual accounts, 156–57

Adverse selection, 72–73

AIME. *See* Average indexed monthly earnings

Argentina, 43, 161

Average earnings of workers, 18

Average indexed monthly earnings (AIME), 18, 87, 88, 112

Baby-boomers, aging of, 35, 74

"Bankruptcy" of Social Security, 29–30

Baseline issue for benefit and revenue comparisons, 11

Beneficiaries, 14–17. *See also specific beneficiaries*

Benefits, 169–75; baseline issue for benefit and revenue comparisons, 11; and change in life expectancy, 83; charge on payroll taxes and benefits, 92–93, 96, 123, 126, 182–83; current official projections, 28–30; determination of, 17–21; divorced spouse, 23, 45; enhancement for low earners, 102–03; and exhaustion of trust fund, 29–30; for family members, 22–23; full benefit age, 18–21; implications of reform proposal, 116–32; income taxation of, 24–25, 29; individual accounts compared with Social Security, 134–35, 142–47; minimum benefit, 101–03; partial taxation of, 24–25; progressivity, 16–17, 18, 86, 146; protection against inflation, 111–13; and purpose of Social Security, 15–16; reduced, 10, 20,

127–32; and reform proposal changes to, 8–9; retirement and family member benefits, 23; taxation of, 24–25. *See also specific beneficiaries*
Budget, avoiding burdens on, 35–37, 195–96
Burkhauser, Richard, 104
Burtless, Gary, 40
Bush, George W.: estate tax proposal, 5; on Social Security, 1; tax cuts, 125–26. *See also* President's Commission to Strengthen Social Security

Cash flow, 30, 141–42
Children of deceased workers. *See* Young survivors
Chile and retirement accounts, 43, 152, 153, 161
Clawback provisions, 155–56
Clinton administration budget surplus, 195
Combined effects of benefit reductions and tax changes, 127–32, 195
Commission to Strengthen Social Security. *See* President's Commission to Strengthen Social Security
Cost-of-living adjustment (COLA), 18, 112; super-COLA for younger disabled workers, 109–11, 130, 171; super-COLA for young survivors, 172
Cutler, David, 160

Deficit. *See* Long-term deficit
Defined-contribution plans, tax-favored, 43, 210–13. *See also* Individual accounts; *specific plans*
Determination of benefits, 17–21
Disabled workers: benefits, 15; combined effects of benefit reductions and tax changes, 129–30; determi-

nation of benefits, 21–22; eligibility for benefits, 91; family member benefits, 22–23; incentive to claim, 107; life expectancy, 61–62; poverty rates, 106; protection as Social Security purpose, 45; reform plan provisions, 8, 106–11, 170–72; super-COLA for younger disabled workers, 108–11, 171
Divorced spouse benefits, 23, 45

Earnings inequality: and improving mortality, 67–69; increase in, 64–67; and long-term deficit, 64–69; and reform plan, 3–4, 84–88, 120–23
Economic Growth and Tax Relief Reconciliation Act of *2001*, 94
Education level and mortality rates, 68–69
Estate tax: as alternative revenue source, 5, 93–96, 181; phasing out of, 94

Family members: determination of benefits, 22–23; of disabled workers, 22–23; and retirement benefits, 23. *See also* Young survivors
Fertility rates: and actuarial deficit, 56; and legacy debt, 34, 74–77; and payroll tax increases, 93
Financing of Social Security, 23–25; from federal budget, 35–37, 195–96. *See also* Revenue
Fiscal soundness, 27–35; avoiding burden on federal budget, 35–37, 195–96; current official projections, 28–30; *75*-year actuarial balance, 8, 30–34, 97, 114; terminal-year problem, 34–35, 56, 84, 96, 168
401(k) plans, 137, 211; amendment of legislation, 43; contribution levels, 138; investment choices of workers

in, 150; preretirement withdrawals,
145–46; SIMPLE *401*(k), 212
403(b) plans, 137, 212
457 plans, 137, 212
Full benefit age, 18–21; effect of gradual increase, 28, 82; and reform
proposal, 84

Goals for reform, 27–54, 193–98;
avoiding burden on federal budget,
35–37, 195–96; fiscal soundness,
27–35; legacy debt spread fairly,
37–39; macroeconomic performance, 45–51; 75-year actuarial balance, 8, 30–34, 97, 114; social
insurance, 39–45
Gramlich, Edward, 151
Greenspan, Alan, 8
Greenspan Commission. *See* National
Commission on Social Security
Reform

Higher income workers: combined
effects of benefit reductions and
tax changes, 127, 129; growth of
untaxed earnings, 85, 183; longer
life expectancies, 3, 68; and payroll
tax changes, 3, 180; and PIA, 18;
reduction of benefits, 8, 88, 131;
and tax-deferred retirement
accounts, 137. *See also* Maximum
taxable earnings base
Hospital Insurance. *See* Medicare

Immigration rates: and actuarial
deficit, 56; and legacy debt, 34,
74–77
Indexation in Social Security, 16, 19.
See also Inflation
Individual accounts, 133–63, 194–95;
add-on voluntary accounts, 140,
194; administrative costs, 156–57;
and aggregate risk taking, 161–62;

benefit comparison, 134–35,
142–47, 183; cash-flow problem,
141–42; economic effects, 157–62;
future legislation, 152–55; identical
portfolio comparison, 144–47;
inclusion in Social Security reform
plan, 133–34, 139–41, 162–63,
194–95; and increasing life expectancy, 81; links to traditional benefit reductions, 155–56; mandatory
accounts, 158–60; and national
saving, 157–61, 160–61; portfolio
diversification, 147–51; preretirement withdrawals, 145; retirement
security and, 136–39; revenue
implications, 141–42; revenue
sources, 151–52; and risk, 143,
146, 148–50, 161–62, 184; Shaw
plan, 156; voluntary accounts,
158–60; and work effort, 161. *See
also specific plans*
Individual Retirement Accounts
(IRAs), 137, 210–11; amendment
of legislation governing, 43; nondeductible, 211; Roth IRAs, 211;
SIMPLE IRAs, 212; taxpayers'
contribution level to, 138; withdrawals from, preretirement, 154
Inflation: benefits adjusted for, 11, 16;
consumer price index, used to
adjust benefits for, 113; indexation
for, 18, 19; protection of benefits
against, 8, 111–13
IRAs. *See* Individual Retirement
Accounts

Keogh accounts, 137
Kolbe, Jim, 102
Kolbe-Stenholm proposal (*2001*), 102

Labor market incentives, 46, 48–49
Latin America, 161. *See also specific
countries*

Legacy debt: adjustments for legacy costs, 88–93; burden of, 4–5, 69–74, 182–83; charge on payroll taxes and benefits, 92–93, 96, 123, 126, 182–83; explanation of, 6–7, 208–09; fertility and immigration rates and, 34, 74–77; implications of, 72–73; increase in payroll tax for, 92–93; and long-term deficit, 69–77; and reform plan, 4–5, 123–27, 197; sharing fairly, 37–39, 89–90, 131, 183, 197; tax on earnings above maximum taxable earnings base, 5, 92, 123, 177, 180; universal coverage to offset, 5, 89, 90–92, 123, 191–92

Life expectancy: and actuarial deficit, 56; and career length, 63, 81; of disabled workers, 61–62; and earnings inequality, 67–69; of higher income workers, 3, 68; and long-term deficit, 58–64; of minorities, 174; projections, 82; and reform plan, 2, 119–20

Local government employees. *See* State and local government employees

Long-term deficit, 1, 55–77, 167–68; changes in actuarial deficit since *1983*, 56–57; and increasing earnings inequality, 64–69; and increasing life expectancy, 58–64; and legacy debt burden, 69–77

Low lifetime earnings, workers with: benefit enhancement for, 102–03; combined effects of benefit reductions and tax changes, 127–28; increase in benefits, 8, 10; and individual accounts, 146; minimum benefit for, 101–03; PIA, 18; protection as Social Security purpose, 45; reform plan provisions, 8,

100–03, 172–73; and years of covered work, 101. *See also* Earnings inequality

Macroeconomic performance: improvement of, 45–51; labor market incentives, 46, 48–49; national saving, 47, 50–53

Mandatory individual accounts, 158–60

Maximum taxable earnings base, 24, 65–66; increase of, 85–86, 120, 121–23, 177; taxes on earnings above, 5, 92, 123, 177–78, 180

Medicaid, 35, 106

Medicare: payroll tax, 66–67, 92; premiums subtracted from Social Security payments, 44; reform of, 35

Medicare Hospital Insurance Trust Fund, 25

Minimum benefit, 101–03

Minorities and reform plan, 173–75

Mitchell, Olivia, 184

Monthly benefit amount, 18–19

Mortality rates. *See* Life expectancy

National Commission on Social Security Reform (Greenspan Commission), 8, 56, 57

National saving, 47, 50–53, 199–204; and individual accounts, 157, 160–61; and Social Security trust fund, 51–53

Normal retirement age, 21

Office of the Chief Actuary: adjusting for improved life expectancy, 83; income and cost rate estimates, 118; scoring of stock market investments, 42; on voluntary accounts, 158

O'Neill, Thomas P., 8
Overview of Social Security, 14–26

Paine, Thomas, 95
Payroll tax: current official projections, 28–30; as funding source of Social Security, 24; increase in, 5, 11–12, 12, 70, 120, 130, 176–79; Medicare share, 66–67, 92; and reform plan, 3–4, 11–12, 12, 176–80; and seventy-five-year actuarial balance, 30–34; as sole source of Social Security funding, 79; taxable payroll defined, 28; used to cover legacy cost, 92–93. *See also* Maximum taxable earnings base
Pensions, 136, 137
PIA. *See* Primary insurance amount
Political economy and reform plan, 185–86
Political risk and Social Security, 41, 43, 186
Portfolio diversification in individual accounts, 147–51
Pozen, Robert, 92
President's Commission to Strengthen Social Security: against payroll tax increases, 195; compared with reform plan, 186–90, 217–27; general revenue for Social Security deficit, 195; increased benefits for lower earners, 102; individual accounts linked to traditional benefits reduction, 155, 158; and life expectancy adjustments, 82, 83; reduction in benefits, 88
Primary insurance amount (PIA), 18–20, 83, 87, 108, 120, 131
Primus, Wendell, 102
Progressivity of benefits, 16–17, 18, 86, 146

Purpose of Social Security, 15–16, 193. *See also* Social insurance role of Social Security

Railroad Retirement Fund investment in equities, 149
Reagan, Ronald, 8
Reduced retirement benefit, 10, 20
Reform plan, 79–98; benefits of, 12–13; combined effects of benefit reductions and tax changes, 127–32, 195; compared with President's Commission to Strengthen Social Security, 186–90, 217–27; estate tax as alternative revenue source, 5, 93–96, 181; Kolbe-Stenholm proposal, 102; need for, 1–2; other recent proposals, 98, 115, 155–56; and political economy, 185–86; questions and answers about, 164–92; Shaw plan, 156; summary of effects, 9. *See also* Goals for reform; *specific aspects of plan*
Replacement rates: at retirement, 43–45; for survivors, 104, 105
Retirement age: incentives, 46; normal, 21; reform plan on, 175–76; trends in, 205–07
Retirement role of individual accounts vs. Social Security, 136–39
Revenue, 180–82; baseline issue for benefit and revenue comparisons, 11; budget surplus to fund Social Security, 195; current official projections, 28–30; estate tax as alternative source, 5, 93–96, 181; implication of reform plan for, 116–32; individual accounts creating cash-flow problem, 141–42; sources of, 23–25, 151–52

Risk: accounting for, 39–43; aggregate risk taking, 161–62; and individual accounts, 143, 146, 148–50, 184
Roth IRAs, 211

Salary reduction simplified employee pension plans (SARSEPs), 213
Shaw, Clay, 156
Shaw plan, 156
SIMPLE *401*(k), 212
SIMPLE IRAs, 212
Smeeding, Timothy, 104
Social insurance role of Social Security, 39–45, 193; individual accounts and, 145; inflation protection of benefits, 111–13; other recent proposals, 115; preserving and improving, 39–45, 99–115; and progressivity of benefits, 16–17, 18, 86, 146; risk factors, 39–43. *See also specific beneficiaries*
Social Security trust fund: actuarial effects of reform proposal on, 117–19; cash-flow surpluses, 25; current official projections, 28–30; exhaustion of, 29–30, 200–04; interest earnings, 25; and national saving, 51–53, 199–204; as source of revenue for benefits, 25; and stock market investment, 184–85, 214–16; interest rates on, 113. *See also* Revenue
Spousal benefits. *See* Divorced spouse benefits; Widows and widowers
SSI. *See* Supplemental Security Income
State and local government employees: extending Social Security coverage to, 5, 89, 90–92, 123, 191–92; Government Pension Offset and the Windfall Elimination Provision, 191–92; nonparticipa-

tion of, 5; shortcomings of present system for, 91
Stenholm, Charlie, 102
Stock market: fluctuations and worker investments, 40; individual accounts and portfolio diversification, 147–51; individual returns and actuarial solvency, 42; and trust fund investment, 184–85, 214–16
Super-COLA: for younger disabled workers, 109–11, 130, 171; for young survivors, 172
Supplemental Security Income (SSI), 106
Surviving children. *See* Young survivors
Surviving spouses. *See* Widows and widowers
Sweden, 82, 83

Taxable payroll defined, 28
Taxation: Bush administration cuts, 125–26, 181; charge on payroll taxes and benefits, 92–93, 96, 123, 126, 182–83; current official projections, 28–30; and defined-contribution plans, 210–13; of earnings above maximum taxable earnings base, 5, 92, 123, 177–78, 180; estate tax as alternative revenue source, 5, 93–96, 181; income taxation of benefits, 24–25, 29; legacy costs, 123–27; and reform plan, 127–32; of Social Security benefits, 24–25. *See also* Legacy debt; Payroll tax
Terminal-year problem, 34–35, 56, 84, 96, 168
Thrift plans, 213
Trust funds. *See* Medicare Hospital Insurance Trust Fund; Social Security trust fund

United Kingdom, 158, 159, 194
Universal coverage. *See* State and local
  government employees
Universal legacy charge on payroll
  taxes, 92–93, 96, 123, 126,
  182–83
Urban-Brookings Tax Policy Center
  tax model, 121

Voluntary individual accounts,
  158–60

Widows and widowers: benefits, 15;
  and minorities, 175; poverty rate,
  103–04; protection as Social Security purpose, 45; reform plan provisions, 8, 103–06; replacement
  rate for survivors, 104, 105
Women: reform plan provisions, 173;
  shortened careers, 45

Young survivors: benefits, 15, 23;
  reform plan provisions, 8, 106–11,
  172